Donizetti's opera, based on Walter Scott's novel, is a staple of the *bel canto* operatic repertoire and famed above all for its vocally challenging and frequently reinterpreted 'mad scene' that precedes the lead character's death. This handbook examines the impact *Lucia* has had on opera studies and investigates why, of all of Donizetti's seventy-plus operas, this particular work has inspired so much enthusiastic interest among scholars, directors and singers. A key feature is the sheer mutability of the character Lucia as she transforms from a lyric *bel canto* figure in the first half of the nineteenth century to a highly charged coloratura *femme fatale* by century's end, fascinating not just to opera historians but also to those working on literary theories of horror and the gothic, the science of the mind, sound studies, gender theory and feminist thought. The book places *Lucia* within the larger contexts of its time, while underlining the opera's central dramatic elements that resonate in the repertoire today.

MARK A. POTTINGER is Professor of Musicology and Chair of the Communication, Sound and Media Arts Department at Manhattan University. Winner of the prestigious Berlin Prize in 2017, he is the author of numerous publications on the music and cultural life of nineteenth-century Europe and the contemporary listening environment.

NEW CAMBRIDGE MUSIC HANDBOOKS

Series Editor

NICOLE GRIMES, TRINITY COLLEGE DUBLIN

The New Cambridge Music Handbooks series provides accessible introductions to landmarks in music history, written by leading experts in their field. Encompassing a wide range of musical styles and genres, it embraces the music of hitherto under-represented creators as well as reimagining works from the established canon. It will enrich the musical experience of students, scholars, listeners and performers alike.

Books in the Series

Hensel: String Quartet in E flat
Benedict Taylor

Berlioz: *Symphonie Fantastique*
Julian Rushton

Margaret Bonds: The *Montgomery Variations* and Du Bois *Credo*
John Michael Cooper

Robert Schumann: Piano Concerto
Julian Horton

Schoenberg: 'Night Music' – *Verklärte Nacht* and *Erwartung*
Arnold Whittall

Bach: The Cello Suites
Edward Klorman

Donizetti: *Lucia di Lammermoor*
Mark A. Pottinger

Forthcoming Titles

Schubert: The 'Great' Symphony in C major
Suzannah Clark

Clara Schumann: Piano Concerto in A minor Op. 7
Julie Pedneault-Deslauriers

Beethoven: String Quartet Op. 130
Elaine Sisman

Louise Farrenc: Nonet for Winds and Strings
Marie Sumner Lott

Cavalleria rusticana and *Pagliacci*
Alexandra Wilson

DONIZETTI: *LUCIA DI LAMMERMOOR*

MARK A. POTTINGER
Manhattan University

CAMBRIDGE
UNIVERSITY PRESS

Shaftesbury Road, Cambridge CB2 8EA, United Kingdom

One Liberty Plaza, 20th Floor, New York, NY 10006, USA

477 Williamstown Road, Port Melbourne, VIC 3207, Australia

314–321, 3rd Floor, Plot 3, Splendor Forum, Jasola District Centre,
New Delhi – 110025, India

103 Penang Road, #05–06/07, Visioncrest Commercial, Singapore 238467

Cambridge University Press is part of Cambridge University Press & Assessment,
a department of the University of Cambridge.

We share the University's mission to contribute to society through the pursuit of
education, learning and research at the highest international levels of excellence.

www.cambridge.org
Information on this title: www.cambridge.org/9781009374484

DOI: 10.1017/9781009374507

First published 2025

A catalogue record for this publication is available from the British Library

*A Cataloging-in-Publication data record for this book is available
from the Library of Congress*

ISBN 978-1-009-37448-4 Hardback
ISBN 978-1-009-37449-1 Paperback

CONTENTS

FIGURES

MUSICAL EXAMPLES

INTRODUCTION: WHY *LUCIA*?

Let us face it: 'Lucia' is a vehicle for the soprano, and the audience was there to hear Miss Callas. In the Mad Scene she did not let it down.

The New York Times, 1956[1]

On 9 November 1834, Donizetti signed a contract to write three new operas for the royal theatres of Naples, which included the Teatro di San Carlo and the Teatro di Fondo. The first of his contracted operas was to be ready for one of these two stages by July 1835.[2] Although his contract stipulated that he would receive a libretto 'at least four months prior to the first performance', he did not receive an approved libretto from the Napoli authorities until late May 1835. The libretto was Salvadore Cammarano's *Lucia di Lammermoor*.[3] Cammarano, who was initially trained as a painter and sculptor, was appointed as poet and stage director for the royal theatres in Naples in 1834. When he began sketching the libretto to *Lucia*, the Walter Scott novel (*The Bride of Lammermoor*, 1819) had already been set by a handful of Italian librettists, including Giuseppe Balocchi's libretto for Michele Carafa's *Le nozze di Lammermoor* (Paris, 1829), Carlisto Bassi's libretto for Luigi Rieschi's *La fidanzata di Lammermoor* (Trieste, 1831) and Pietro Beltrame's libretto for Alberto Mazzucato's *La fidanzata di Lammermoor* (Padua, 1834).[4] Cammarano's libretto proved more popular, however, which established the author as one of the more successful Italian librettists in the first half of the nineteenth century.[5]

Donizetti began sketching ideas for *Lucia* soon after he and Cammarano met to discuss the opera subject (sometime in early or mid-May). Although we do not know for certain when composition began, the last page of his autograph score is dated 6 July, which means that the bulk of the manuscript was completed in approximately six weeks. It would not be until late September, however, that the work would first be performed at the San Carlo.

The reason for this delay was that the theatre management ran out of money, forcing the theatre to put on low-cost productions to shore up funds.[6] When the rehearsals for *Lucia* finally began in early September, the San Carlo was again struggling to pay its bills, so much so that the *prima donna* who created the role of Lucia, Fanny Tacchinardi-Persiani, refused to rehearse until she was paid.[7] After some negotiation, the rehearsals resumed, allowing the opera to be performed on 26 September for the first time.[8]

Every opera guide published from the twentieth century to today has something to say about Donizetti's most famous tragic opera. Every professional opera singer knows of the 'mad scene' in the final act and understands the technical demands this aria poses for the female voice. Any operagoer introduced to just one opera season at any major opera house will have heard the opera or at least come to know of the work in a season or two. But why? What is so special about *Lucia*?

The answer lies partly in the sheer mutability of the character Lucia to be transformed in performance after performance from a lyric *bel canto* figure (whose madness was often dismissed at the time of the premiere) to a coloratura *femme fatale* with such charged energy that the opera has become the voice piece of several subject areas within academia, including sound studies, literary theories of horror and the gothic, the science of the mind, gender theory and feminist thought.[9] Such research has inspired *Regietheater* productions since the 1990s by some of the biggest names in and outside the opera hall, including Francesca Zambello (Dublin Grand Opera, 1991), Mary Zimmerman (The Metropolitan Opera, 2007), David Alden (English National Opera, 2008), Sandra Leupold (Hamburg State Opera, 2010), Katie Mitchell (The Royal Opera House, 2016) and Amélie Niermeyer (Hamburg State Opera, 2021). Dare I say, there is no other opera from the first half of the nineteenth century that has inspired so much enthusiastic interest among scholars and directors, not to mention world-class singers, such as Lily Pons, Maria Callas, Joan Sutherland, Beverly Sills, Natalie Dessay, Diana Damrau, Nadine Sierra and Pretty Yende.

The main goal of this handbook is to place *Lucia* within the larger crosscurrents of contemporary thought while underlining at the same time the central dramatic elements within the work that have allowed it to remain in the repertoire today. These key elements or points of contact for the listener include the sources for the libretto and production (Chapter 1), the *bel canto* genre (Chapter 2), the sonic landscape of the opera (Chapter 3), the musico-dramatic structure (Chapters 4, 5 and 6) and the overall reception of the work (Chapter 7). In addition, the reader will also find three appendixes at the back of the book, which place the opera within the context of Donizetti's life and compositional activity (Appendix A), the overall compositional structure of the work (Appendix B) as well as the opera's presence in film (Appendix C).

Chapter 1 discusses the many dramatic elements within the opera's libretto, which include the rich Scottish setting, the gothic genre, the persistence of death and the world of nineteenth-century female madness. Madness in particular is of great interest to scholars today, for *Lucia* premiered at a time when female madness was frequently seen and heard on the stages of Italian opera and in nearby asylums. Thus, through an examination of the sources that define the libretto, we can perceive the sociocultural environment of Cammarano in particular and Italian opera in general in the early nineteenth century.

Chapter 2 places *Lucia* within the context of *bel canto* opera in the first half of the nineteenth century and discusses the dramaturgy, voice types and fixed vocal forms that are often found in this style of opera. In addition, going beyond the mere definition of 'beautifully sung', Chapter 2 argues that *bel canto* reflects an operatic work where the singer's vocal agility (i.e., their *coloratura*) is the main vehicle that defines the character's dramatic persona and climactic journey, from an unfortunate individual who, at first glance, is powerless to change their situation, to a fully rounded character with a certain heroic potential. *Lucia* is unique in this regard owing to the main character's ability to shape-shift from a quiet and somewhat naïve lover and dutiful daughter to a murderer and usurper of family values. This malleability between a tasteful showpiece for the female voice and a tragic *tour-de-force* is one of the many factors that keeps *Lucia* in the repertoire today.[10] Such versatility places Donizetti's opera more in line with the psychologically rich and often violent works of Verdi and Puccini at the end of the century rather than the operatic works of the 1830s.

Chapter 3 reflects upon the sonic landscape within the opera. In a romantic opera, the orchestra is the cementing agent between the separate dramatic forces of the text and the voice as it often serves as an omniscient narrator, detailing to the listener not only the actions of the characters on stage and the external environment but also the unspoken and unseen world of internal thoughts and desires. By listening to the orchestra, the audience can interpret the sounds they hear as reflective of the overall goals of the principal characters on stage. For example, the ominous use of *pianissimo* timpani paired with bass drum at the start of the orchestral prelude foreshadows for the listener the death of Lucia, as this is the same music heard in the opera's final scene. The opening sounds of the prelude remind us that this work is indeed a tragedy where death is the prescribed outcome not only for Lucia but also for her lover, Edgardo. Of particular interest in this chapter is the glass harmonica, originally planned by Donizetti to be used in the 'mad scene' of Act III but later replaced with the flute. Donizetti's original intent of using this high-pitched resonant instrument to depict female madness has resurfaced in modern productions of the work. The playing of this curious instrument presents audiences with contemporaneous sounds of horror, violence and mystery commonly found in fantasy and sci-fi films today.

After discussing the opera's overall literary and sonic environment, Chapters 4, 5 and 6 examine each of the three acts in *Lucia*. Chapter 4 discusses Act I, where the action occurs outside the walls of Ravenswood Castle. We learn during the opera that the castle changed hands a generation earlier from the Ravenswood family to the Ashton family, which is ruled by Lucia's brother Enrico. Early in the act, he tells us of his hatred for the Ravenswood family. And when he finds out that Lucia has fallen in love with Edgardo, the last surviving Ravenswood, Enrico is doubly enraged, for not only is Lucia in love with a mortal enemy but she is also destroying his plans to marry her off to a wealthy benefactor (Lord Arturo Bucklaw). We also learn in Act I that a ghost appeared to Lucia at the mouth of a fountain. Although we never see or hear the ghost, only what Lucia sings of it in her gothic-tinged *cavatina* 'Regnava nel silenzio' ['At dead of night'], the ghost nonetheless haunts Lucia to such a degree that the aria's melody returns in Act III, when Lucia is near death. In short, the opening scenes of Act I reveal the power of vengeance and death that will engulf Lucia throughout the opera.

In addition to the aria sung by Lucia, Chapter 4 also discusses the famous love duet that ends the act, 'Verranno a te sull'aure' ['On the breeze will come to you my ardent sighs']. The duet presents the promise of eternal love, forsworn in front of the same fountain where the ghost appeared to Lucia. The dramatic potency of this duet is quite profound as it parallels the betrayal of the ghost by her Ravenswood lover to Lucia's betrayal in Act II. Both betrayals end in death, so the coupling of the two events helps to embody what is referenced throughout the opera, namely the deadly curse that befalls anyone who breaks a solemn vow. The chapter thus presents the musico-dramatic structure of the entire opera through an analysis of the opening act.

Chapter 5 discusses the events of Act II, which begins with Enrico alone in his study and ends with Lucia signing a marriage contract to marry Arturo, the only one who has the power to rekindle the Ashton family fortune. The dramatic pacing of this act quickens from one scene to the next, culminating in a spectacular *finale*. The main vocal number of the *finale* is the celebrated sextet, 'Chi me frena in tal momento?' ['Who stops me at this moment?'], a slow vocal number that presents the sentiments of all the principal characters following the sudden arrival of Edgardo at the nuptial agreement ceremony. Curiously, Donizetti sets this dramatically explosive moment in a dance-like rhythm with pizzicato strings in major, as if the shock-filled reality of the situation is suspended and we enter a collective 'stop frame' moment in which all the characters appear to be frozen in place as thoughts of betrayal, vengeance and remorse mingle together. The sextet begins as a duet between Edgardo and Enrico, who, after seeing Lucia faint, express guilt and regret for causing Lucia such emotional distress. The duet soon moves to a quartet as Lucia and Raimondo (her confidant and minister) join Edgardo and Enrico with the singing of the same melody and its accompanying lines. The whole ensemble then comes together as Alisa (Lucia's handmaiden), Arturo and the chorus, accompanied now by the full orchestra, express concern over Lucia's health, fearing that she is 'between life and death'. In essence, Donizetti builds the emotional energy of this sextet into a musical maelstrom, all centred on the life of a young woman at her wit's end. Perhaps this is the reason why the music of the sextet appeared in films more often than any other number in the score – a quintessential Italian vocal number in the midst of a *cantabile–cabaletta* format, with duelling melodies that tug at the emotional heartstrings of the listener (see Appendix C).

Discussion of Lucia's declining mental state continues in Chapter 6. In Act III, following the challenge presented to Edgardo by Enrico to fight at dawn, Donizetti composes a multi-sectional aria interspersed with the chorus that begins with Lucia's memory of Edgardo's voice ('il dolce suono' ['The sweet sound']) and ends with a show-stopping *cabaletta* ('Spargi d'amoro pianto' ['Shed bitter tears']). The orchestral accompaniment to this long multi-part aria (over 20 minutes in length) recalls the music found earlier in the opera, including Lucia's *cavatina*, the love duet from Act I and the nuptial music of Act II. Lucia's madness is rationalized here for the listener as we hear what Lucia hears and yet, it remains a complete mystery for the other characters on stage. In addition, in no other *bel canto* opera in the first half of the nineteenth century, which contains female madness, does the lead woman commit murder. This plot twist therefore connects with more naturalistic tales of domestic violence made popular in the second half of the nineteenth century, such as in the operas of Verdi, Bizet and Puccini.

The final chapter discusses the opera's initial reception by nineteenth-century audiences and its future legacy. As many scholars have shown, regardless of its popularity today, the 'mad scene' in Act III was not popular in the years following the premiere in 1835.[11] In fact, it was the character Edgardo and his music that received the most praise from audiences and critics alike. Chapter 7 sets out to answer why this was the case by presenting key critical reviews of the work, including those in Naples and Paris. Paris is a rather telling example, for *Lucia* appeared in three different versions: the original Italian work at the Théâtre-Italien (1837), a French-language version at the

Théâtre de la Renaissance (1839) and a French *grand opéra* version with ballet at the Paris Opéra (1846). In addition to its reception in the press, Chapter 7 also discusses *Lucia*'s popularity with publishers of opera selections for the salon and the opera's auspicious appearance in Gustave Flaubert's *Madame Bovary* (1857). Such reception points to the extent of the opera's success outside the opera hall and serves as further evidence of *Lucia* in the everyday consciousness of European audiences.

But once again, in all such performances, Edgardo's death created a more lasting impression on audiences than Lucia's. This all changed when the 'mad scene' was extended to accommodate several extreme vocal performances (both in concert and in the context of the opera) near the end of the nineteenth century. When this change occurred, the opera entered a new mode of expression, reflecting Lucia's inner strength in the face of weakness. Such a change brought renewed focus on the character of Lucia, whereby her actions throughout the opera are now viewed and heard as those of a woman who reflects a kinship with the *femme fatale*, a late nineteenth-century outgrowth of the fears surrounding the rise of women who are independent of men and the subsequent loss of patriarchal control. This late-nineteenth-century version of *Lucia* continues to inspire new productions of the opera, endearing the work further to those who wish to challenge common (mis)perceptions of femininity and female madness. For example, in Simon Stone's recent production for The Metropolitan Opera (April 2022), the Australian director depicted Lucia as 'a woman trying to survive, to create a future for herself, to be independent, but being ground to dust by the patriarchy around her'.[12] The opera is set in present-day America in the 'Rust Belt', an area of the United States that was hollowed out by industry. In the 'mad scene', Lucia wears a blood-soaked wedding dress (resonating with Brian De Palma's *Carrie*, 1976) as she sings the extended aria cadenza with glass harmonica. Presented in this way, female madness is seen and heard as the outcome of masculinity gone awry.

Taken as a whole, *Lucia di Lammermoor* remains a testament to a time when colourful orchestration, tuneful melodies, intimacy with literature, an exotic setting, a connection to real-life passions and, most importantly, the virtuosity of performance were viewed as necessary ingredients to capture the audience's attention for a new operatic work. What has made the opera stand out then and remain so compelling today is its ability to combine these elements seamlessly to present a true reflection of human emotion and desire through horror and violence, death and the hope of new life. In the end, *Lucia* is a work that celebrates the life of a defenceless woman and an ill-fated man, two of the unlikeliest of individuals to meet and to fall in love. This handbook, therefore, is a guide to the treasures within *Lucia* that make it the *nonplus ultra* of *bel canto* opera, providing further evidence for its popularity among singers, audiences and directors today.

Notes

1. Howard Taubman, 'Music: "Lucia" at the "Met"; Maria Callas in Her Third Title Role', *The New York Times*, 4 December 1956, L51. American-born soprano Maria Callas (1923–77) is largely considered the finest interpreter of Lucia in the twentieth century. Ever since her debut performance of the role in Mexico City in 1952, Callas paved the way for full-voiced sopranos to sing Lucia not only as a showpiece for vocal agility but for its overall dramatic potential to convey true human emotion. In fact, due to her unique vocal timbre, Callas is often cited as the one who redefined coloratura in the twentieth century as a 'vocal allegory of passion and pain' and not simply as 'an instrumental virtuosity [or] a vocal frill' (Rodolfo Celletti, 1978); quoted in Marco Beghelli, 'Maria Callas and the Achievement of an Operatic Vocal Subjectivity', in *The Female Voice in the Twentieth Century: Material, Symbolic and Aesthetic Dimensions*, eds. Serena Facci and Michela Garda (New York: Routledge, 2021), 45.
2. William Ashbrook, *Donizetti and His Operas* (Cambridge: Cambridge University Press, 1982), 95.
3. It is questionable whether Donizetti received approval to work on Cammarano's libretto by May 1835. The libretto was officially submitted to the censors for approval on 10 August 1835, which would mean that Donizetti went against protocol and began setting the opera well before it was approved by theatre administrators on 12 September 1835. As gleaned from Donizetti's personal correspondence, however, the composer was quite frustrated with the delay from theatre officials and thus took matters into his own hands; see *Lucia di Lammermoor: drama tragico in tre atti di Salvadore*

Cammarano [critical edition], ed. Gabriele Dotto and Roger Parker (Milan: Casa Ricordi, 2021), I, xxv–i.

4. Dotto and Parker, I, xxv.
5. The two other well-known Italian librettists at the time were Felice Romani (1788–1865) and Gaetano Rossi (1774–1855), who wrote librettos for the operas of Rossini, Bellini, Donizetti and many others. For an assessment of Cammarano's career and where Lucia fits within his overall output, see John Black, *The Italian Romantic Libretto: A Study of Salvadore Cammarano* (Edinburgh: Edinburgh University Press, 1984), 291–306.
6. Dotto and Parker, I, xxvi–ii.
7. Ashbrook, 99. Further evidence of the financial and administrative challenges that plagued the San Carlo at this time was the contractual dispute with the glass harmonica player who was set to perform in the 'mad scene' at the premiere (see Chapter 3).
8. For a detailed list of the changes that occurred during rehearsal, see Dotto and Parker, I, xxvi–ii.
9. See, for example, Catherine Clément, *Opera, or the Undoing of Women*, trans. Betsy Wing (Minneapolis, MN: University of Minnesota Press, 1988), 87–90; Susan McClary, *Feminine Endings: Music, Gender, and Sexuality* (Minneapolis, MN: University of Minnesota Press, 1991), 80–98; Mary Ann Smart, 'The Silencing of Lucia', *Cambridge Opera Journal* 4/2 (1992): 119–41; Heather Hadlock, 'Sonorous Bodies: Women and the Glass Harmonica', *Journal of the American Musicological Society* 53/3 (2000): 507–42; Julie Jaffee Nagel, 'Psychoanalytic and Musical Perspectives on Shame in Donizetti's Lucia di Lammermoor', *Journal of the American Psychoanalytic Association* 56/2 (2008): 551–63; Cormac Newark, *Opera in the Novel from Balzac to Proust* (Cambridge: Cambridge University Press, 2011), 78–109; Jessie Fillerup, 'Lucia's Ghosts: Sonic, Gothic and Postmodern', *Cambridge Opera Journal* 28/3 (2016): 313–45; and Mark A. Pottinger, 'Lucia and the Auscultation of Disease in Mid-Nineteenth-Century France', *Nineteenth-Century Music Review* 19/1 (2022): 55–83.
10. Legendary performances by leading sopranos of every generation since the opera's debut have contributed greatly to Lucia's success. Although beyond the scope of this book, the performance history of Lucia is literally a 'who's who' of the opera world; see, for example, Peter Clark, 'From the Archives: Lucia di Lammermoor at the Met', https://www.metopera.org/discover/archives/notes-from-the-archives/from-the-archives-lucia-di-lammermoor-at-the-met/ (accessed 1 December 2024).
11. William Ashbrook, 'Popular Success, the Critics and Fame: The Early Careers of Lucia di Lammermoor and Belisario', Cambridge Opera

Journal 2/1 (1990): 65–81; Romana Margherita Pugliese, 'The Origins of Lucia di Lammermoor's Cadenza', *Cambridge Opera Journal* 16/1 (2004): 23–42; Smart, 'The Silencing of Lucia'; Rebecca Harris-Warrick, 'Lucia Goes to Paris: A Tale of Three Theaters', in *Music, Theater, and Cultural Transfer: Paris, 1830–1914*, eds. Annegret Fauser and Mark Everist (Chicago: Chicago University Press, 2009), 195–227 and Pottinger, 'Lucia and the Auscultation of Disease'.

12. Simon Stone's production at The Metropolitan Opera premiered on 23 April 2022; see Joshua Barone, 'Risking Boos, the Met Opera Puts Present-Day America Onstage', *The New York Times*, 22 April 2022.

ACKNOWLEDGEMENTS

Writing a book on a well-known opera is both thrilling and daunting. *Lucia* is a key work within the *bel canto* repertoire and as such it has been a ready object for analysis, performance, discussion and reception within and outside opera studies, but strangely, the work has never enjoyed a full-length study until now.

I would like to thank the editor of the New Cambridge Music Handbooks series, Nicole Grimes, for trusting me with this project and for her continual encouragement and support throughout the drafting, research and writing. I am also indebted to colleagues who have probed, questioned and supported my thoughts on *Lucia* over the years, including Hilary Poriss and Mary Ann Smart. I am equally indebted to the anonymous reader who read through the book in draft form and provided wonderful insights on nineteenth-century Italy, Donizetti and the *bel canto* tradition.

The research for this present study has benefitted greatly from the vast resources available to me as a New York Public Library Research Fellow at Columbia University in New York City. I am grateful to the librarians and to the staff who helped me track down various nineteenth-century sources that appear in print or within online depositories. I am also grateful to the Joseph Kerman Fund and General Fund of the American Musicological Society, supported in part by the National Endowment for the Humanities and the Andrew W. Mellon Foundation. Their financial support has helped to offset the cost for the use of the Ricordi critical edition, whose examples are reproduced throughout the book.

Thanks also go to my student assistant for his many hours of scanning scores and illustrations and to my colleagues at Manhattan University, who afforded me the necessary time to complete the book. Last and certainly not least, I thank my wife Kristine, my family and the many dear friends who accompanied me on numerous nights to the opera. This handbook is dedicated to all who find opera an art form like no other, a rich resource for cultural contemplation, sonic amusement, visual wonder and the celebration of the sheer power of the human voice.

A NOTE ON EDITIONS AND TRANSLATIONS

A definitive autograph score is elusive in early nineteenth-century Italian opera. The score of an Italian opera at this time was viewed as a working document, written very quickly. It would principally rely upon the singer's ability and the various instrumentalists on hand to define the work for audiences and publishers alike. *Lucia* is no exception. Thankfully, a modern edition of *Lucia di Lammermoor* appeared in 2021 published by Casa Ricordi and edited by Gabriele Dotto and Roger Parker. This two-volume critical edition of the orchestral score and libretto gathered all known sources of the opera and brought together what can arguably be said to be the most trusted source in defining the notes, rhythms, words and performance practice (e.g., slurs, instrumentation, dynamics, tempo) heard at the time of the premiere and presented in subsequent revivals throughout the nineteenth century. Therefore, the Dotto and Parker edition is used throughout this handbook and is referenced frequently, especially the 'Historical Introduction' and 'Critical Commentary' found in volumes 1 and 2, respectively.

An early English-language version of the libretto provides the majority of the translations.[1] In addition, owing to its common presence in libraries and its frequent use by singers in the English-speaking world, the G. Schirmer piano-vocal score (1898) in Italian with English translation by Natalia Macfarren is used to enrich the translation of the libretto and to provide several musical examples of *Lucia* where needed. The Schirmer score is in fact a reprint of the 1871 London-based Novello, Ewer and Co. edition but with an additional introductory essay by E. Irenaeus Stevenson, an American author and music critic for *Harper's Weekly*. Musical examples also appear from a Ricordi edition of the piano-vocal score, which first appeared in 1835 and was later edited by Mario Parenti (1960) and reprinted in 1973.

Note

1. 'Lucia di Lammermoor' Salvadore Cammarano, [sic]: Salvadore Cammarano, *'Lucia di Lammermoor' di Salvatore Cammerano [sic]: Lucy of Lammermoor, a Tragic Drama in Three Acts, the Music of Donizetti, as Represented at Palmo's New York Opera House, January 1847*, trans. Joseph Attinelli (New York: Piercy & Houel, 1847). (New York: Piercy & Houel, 1847).

OPERA SUMMARY[1]

Characters

Lucia Ashton: Soprano
Enrico Ashton (brother of Lucia): Baritone
Edgardo Ravenswood (lover of Lucia and last surviving
Ravenswood): Tenor
Lord Arturo Bucklaw (bridegroom of Lucia): Tenor
Raimondo (tutor, chaplain and confidant of Lucia): Bass
Alisa (Lucia's friend and handmaid): Mezzo-Soprano
Normanno (captain of the castle guard): Tenor
Historical Setting: Lammermoor, Scotland, Late Sixteenth Century

Part One in One Act[2]

The Departure [Act I]

(Scenes 1–3, near the castle grounds): An intruder has been spotted near the Ashton family home (formerly the home of the Ravenswood clan). Normanno sends soldiers off in search of the stranger. Enrico arrives on the scene troubled. His family's fortunes are in danger; only the arranged marriage of his sister, Lucia, with Lord Arturo Bucklaw can save the family. Raimondo, Lucia's tutor and confidant, reminds Enrico that Lucia is still mourning the death of their mother. But Normanno reveals that Lucia is concealing a love for Edgardo Ravenswood, the mortal enemy of the Ashton clan. Enrico is furious and swears revenge. The search party returns and explains that they have seen and identified the intruder; it is Edgardo. Enrico's fury increases.

(Scenes 4 and 5, near a fountain): At dusk, just as the sun sets and the moon begins to rise, Lucia and her companion Alisa are waiting for Edgardo. Lucia tells Alisa that in this very spot, near the fountain, she saw the ghost of a woman. Lucia explains that the woman was murdered by a jealous lover, a member of the

Ravenswood clan. Alisa urges her to forget Edgardo, but Lucia insists that her love for Edgardo can overcome all, even ghostly visions. Edgardo arrives and explains that he must depart for France on a political mission to secure Scotland's future. Before he leaves, he wants to make peace with Enrico. Lucia, fearing her brother's anger, asks Edgardo to keep their love a secret. Edgardo agrees and they exchange wedding rings by the fountain under a full moon. Edgardo departs for France, while Lucia returns to the castle.

Part Two in Two Acts

Act I: The Nuptial Agreement [Act II]

(Scenes 1–3, Enrico's residential apartments): Some months have passed. It is the day of Lucia's wedding to Lord Bucklaw. Normanno assures Enrico that he has successfully intercepted all correspondence between Lucia and Edgardo and has taken the liberty to create a forged letter, which indicates that Edgardo has fallen in love with another woman. As Normanno leaves to welcome the wedding guests, Lucia enters. Although she is starting to lose her grip on reality, Lucia remains resolute in her refusal to marry Lord Bucklaw. Enrico, out of desperation, shows Normanno's forged letter to Lucia. Seeing that Lucia is affected by the letter, Enrico insists that she must marry Arturo to save the family. As Enrico leaves, Raimondo enters and urges Lucia to think of her late mother and to fulfill her duty to her family. Lucia finally agrees to marry Arturo.

(Scenes 4–6, a gathering hall in the castle): As the wedding guests arrive, Enrico explains to Arturo that Lucia is still mourning their mother's death. Lucia enters and reluctantly signs the nuptial agreement. Suddenly, Edgardo bursts into the hall, claiming his bride, which causes Lucia to faint. The entire wedding party is outraged. Arturo and Enrico order Edgardo to leave but he insists that he and Lucia are already married. When Raimondo shows him the wedding contract with Lucia's signature, Edgardo curses her, takes off his ring and gives it back to Lucia. This prompts Lucia, who is still confused after waking from her faint, to give Edgardo back his ring. He seizes the ring from Lucia and tosses it at her feet, stepping on it in disgust. Edgardo leaves. Lucia is overcome with emotion and faints a second time.

Act II: [After] The Nuptial Agreement [Act III]

(Scenes 1 and 2, Edgardo's broken-down home on the Wolf's Crag, near the sea): It is night, a powerful storm rages outside. Enrico visits Edgardo and taunts him with news that Lucia and Arturo are in bed together. Enrico continues his insults and challenges Edgardo to a duel to take place at dawn 'among the icy tombs of Ravenswood'. Edgardo agrees.

(Scenes 3–6, a banqueting hall in the castle): Raimondo interrupts the wedding festivities with news that Lucia has gone mad and killed Arturo. Lucia enters the hall in her nightdress, covered in blood. Moving between joy and horror, she recalls her meeting with Edgardo at the fountain and hallucinates that she is now with him on their wedding night. She vows that she will never be happy without him and that she will see him in Heaven. When Enrico enters, he moves to strike Lucia but soon realizes she has lost her mind. After some exchange, Lucia collapses and is taken to her bedroom.

(Scenes 7–9, the Ravenswood graveyard): It is dawn. Edgardo laments the loss of Lucia's love and awaits his duel with Enrico, who he hopes will end his life and bring him peace. Guests leaving the castle tell Edgardo that Lucia is near death and has called out his name. As he rushes to the castle to see her, Raimondo appears and tells him that Lucia is already dead. Determined to join her in Heaven, Edgardo kills himself with a knife. Raimondo and the men of Lammermoor pray for his soul.

Notes

1. The opera summary is compiled from the original published libretto by Salvadore Cammarano, *Lucia di Lammermoor, dramma tragico in due parti* (Naples: Tipografia Flautino, 1835) as well as *Lucy of Lammermoor, a Tragic Drama in Three Acts*, trans. Joseph Attinelli (New York: Piercy & Houel, 1847). The story and characters are adapted from Sir Walter Scott's historical novel, *The Bride of Lammermoor* (1819).

2. The libretto was originally divided into two parts: part one was titled 'The Departure' and part two was titled the 'Nuptial Agreement', which was constructed as two co-dependent acts – the before and after. The opera is customarily performed today as three independent acts.

SOURCE STUDIES

Scour the grounds . . . the sprawling ruins of the tower . . .
tear away the veil of this terrible mystery.

(Act I, Normanno)[1]

The Scottish Setting

In early nineteenth-century Italy, Scotland was often depicted in opera as a distant sea-swept land filled with mystery and ancient tales, a picturesque setting for popular works such as Johann Simon Mayr's *Ginevra di Scozia* (1801) and Rossini's *La donna del Lago* (1819). Scotland was also a well-used location by Cammarano, the librettist of *Lucia*, especially when problems with the Neapolitan theatrical censors arose. For example, in an effort to defuse the political elements within the French play *Le proscrit* ['The Outcast'] (1839) when turning it into the Italian opera *Il proscritto* (1842, with music by Saverio Mercadente), Cammarano changed the action from France (around the time of Napoleon's defeat) to Scotland in the 1650s and the time of Lord Oliver Cromwell (1599–1658). As John Black speculates, 'perhaps this was considered so far-flung and outlandish a country that any degree of treason could be perpetuated without threatening the security of the Bourbon occupancy of the throne or the moral welfare of the people'.[2] Fortunately, for *Lucia*, which is set in Scotland, no geographical changes were requested by the Neapolitan censors. The only alteration required of the original text was the change of Raimondo's profession from a Presbyterian minister to a 'tutor and confidant', presumably because the censors did not wish to see a member of the Church of Scotland depicted on an Italian stage.[3]

The historical setting of the opera was a different matter. Part of a collection of historical novels that highlight Scottish rural life in the late 1600s and early 1700s, *The Bride of Lammermoor* is set during the time of the Treaty of Union (1707), when Scotland and England became one state, the United Kingdom of Great Britain. Although Walter Scott's historical setting has little to do with the actual action within the novel, the book is framed by the setting nonetheless, so much so that at the start of the book, the Ravenswood clan is stripped of its lordship and lands after supporting the deposed King James VII (1688), the last Catholic monarch of England, Scotland and Ireland. The Scottish throne thus went to the Protestant William of Orange (William III) and Mary II, Queen Regent, who were supported by the Ashton clan. As the Ravenswood estate came up for sale, Sir Ashton purchased the land and took control of the castle and all its contents. He even tried to prevent Edgar Ravenswood, the last surviving member of the Ravenswood clan, from burying his father in the family crypt. Hence, the bitter conflict that ensues when Edgar (Edgardo) and Lucy Ashton (Lucia) become lovers.

Cammarano's libretto is set at the end of the sixteenth century, a whole century before the action of Scott's novel.[4] If we are to take Cammarano's historical backdrop at face value, then the opera takes place during the time of Mary, Queen of Scots, or Mary Stuart (1542–87) the daughter of James V of Scotland. When James died, Mary inherited the throne before her first birthday. Ruled by regents until she was old enough to claim the Scottish throne, Mary was sent to France, her mother's birthplace, where she was raised a Catholic and married Francis II, King of France. When Francis II died in 1560, Mary returned to Scotland a year later to claim the throne. Scotland had become decidedly Protestant in her absence, breaking with the Roman Catholic Church. Mary was eventually forced to abdicate the throne in 1567 and sought refuge with her cousin Queen Elizabeth I. Suspecting her of treason, Elizabeth had Mary beheaded in 1587.

Following her death, Mary Stuart was a popular subject among European Catholics, with books and plays appearing soon after her death.[5] She was viewed by many as a martyr of the faith – the legitimate ruler of England and Scotland owing to Henry VIII's break with the Catholic Church to marry Anne Boleyn, the mother of Elizabeth I. Mary Stuart was also the subject of a number of operas throughout the nineteenth century, especially in Italy, where Donizetti even set a version of the tale that premiered at La Scala on 30 December 1835 as *Maria Stuarda*, just a few months after the premiere of *Lucia*.[6] Although it did not achieve great success in the nineteenth century, Donizetti's opera on the Scottish queen is a familiar work among opera fans today, who often refer to it as one of the three 'Tudor Queens' of Donizetti, which also includes *Anna Bolena* (1830), second wife of Henry VIII, and *Roberto Devereux* (1837), lover of Queen Elizabeth I.

Serving neither as a mistaken translation nor a mere coincidence, I believe the historical backdrop to *Lucia* was intentionally set by Cammarano to the time of Mary Stuart. There are two examples in the libretto that support this conclusion, namely in Act I, scene 5, as Edgardo mentions to Lucia that he has a political mission in France to secure Scotland's future, and in Act II, scene 2, as Enrico voices his frustrations to Lucia that if Mary ascends the throne, it would be disastrous for the Ashton family.[7] The implication here is that the Ravenswood family is Catholic (in compliance with the Scott original) and a supporter of Mary's reign, while the Ashton family is Protestant and a supporter of a Scotland independent of continental influences. (Note that Raimondo, Peter Bide-the-Bent in Scott's novel, is a Presbyterian minister who serves the Ashton clan.) In addition, situating Edgardo as the only supporter of Mary in the opera helps to endear him to Catholic audiences. His departure from Lucia at the end of Act I to take up his mission in France is thus better understood and perhaps excused owing to its importance to Scotland's future and the Catholic cause. And coupled with the fact that he remains the last surviving Ravenswood – living in a broken-down tower on his former family estate – Edgardo's departure highlights a sympathetic connection to Mary Stuart and her fight for legitimacy.

The Gothic

The gothic, as a literary genre or style of writing, was richly defined in the late eighteenth and early nineteenth centuries, representing a varied response to the irrational, unseen and superstitious elements within nature and the human soul.[8] Matthew Gregory Lewis's gothic novel *The Monk* (1796), for example, presents an understanding of human moral truth that is attained through supernatural horror and extreme sexual desire, all set within the context of the Spanish Inquisition in the fifteenth century.[9] Ann Radcliffe, the famous author of many gothic novels in her day (e.g., *The Mysteries of Udolpho*, 1794 or *The Italian*, 1796) often sought to rationalize the terror-filled elements in her works by revealing the cruelty of Catholic institutions or of wanton men.[10] Although first arising in the British Isles and then spreading throughout Europe, the gothic came slowly to Italy owing much to the fact that 'in the absence of a unified nation and in a context of linguistic de-territorialisation, literate élites [e.g., Alessandro Manzoni] conceptualise[d] Italianness as the un-mediated legacy of Classical tradition in the name of "reason"'.[11] One of the consequences of such a position, as the Italian literary scholar Fabio Camilletti argues (quoting Manzoni), 'is the unappealable refusal ... of the "irrational" and "superstitious" drives of the "Northern" cultures ... [which] Italian literature should irrevocably reject [and] find an "Italian way" to literary modernity based, instead, on rationalism, aesthetic measure and avoidance of excess'.[12] However, despite the lack of a true gothic tradition in Italy, the country still remained the setting of many gothic novels, owing to its strong connection to the Classicism of the past and the Catholic Church, which was viewed by gothic writers in Northern Europe as an institution filled with cruel and ancient mysteries. In fact, gothic writers strengthened the stereotype of Italy as a violent and backward environment by 'creating and exploiting what would soon become the typical gothic paraphernalia, made of ruined castles, ghosts, dark forest, sentimental heroines, wicked villains and the dramatic landscapes of the Alps and Apennines'.[13] Thus, although the gothic was not prevalent in Italian writing in the first half of the nineteenth century, the gothic was still known to many Italians owing to the proximity between the fictional Italy of the past and the real Italy of the present in the work of gothic writers. Indeed, the very notion of the gothic is one that appears to focus on the liminal space between the irrational and the rational, the performative and the real, making Italy a ripe space in the early nineteenth century for the reception of the gothic in opera.[14]

Although it was never performed during the composer's lifetime, Donizetti's first attempt at the horror-filled conventions of the gothic was the opera *Gabriella di Vergy* (1826), from a libretto written by Andrea Leone Tottola and based on a late eighteenth-century French play of the same name.[15] The opera is set in France during the time of the Crusades, where false love, imprisonment, murder, madness and a blood-soaked heart ripped from a lover's chest all make an appearance. The use of violent medieval settings and various horrific plot elements was somewhat new to Italian opera librettos in the 1820s (e.g., Rossini's *Matilde di Shabran*, 1821) and thus created the opportunity for composers like Donizetti to experiment with the loosening of conventional forms and musical gestures in their works for the stage.[16] This was certainly the case with *Lucia*, where one finds several gothic elements that serve to haunt Lucia and thus become a powerful resource in relaying the dramatic potential of Donizetti's music (see Chapter 3 for a discussion of the score in relation to the sound of the gothic).

In keeping with the gothic elements in *The Bride of Lammermoor*, Scott indicates in the introduction to the novel that the story of Lucy Ashton was based on a tale he heard as a child about Janet Dalrymple (d. 1669), the daughter of James, First Viscount of Stair and Dame Margaret Ross, who apparently practiced witchcraft.[17] In spite of her secret engagement to a Lord Rutherford, 'who was not acceptable to them either on account of his political principles or his want of fortune' (ix), Janet Dalrymple was forced by her mother to marry a David Dunbar of Baldoon (in Southeast Scotland). On the night of Janet's wedding to David, she stabbed him and was quickly taken away and deemed insane. David survived but Janet died some weeks later.[18]

Scott expanded the story of Janet Dalrymple and filled it with much of the gothic machinery that appeared in British novels since the late-eighteenth century, including a persecuted heroine, a brooding lover, an ancient castle, prophesies of death and foreboding, three witches, a ghost and a fountain that bears a legend of a murdered watery nymph (see Figure 1.1).[19] Many of these same

RAVENSWOOD AND LUCY AT THE MERMAIDEN'S WELL.

As they arose to leave the fountain which had been the witness of their mutual engagement, an arrow whistled through the air, and struck a raven perched on the sere branch of an old oak.—PAGE 193.

Figure 1.1 Charles Robert Leslie, 'Ravenswood and Lucy at the Mermaiden's Well', illus., in Walter Scott, *The Bride of Lammermoor* (Edinburgh: Adam & Charles Black, 1886), 193.

plot elements appear in Cammarano's libretto, where they all coalesce around a so-called Siren Fountain, which makes its first appearance in Act I, scene 4; the stage setting is as follows:

A park. At the back of the stage, a side of a castle with a passable small door. At the front of the stage is the so-called 'Siren Fountain', which was once covered by a beautiful structure, decorated with architectural ornaments of a Gothic character, but it is now surrounded by the remnants of that construction. The top has fallen in, the sides are all ruined and the spring that gushes out from under the ground has opened a gap between the stones and the rubble, creating a small stream. It is dusk. The moon rises.[20]

The fountain has an auspicious history within the novel (chapter 5) for it is the location where a member of the Ravenswood clan (Raymond Ravenswood) fell in love with a young watery nymph, a naiad, who would appear every Friday to greet him. After spending the day together, the woman would depart at the sound of a bell from a nearby hermitage that would toll at the start of vespers. In his attempt to retain the mysterious woman and to determine her true intentions, Raymond conspired to have the bell toll a half hour later. When the next Friday came, she appeared and greeted Raymond as before. Later, as she began to perceive shadows growing on the ground and the sun nearly set, the naiad shrieked and ripped herself from Raymond's arms and dove down into the fountain. As Raymond looked to find her, a pool of blood appeared in the water, evidence to Raymond that she had died a gruesome death.

In an effort to memorialize her, Raymond adorned the fountain with symbols of sirens and built a protection around the fountain to secure it from harm. Filled with grief and remorse, Raymond later sought death in battle. From this point on in the telling of the tale, Scott writes, 'the house of Ravenswood was supposed to have dated its decay'.[21] However, as Scott further explains, which is a true sign of the gothic, where the perception of truth and fiction are deliberately confused in the telling and retelling of the tale, the supernatural origins of the fountain were eventually explained away by some who believed Raymond fell into a jealous rage and killed his lover who he suspected of betrayal. And yet, according to Scott:

All agreed that the spot was fatal to the Ravenswood family; and that to drink of the waters of the well, or even approach its brink, was as ominous to a descendant of that house as for a Grahame to wear green, a Bruce to kill a spider, or a St. Clair to cross the Ord on a Monday.[22]

In the novel, when Edgar rescues Lucy from the wild bull near his ancient home, he brings her to the fountain so she may gather her wits and catch her breath. And it is here, of course, that he and Lucy fall in love and later declare themselves husband and wife. The fountain, therefore, similar to its appearance in the opera, has a clear ominous connection to the past, bringing forth an ancient legend in order to make it relevant to the present-day lives of the characters in our story, a sure sign of the gothic.

Returning to the opera and picking up from where Scott's legend ends, the scene at the fountain has Lucia and Alisa looking for Edgardo. While scanning the area, Lucia sees the fountain and tells Alisa that at this very spot she saw the ghost of a dead woman, murdered by a jealous lover, a member of the Ravenswood clan:

> At dead of night,
> in the silent darkness,
> as a pale beam of eerie moonlight
> fell upon the fountain,
> a low groan was heard on the breeze,
> and there on the verge, ah!
> the spectre appeared to me ... Ah!
>
> I saw her lips move
> as if she were speaking,
> and with her lifeless hand
> she seemed to beckon me to come;
> for a moment she stood motionless,
> then suddenly vanished,
> and the waters, so clear before,
> were reddened with blood.[23]

Lucia is the only one who has seen the ghost and thus is the first and only individual to speak of its existence. Alisa, the only other character in the opera who knows of Lucia's vision, believes that Lucia's ghost is a sign, a supernatural omen or a warning that her relationship with Edgardo is doomed. Nonetheless, Lucia's vision of a woman murdered by the hand of a jealous lover (and a Ravenswood lover at that) makes Lucia even more desperate to place her hope in Edgardo, who, she believes, will save her from a similar fate.

In contrast to the opera, the ghost in the novel is that of 'Old Alice', a blind former servant of the Ravenswood clan who has the ability to see the future.[24] Earlier in the book, Alice warns both Lucy (Lucia) and Edgar (Edgardo) that their relationship will fail (chapter 19). When Alice later dies (presumably from old age), her ghost appears to Edgar at the same fountain where he and Lucy were engaged (chapter 23). And, similar to the ghost story in *Lucia*, when the ghost appears, she motions with a raised hand, a possible warning, but does not speak before disappearing. Not knowing if what he saw was real, Edgar rushes off to see if Alice is still alive. When he arrives at her cottage, he sees Alice's dead body attended by three witches. This is the last we read of the ghost in the novel. The same can be said for the opera, for the ghost never truly 'appears' on stage, only within the mind of Lucia (in both Acts I and III). Whether the ghost is real or not is never questioned by Lucia or Alisa but understood and accepted as a possible reality within their gothic environment. And yet, although the ghost does not have any lines in the original libretto, nor is it discussed in reviews of the opera from the first half of the nineteenth century, in modern productions of *Lucia* it is customary to have the ghost mimed on stage to remind the audience of what Lucia is seeing. For example, the opera director Mary Zimmerman's 2007 popular production of *Lucia* at The Metropolitan Opera has the ghost appear twice on stage as a blue-lit, pale-faced visitor who motions to Lucia.[25]

Cammarano's libretto also retains Scott's original curse of divine retribution when a solemn vow is broken. In chapter 20 of Scott's novel, Edgar and Lucy exchange two halves of a broken coin, a symbol of their union. In Act I of the opera, Cammarano has the couple exchange rings, which he explains in the published libretto with the following note:

During the period in which this story is set, it was a general belief in Scotland that whoever broke a ceremoniously sworn vow was liable to divine punishment, which would be carried out almost at the same time as the breaking of the vow.

For this reason, lovers' oaths were not things to be taken lightly at the time; they had at least the significance of a wedding. The most common of these ceremonies was that the lovers broke a coin in two and each kept one half. That has, however, been substituted here for an exchange of rings as it is more suitable for the scene.[26]

The fact that Cammarano felt the need to include this note is indicative of his desire to stay true to Scott's original text but also, and more importantly, to have the audience register the significance of the curse to the plot.

Twice in the libretto we are reminded of the curse. The first time is at the end of Act I, when the lovers say their goodbyes, which prompts Edgardo to remind Lucia that 'we are now bound by Heaven' (see Example 1.1). We see in the orchestral score that the majority of the orchestra is silenced as the brass and woodwinds (trumpets, horns and bassoons) alone accompany Edgardo's fateful reminder, which when combined with a syllabic vocal line set to a high G4, gives the curse a strong foreboding sonic presence. The implication is that if they break their vows, they will invite God's wrath.

The second time the curse appears is in Act II, when Lucia tells Raimondo that she cannot marry Lord Bucklaw because of her vow to Edgardo. Raimondo rebuffs this claim by reminding Lucia that 'neither Heaven nor the world recognizes wedding vows that God's minister does not bless'.[27] In the next scene, when Lucia does sign the nuptial agreement to marry Lord Bucklaw, she proclaims, 'I have signed my death warrant', an acknowledgement perhaps of the curse itself. This fear is quickly realized by the arrival of Edgardo, who, after verifying Lucia's signature on the marriage contract, pronounces the curse: 'Heaven and love you have now betrayed . . . may the angry hand of God destroy you.'[28] Musically, Edgardo's words are set in the high register of the voice; the climax of the phrase (A4) is on the words 'cursed' [maledetto] (see Example 1.2). Accompanied once again by brass and woodwinds, the curse takes on a truly gothic presence here. In fact, in Donizetti's letter to Ricordi, he was surprised by the audience's immediate reaction to it (sung by Gilbert Duprez) in the midst of an ensemble number, which is further evidence of the

Example 1.1 Gaetano Donizetti, *Lucia di Lammermoor* [Orchestral Score], Act I, scene 5, No. 3: Scena e Duetto Finale, bb. 351–61. **Lucia di Lammermoor**. Words and Music by Gaetano Donizetti; Critical Edition by Gabriele Dotto and Roger Parker. Copyright © 2022 Casa Ricordi Srl, part of Universal Music Publishing Classics & Screen. This arrangement Copyright © 2024 Casa Ricordi Srl, part of Universal Music Publishing Classics & Screen All Rights Reserved. Used by Permission. *Reprinted by permission of Hal Leonard LLC.*

Example 1.2 Gaetano Donizetti, *Lucia di Lammermoor* [Orchestral Score], Act II, scene 6, No. 6: Finale Alto Secondo, bb. 348–52. **Lucia di Lammermoor**. Words and Music by Gaetano Donizetti; Critical Edition by Gabriele Dotto and Roger Parker. Copyright © 2022 Casa Ricordi Srl, part of Universal Music Publishing Classics & Screen. This arrangement Copyright © 2024 Casa Ricordi Srl, part of Universal Music Publishing Classics & Screen All Rights Reserved. Used by Permission. *Reprinted by permission of Hal Leonard LLC.*

dramatic importance of the curse to the libretto and its appreciation in the score.[29]

Filled with religious superstition, ancient tales of watery nymphs, forbidden love and murder, Scott's novel is one that Cammarano exploits to provide a gothic setting to the libretto. His use of the legend of the fountain, the marriage vow, the promise of God's wrath if it be broken and the lone appearance of the ghost of a woman, who (legend has it) a Ravenswood killed, all create a dark mystery within the opera and one that presents a competing narrative to the family rivalry between the Ashtons and the Ravenswoods. This mystery is never truly answered in the opera but is left open for interpretation by both the characters in the opera and the audience. We never truly know if the ghost is real, nor if Lucia dies due to the curse or whether the fountain is filled with such potent energy that any vow made near it is in direct response to the wrongs of the past. And so the libretto to *Lucia* remains a true reflection of the gothic genre, a mixture of both the real and unreal, the past and present, the internal and external, which, although centered on the fountain, are all conveniently located within and around Lucia, making her perception of reality the main psychological focus for the work.

The Persistence of Death

It was not uncommon in Italian *bel canto* to be reminded of the persistence of death in everyday life. Death finds its way in many Italian works of the time, including (to name a few) Bellini's *I Capuleti e I Montecchi* (1830), *Norma* (1830) and Donizetti's own *Anna Bolena* (1830), *Lucrezia Borgia* (1833), *Rosmonda d'Inghilterra* (1834) and the forementioned *Maria Stuarda* (1835). In *Music in the Present Tense: Rossini's Italian Operas in their Time* (2019), Emanuele Senici argues that the Napoleonic wars 'constituted for a number of Italians a profoundly traumatic experience … a spiritual and moral death', whereby the theatricality of opera and its glorification of a 'good death' was a necessary cathartic resource to comprehend the present.[30] By the 1830s, death appeared to be a constant reality for many Italians, either through the suppression of Italian revolutionary sentiment (e.g., the *carbonari*) by the Austrian army, which resulted in several deadly skirmishes across the peninsula, or the raging cholera epidemic that swept across Europe, the latter of which by 1837 claimed 19,470 lives in Naples alone (18 per cent of the total population).[31] And so, it is not surprising that when Donizetti's opera begins, we are told in the opening scene that Lucia is in mourning, grieving her mother's death, whose grave she often visits.[32]

In Act I, scene 2, Raimondo chides Enrico for trying to marry Lucia off before she is ready: 'Can a mourning virgin, who weeps over a dear mother's recent passing bend her thoughts to the marriage bed? Ah! Let us respect a grieving heart ... when oppressed with such sorrow one cannot feel love.'[33] But then, in Act II, after telling Lucia that he has received no word from Edgardo, Raimondo advises Lucia to marry the man whom her brother has arranged for her, and he does so by using the memory of her dead mother: 'Surrender, or more misfortunes will come to you ... be moved by my tender care, the death of a parent and the impending peril of your brother ... or your mother will turn over in her grave.'[34] To such words, Lucia responds: 'You win ... life will be a long and cruel torment for me'.[35]

The link between Lucia and death continues in the next scene at the wedding ceremony. At the start of scene 4, Arturo is concerned about Lucia's well-being. Enrico assures him that she is fine but advises him not to 'be surprised by her appearance; she still mourns her mother's death'.[36] After Lucia enters the hall and signs the marriage contract, she complains of feeling ill. When Edgardo suddenly appears, Lucia faints and falls into the arms of Raimondo and Alisa. As she slowly recovers, falling in and out of consciousness, Lucia remarks 'with fear I had hoped that my life had ended but death is no help for me; I still live on in torment ... No peace is found in Heaven nor on Earth; both have betrayed me! I would like to cry but I cannot; Ah! even tears are denied me'.[37] No more talk of mourning is heard at this point in the opera, for everyone now sees that the true reality of Lucia's grief is not her mother's death but her own, hastened by the loss of Edgardo, which prompts everyone on stage to proclaim: 'she is like a withered rose, standing between life and death'.[38]

In the penultimate scene of the opera, Lucia appears as a ghost, a 'mostly-dead' woman walking among the living.[39] The libretto states:

Lucia is in a simple white dress: her disheveled hair and the look of death on her face give her more the appearance of a ghost than of a living creature. Her fixed gaze, her convulsive movements and her malevolent smile disclose not only a frightening insanity but also the signs of a life that is drawing to a close.[40]

Her deathly appearance (as seen in similar performances of Ophelia in Shakespeare's *Hamlet* at the time; see Chapter 6) is evident to the wedding party, who collectively respond: 'she looks as if she has risen from the grave'![41] Lucia then sings of her love for Edgardo, but all along, she remains fearful that the ghost from the fountain, a symbol of a lover's betrayal, will separate them. Lucia's final words are, 'I am near the tomb … Already, I feel death's cold breath, but my heart languishes … one heartbeat remains; it is a heartbeat of love! Shed bitter tears on my grave [Edgardo], while up in Heaven, I will pray for you … Only with your arrival will Heaven be a place of beauty for me.'[42]

Death is also a constant companion to Edgardo, the other main victim of this tragic tale. Edgardo first appears in Act I, scene 5, soon after Lucia mentions the ghost to Alisa. He tells Lucia he has to leave Scotland, but before he leaves, he wants to make peace with Enrico and forgive him for killing his father. When Lucia hears Edgardo's anger towards Enrico grow, she tries to calm him, but Edgardo insists on telling her why he is so upset:

> Hear me, and tremble!
> On the grave,
> which entombs the betrayed ashes of my father,
> I, in my fury, swore an eternal war against thy blood –
> but then I saw you,
> in my heart another affection was born,
> and my anger was silent …
> Yet that vow is not broken;
> I may still fulfil it![43]

Donizetti sets Edgardo's lines in a slow, dance-like rhythm within a mixed minor–major mode, which serves as a foil to Lucia's *cavatina* ('Regnava nel silenzio' ['At dead of night']) presented in the previous scene (Lucia's *cavatina* is discussed in Chapter 4). By setting Edgardo's most intimate thoughts in this way, we come to hear the dueling forces on Edgardo's conscience: his love for Lucia and his father's death. Following his opening aria, Edgardo and Lucia agree to exchange wedding rings, promising the other that 'only the icy hand of death shall end our love'.[44] This promise, of course, unites the two lovers both in life and in death and reflects the connection that the opera shares with Shakespeare's *Romeo and Juliet*, namely that their love can only exist in death as familial forces and acts of revenge conspire to keep them apart.

The full circle of Edgardo's death vow comes at the end of the opera as he stands among the tombstones of his dead relatives to take his own life:

> You, who have spread your wings to God,
> O beautiful soul, look not upon me with anger.
> Let thy faithful lover ascend to thee.
> Ah, if on Earth the anger of mortals waged a war against us,
> and kept us divided,
> let God unite us in Heaven.
> I follow you.[45]

It is strange that an opera about a female bride ends with the male lover's death in a kind of reversal of Shakespeare's play, where instead of Juliet killing herself after seeing Romeo's dead body, Edgardo, after hearing of Lucia's death, kills himself with the hope of seeing her again. A possible reason, however, for not having Lucia's death end the opera might simply be in keeping with Scott's original text. In the final chapter of *The Bride of Lammermoor*, after the death and funeral of Lucy, Edgar rides off on horseback to fight Colonel Douglas Ashton (Lucy's older brother).[46] While crossing the beach, an area known as Kelpie's Flow, Edgar is swallowed up in quicksand and dies, which fulfils the prophecy and warning spoken earlier in the book by Edgar's servant.[47] Anyone familiar with Scott's novel would certainly expect the opera to have an ending where Edgardo dies while fulfilling his vow to fight for Lucia. All of which seems to suggest Donizetti and Cammarano, in their effort to be faithful to the source text, cast aside the conventions of Italian opera and ended *Lucia* with Edgardo's death and not the death of the *prima donna*, which was common practice at the time (see Chapter 2 for a discussion of the conventions of Italian *bel canto*).

As we examine the life of Lucia and Edgardo, two lovers at war with themselves and the world, we see that they both greet death with hope. According to Vijay Mishra, the 'gothic sublime' is a type of enlightenment or emotional release from internal forces that enslave one, which are often materialized outside the individual in the form of a ghost or death itself. Only by conquering the 'thing' that has haunted them will one be free of what has held them back, their conscience clear of regret, guilt and fear.[48] If we apply this theory to the opera, we see that Lucia's grief over the death of her mother and Edgardo's grief over the death of his father persist throughout the opera, pulling the lovers apart from their destiny to be together. By conquering death, they are able to transcend the burdens of their past and free themselves to love. However, the price is severe. Lucia kills the man she is forced to marry and dies from the strain, while Edgardo takes his own life. Similar to other lovers in operas before them (e.g., Romeo/Juliet and Norma/Pollione), death is the doorway to a new and happier life, one they both embrace.

Female Madness and Murder

In Scott's novel, it is Lady Ashton, Lucy's mother, who has a tight grip on her daughter's emotions and actions, an abusive relationship that does not allow Lucy to have any independence of action or thought, hence all the misunderstandings, violence and death that occur at the end of the novel. It would seem that the only way out for Lucy is madness, allowing her to break with the reality around her and to escape into her own mind, where she is finally able to take control of her life, albeit a life that swiftly leads to her death. The novel's signature plot element of female madness has a long history within literature, especially gothic literature. It also features strongly in opera, and it is precisely what Cammarano uses to define Lucia's retreat from a world where, in her words, as spoken at the nuptial agreement in Act II: 'I am betrayed by both Heaven and Earth'.[49]

When she first appears on stage, Lucia tells us she had a vision. Although such a vision reflects elements of the gothic (as mentioned earlier), from a medical point of view, Lucia hallucinated. Coupled with the fact that her vision of the ghost does not materialize for the audience nor for any of the principal characters on stage, evidence is clear that Lucia is having severe delusions. Indeed, throughout the opera, Alisa, Enrico, Raimondo, Arturo and Edgardo all voice their concerns over Lucia's mental state and so when she appears at the end of the opera – pale, disheveled, splattered with her victim's blood, convulsing, uttering scattered thoughts – it is no surprise; they all saw it coming.

In the nineteenth century, madness in women was seen more often than not as a symptom of hysteria, understood at the time to be a particular female ailment with a long history of documentation in society.[50] Hysteria was a disease that had both physical and emotional symptoms. If untreated, the individual suffering from the disease would experience muscle contractions, shortness of breath, fever, hallucinations and vocal fits of anger; in short, madness.

One of the more important studies on hysteria in the first half of the nineteenth century was written by the French physician and medical historian Frédéric Dubois d'Amiens (1799–1873), who published *Histoire philosophique de l'hypochondrie et de l'hystérie* [*A Philosophical History of Hypochondria and Hysteria*] in 1833.[51] In this 551-page, award-winning medical treatise, Dubois d'Amiens states that hysteria results from an anemic condition within menstruating women, whereby sudden emotional swings, such as joy, grief, fright or surprise further induce the symptoms of the disease.[52] With this description in mind, one notes that throughout the opera, Lucia is continually referred to as being quite pale and physically frail, which were possible signs to many in the nineteenth century that Lucia, a young woman, ready to bear a child, was menstruating and thus more susceptible to hysteria. For example, in Act II, scene 2, Lucia enters her brother's chambers, lingers by the door and is described in the libretto with a quasi-medical description: 'the

18

paleness of her face, a bewildered expression, everything about her highlights an internal suffering and the first symptoms of mental derangement'.[53] During the ensuing dialogue, she suffers a succession of shocks and is seized by tremors after reading the supposed letter from Edgardo. The libretto describes her appearance: 'surprise and the most excited breathlessness are expressed on her face, followed by a tremor that shakes her from head to toe'.[54] But it is during the *finale* of Act II, just after having signed the nuptial agreement, that she complains of faintness, which indeed occurs right as Edgardo appears. After the *finale*, Lucia loses the strength once again to stand and faints as the curtain falls to end the act. The fact that the libretto continues to define her physical condition, symptoms once again to be diagnosed by the audience and those on stage, highlights the failing health of Lucia.

Decisively, in the last act, in the 'mad scene', Lucia, after murdering her husband, lurches from one hallucination to another: first, she believes she sees Edgardo; then the ghost, who separates her from Edgardo; and then, she senses the presence of enemies who want to destroy her happiness with Edgardo. Next, believing herself safe with Edgardo, Lucia begins to tremble with joy as she hallucinates that she is with him in paradise. This idyll is then shattered by her brother's sudden arrival on stage, triggering a new set of hallucinations in which Lucia relives the moment when Edgardo stomps on the ring and curses her.

The hallucinations that Lucia experiences are what d'Amiens refers to as *hallucinations singulières* [a focused or particular hallucination], an affliction often diagnosed in hysterics.[55] 'The sweet sound' ['il dolce suono'] of Edgardo's voice heard in Lucia's head and sung throughout the 'mad scene' becomes an obsession, a singular focus that helps to rationalize the condition she is facing. When Lucia's 'mad scene' ends, she is taken off to her bedroom, where she quickly succumbs to the final stages of the disease by falling into a state of muteness, where only moans and inarticulate mumblings of Edgardo's name can be heard. According to d'Amiens, *mâchoire de verrouillage* [lock jaw] would have set in and her muscles contracted, leading one to believe that her heart will soon stop.[56]

In this state, Lucia remains at the end of the opera past any hope of medical treatment and dies. In fact, the common cure for female hysterics in the nineteenth century was marriage or rather the so-called 'marriage bed', whereby coitus was generally understood by the medical community as a way to alleviate the symptoms of the disease.[57] Marriage, of course, is the lynchpin to the dramatic action within *Lucia*. It is in marriage that Lucia is defined by her brother and by Raimondo, who both argue in Act II that Lucia must give up her own desires so that others can live. When Lucia kills Arturo, however, she ceases to have value for the men around her. She thus becomes an uncured female hysteric, destined to remain unwed (now widowed), a murderer, a ghost among the living.

In defining her appearance and actions as a madwoman in both the novel and the opera, Scott and Cammarano created a woman who was not simply a diversion from everyday life nor a mere tragic figure, but someone who could be found on the stages of many Italian theatres at the time (e.g., Bellini's *Il Pirata*, *La Sonnambula* and *I Puritani*) or within a nearby asylum, such as the Maddalena Lunatic Asylum in Aversa, just north of Naples.[58] Cammarano knew this to be true as evidenced in a stage manual he wrote for an outside theatre: 'Let the chorus be sure to show themselves full of pity and terror over Lucia's ordeal, and Alisa to keep herself always near at hand, following her with her eyes, as we usually do with unfortunate people who have gone out of their minds.'[59] Mad women were thus pure voyeuristic entertainment or, at best, observed education for those who desired a deeper understanding of what defines health and well-being within society.

Those who visited asylums in the nineteenth century (often on Sundays) included family and friends of the patient, clergy, tourists, actors, philanthropists, subscription holders and government inspectors, who would report on the gender, age and general cause of the patient's malady.[60] A particular example is an 1838 report published from the Maddalena Asylum (see Figure 1.2), written at a time and location consistent with the premiere of *Lucia* at the Teatro di San Carlo. One notes from the Maddalena report that there were two hysteria patients in residence (highlighted). Also,

Causes. As far as could be ascertained, these were as follows:

Physical Causes. Masturbation, male 3; blindness, male 1; venereal excess, male 12; excessive drinking, male 27, female 12; starvation, male 4; insolation, male 2; repelled eruptions, male 6; repelled lactation, female 2; suppressed and irregular menstruation, 28; suppressed gonorrhœa, female 2; syphilis, male 1; piles, male 4; gout, male 2; fever, male 3, female 1; hysteria, 2; encephalitis, male 1; apoplexy, male 9; epilepsy, male 25, female 8; congenital idiocy, male 8, female 2; hereditary madness, male 1; chronic headach, male 1.

Moral Causes. Natural insuperable sadness *(tristezza)*, male 48, female 25; wounded vanity, male 8, female 1; disappointed ambition, male 12, female 4; regrets, male 10, female 2; rage, male 3, female 1; despair, male 1; discouragement *(avvilimento)*, male 2, female 1; fear, male 15, female 9; terror, male 13, female 3; hatred, male 5; religious scruples, male 19, female 13; disappointed hope, male 3, female 2; deluded hope, male 4, female 1; remorse, male 1; infidelity, conjugal, male 4, female 1; jealousy, male 21, female 18; disappointed love, male 28, female 21; nostalgia, male 5; excess in study, male 1; excessive labour, male 1; family quarrels, male 11; domestic anxieties, male 2; ruined fortune, male 24; poverty, male 52, female 31; exalted imagination, male 6, female 3; death of relatives, male 5, female 7; attendance on the insane, male 1; depraved habits, male 4; sensuality, male 8, female 11.

The following is a Table of the per centage of Cases, Cures, and Deaths, for the two decennial periods between 1813 and 1832.

	Periods	Jan.	Feb.	Mar.	Apr.	May	June	July	Aug.	Sep.	Oct.	Nov.	Dec.
Cases,	1	$5\frac{4}{10}$	$4\frac{4}{10}$	$6\frac{2}{10}$	8	$9\frac{8}{10}$	$11\frac{2}{10}$	$10\frac{8}{10}$	$12\frac{5}{10}$	$8\frac{8}{10}$	$7\frac{8}{10}$	$6\frac{8}{10}$	8
	2	$5\frac{1}{10}$	$7\frac{3}{10}$	$7\frac{2}{10}$	$7\frac{2}{10}$	$11\frac{1}{10}$	$11\frac{2}{10}$	$12\frac{8}{10}$	$10\frac{8}{10}$	$8\frac{1}{10}$	$8\frac{3}{10}$	$5\frac{1}{10}$	$4\frac{8}{10}$
Cures,	1	$7\frac{8}{10}$	$2\frac{8}{10}$	$6\frac{8}{10}$	$5\frac{8}{10}$	5	$8\frac{1}{10}$	$11\frac{1}{10}$	8	$12\frac{1}{10}$	$12\frac{4}{10}$	9	$10\frac{8}{10}$
	2	$5\frac{8}{10}$	$6\frac{1}{13}$	$11\frac{2}{10}$	$10\frac{1}{10}$	$7\frac{2}{10}$	$5\frac{8}{10}$	$11\frac{1}{10}$	$8\frac{8}{10}$	$8\frac{8}{10}$	$10\frac{2}{10}$	$9\frac{2}{10}$	$4\frac{8}{10}$
Deaths,	1	$14\frac{4}{10}$	$7\frac{1}{10}$	$9\frac{1}{10}$	$4\frac{8}{10}$	$5\frac{7}{10}$	$3\frac{8}{10}$	$5\frac{2}{10}$	$9\frac{2}{10}$	$7\frac{8}{10}$	9	12	$11\frac{2}{10}$
	2	$13\frac{8}{10}$	12	$7\frac{2}{10}$	$7\frac{1}{10}$	$1\frac{8}{10}$	$6\frac{7}{10}$	$7\frac{8}{10}$	$6\frac{8}{10}$	$6\frac{1}{10}$	$6\frac{8}{10}$	$8\frac{1}{10}$	$10\frac{1}{10}$

The admissions, in the course of these twenty years, have been—men 2,775, women 1,122: total 3,897. The readmissions, from relapses, were—men 22, women 39; total 61, (131 in the paper.) There have escaped, of men 70, women 1; total 71. Relieved and intrusted to their friends, men 369, women 179; total 548. Cured—men 1,072, women 442; total 1514. Dead—men 909, women 313; total 1,222. The number admitted, and of those previously in the hospital, are, to the cured, as 1 to $2\frac{67}{100}$ of the males, and as 1 to $2\frac{43}{100}$ for the females: to the dead, as 1 to $3\frac{14}{100}$ for the males, and as 1 to $3\frac{71}{100}$ for the females. [This is evidently a mistake: it should be, the proportion of cures, &c. to admissions and patients already in confinement; but, for want of the latter element of the computation, or even an average of annual admissions, I cannot prove the correctness of the assertion.—*Translator's note.*]

The deaths for one year were—sanguineous apoplexy, males 14, females 8; apoplexy supervening upon a violent epileptic attack, males 7, females 1; serous apoplexy, females 5; aneurism of the heart, male 1, females 2; angina œsophagæa, male 1; convulsive asthma, male 1, females 4; synochus, males 3, female 1; colliquative diarrhœa, males 8, females 2; dysentery, males 7, females 11; nervous phthisis, males 9, (perhaps marasmus is meant;) phthisis pulmonalis, males 10, females 3; phthisis mesenterica, males 8, females 7; intestinal phthisis, (probably ulceration of Peyer's glands,) female 1; hæmoptysis, male 1; gangrene from lying, male 7; pneumonia, males 2, females 2; hydrothorax, male 1, female 1; ascites, male 1, female 1; anasarca, males 3, females 3. Total males 84, females 52.

Filiatre Sebezio. 1836.

Figure I.2 Felippo Volpicella, 'Statistics of the Lunatic Asylum at Aversa (Naples)', *British and Foreign Medical Review, or, A Quarterly Journal of Practical Medicine* 6 (1838): 239.

the report labels hysteria as a 'physical cause' of madness rather than a 'moral cause', such as 'disappointed love' or 'jealousy'. What this report thus shows is that madness was a symptom of a very real disease and one that was common not only to operas and gothic novels but also to public asylums.

In the end, such accounts of the lives of the mentally ill allowed the reader or viewer to sympathize with those individuals whose humanity was on full display for all to see and hear. In fact, in 1838, a few years after the premiere of *Lucia*, several European courts rewrote the laws that defined the treatment and care of the mentally ill. These so-called 'Lunacy Acts' were passed in England, Ireland and France and were soon imitated by regional legislators in Italy.[61] The new laws were designed for the protection of people with mental illness from abuse and mistreatment. They mandated that every asylum provide a framework for the assistance, care and protection of people with mental illness and eliminate the possibility of detention.[62]

'Lunacy Acts' were a part of a larger asylum reform movement that began during the late 1780s and continued well into the nineteenth century. The French physician Philippe Pinel (1745–1826) is credited as the first to develop such humane treatment, which began soon after the French Revolution by freeing the mentally ill from chained imprisonment, famously depicted in Tony Robert-Fleury's oil painting of 1876 (see Figure 1.3). The painting portrays several stock figures in asylums at the time: a woman (on the ground) tearing at her clothing, two huddled melancholics, a tense maniac, and a woman (at the right) with a vacant stare chained to the wall.[63] In the center is a limp and passive woman being freed from her chains as Dr. Pinel looks on with approval.

The success of Pinel's treatment with the mentally ill was well documented and increasingly became the standard for treating patients within insane asylums.[64] Pinel's work was cited throughout d'Amiens's study on hysteria. In particular, in the section 'Thérapeutique', d'Amiens references Pinel's method of treatment, which argues for the patient to be first brought into dialogue with the physician and then, with the power of

Figure 1.3 Tony Robert-Fleury, 'Pinel, médecine en chef de la Salpêtrière, délivrant les aliénés de leurs chaînes', 1876, Photoengraving on paper based on original oil on canvas, Goupil & Co. Image courtesy of The British Museum, London, UK.

suggestion, the hysteric would come to recognize their own malady and begin the process of healing.[65]

Comparing the treatment that Lucia receives in Act III in the opera to that prescribed by Pinel, one notes that the wedding party does not tackle her, restrain her or even arrest her for the murder of her husband. The individuals on stage simply observe her, albeit in horror, allowing Lucia to wander the stage despite her obvious mental derangement. Even when her brother Enrico rushes in to grab her after she appears in front of the entire wedding party in a night dress stained with Arturo's blood, Raimondo pulls him back and argues, 'Stop! Don't you see her [mental] state?'.[66]

This is in contrast to the Scott original, which has Lucy overpowered by those around her with physical force:

Female assistance was now hastily summoned; the unhappy bride was overpowered, not without the use of some force. As they carried her over the threshold, she looked down, and uttered the only articulate words that she had yet spoken, saying, with a sort of grinning exultation, 'So, you have ta'en up your bonny bridegroom?' She was, by the shuddering assistants, conveyed to another and more retired apartment, where she was secured as her situation required, and closely watched.[67]

Published in 1819 and set in the late seventeenth century, the Scott original text has Lucy endure the same brutal handling that was prevalent among the mentally ill in Europe before the nineteenth century, that is to say, treating them as criminals.[68] Although Lucy did attack her husband with a knife, she does not kill him, only injure him. Nonetheless, the difference in treatment between Lucy and Lucia is stark, a further indication that the 1835 operatic version of the story conformed to the moral treatment generally understood by the medical community at the time, which was further supported by Cammarano's instructions to a stage manager mentioned earlier.

On the issue of murder in the opera, it is important to note that of all the leading female characters in Italian opera who succumb to madness, including Imogene in Vincenzo Bellini's *Il Pirata* of 1827, Anna Bolena in Donizetti's own *Anna Bolena* of 1830, Amina in Bellini's *La Sonnambula* of 1831 and Elvira in Bellini's *I Puritani* of 1835, Lucia is the only one who kills.[69] The fact that Lucy/Lucia commits violence against her husband was and remains the most shocking aspect of the story/opera. The original legend on which Scott based his novel was known primarily due to this violent act, which was presumed to have been aided by supernatural forces or witchcraft.[70] Depending on class and station, in France in particular and Europe in general, a woman in the early nineteenth century who murdered her husband was considered a traitor to the state.[71] As the husband was viewed as the king of the household and the household was viewed as a reflection of the state, such murderous acts were a threat to social order and in need of immediate suppression. In the operatic world, for example, when a woman kills, her own death soon occurs, such as with Lady Macbeth in Verdi's *Macbeth* (1847), Marguerite in Gounod's *Faust* (1859) and Puccini's *Tosca* (1900).[72] When a woman is 'mad', however, society appears to be kind to the killer (e.g., Massenet's *Navarraise*, 1894), a kind of 'insanity defense' soon develops among her would-be accusers, as

24

witnessed in the 'mad scene' in *Lucia*, when Raimondo and the chorus stop Enrico from punishing Lucia owing to her obvious display of madness. Because of this madness, Lucia's murderous act is dismissed, leaving others to be blamed for her actions. The pious-minded Raimondo quickly blames Enrico ('Tremble, cruel man, you are responsible for her life') and Normanno ('Wretch, you spilled blood! You are the cause!'), forcing everyone in the opera to look upon Lucia with pity.[73] One notes in the final scene of the opera, the chorus of men who are leaving the castle do not speak of Arturo or his murder but voice concerns for Lucia, referring to her simply as 'Oh, poor one' [Oh meschina!].

By casting blame on others, Lucia remains a vulnerable creature in the opera and not a reflection of the glorious heroine we have often seen in opera productions since the mid twentieth century (e.g., Maria Callas, Berlin State Opera, 1955 or Nadine Sierra, The Metropolitan Opera, 2022). The reception of the 'mad scene', both in the nineteenth century and today, will be discussed in Chapter 7, but for now, suffice it to say, Lucia's madness did not resonate well with audiences in the first half of the nineteenth century, who saw in the character of Lucia a mad woman to be sure but one that was dismissed in favor of her lover, whose act of suicide was far more laudable and desired.

This chapter set out to define how the Scottish setting, the gothic, the persistence of death and female madness play a part in crafting an early nineteenth-century libretto that bears witness to the creative mind of Cammarano and his socio-cultural environment. The gothic genre and female madness in particular are source texts that are often seized upon by opera directors today, who project contemporary notions of horror and mental illness onto the work that make these areas of the opera loom larger than others (e.g., opera directors Mary Zimmerman, The Metropolitan Opera, 2007 and Katie Mitchell, The Royal Opera House, 2016). It would be desirable, however, to see in future opera productions more of an emphasis on the Scottish setting, especially the religious and political strife that exists between the two families, a conflict that resonates all too well in our ever-increasingly polarized world. Such an emphasis would give greater power to the main forces that keep the two lovers apart and further underline the *Romeo and Juliet* tropes that are found throughout the work, including warring families, doomed love, a misplaced/false letter, a religious man who attempts to counsel both sides and the final murder-suicide.[74]

Notes

1. 'Percorrete le spiagge vicine, della torre le vaste rovine: cada il vel di sì turpe mistero'. Cammarano, 5.
2. Black, *The Italian Romantic Libretto*, 25. Cammarano primarily wrote for the theatres of Naples, which was the capital of the Kingdom of the Two Sicilies (1816–61) and a royal seat of the Spanish Bourbon monarchy, under the protection of Austria.
3. Black, 224, 234–5.
4. Cammarano, 4. Gaetano Barbieri's Italian translation of the Scott novel was used by Cammarano. The translation was published as *La promessa sposa di Lammermoor o Nuovi racconti del mio ostiere* (Milan: V. Ferrario, 1824). Barbieri's translation does adhere to the Scott original and presents the setting of the work as 1689, the time of the Jacobite Rising in the Scottish Highlands (Barbieri, 11). For a summary of the changes or additions to the libretto that depart from Scott's original text, see Joël-Marie Fauquet, *L'Avant-scène opéra*, no. 233: *Lucia di Lammermoor, Donizetti* (Paris: Éditions Premières Loges, 2006), 27–30.
5. See, for example, Rosalind K. Marshall, *Mary Queen of Scots: Truth or Lies* (Edinburgh: St. Andrew Press, 2010) and Allan Massie, *The Royal Stuarts: A History of the Family that Shaped Britain* (New York: St. Martin's Griffin, 2013).
6. See Alexander Weatherson, 'The Stuarts and their Kith and Kin', *Donizetti Society Newsletter* 106/2 (2009): 13–20 and Mary Ann Smart, *Waiting for Verdi: Italian Opera and Political Opinion, 1815–1848* (Oakland, CA: University of California Press, 2018), 60–101, who lists twenty-two works on Tudor subjects read and performed in Italy from 1809 to 1845.
7. More specifically, Enrico proclaims: 'Spento è Guglielmo … a Scozia Comanderà Maria' [William is dead … and Mary will [soon] control Scotland] (Cammarano, 17). Although the pairing of William and Mary in the libretto does appear to reference the late seventeenth-century setting of Scott's novel, Queen Mary II died in 1694, several years before William III's death in 1702. As an alternative, the libretto might be referring to one of several Williams that were members of a group of Protestant Scottish nobles, the so-called Lords of the Congregation, who were opposed to the ascension of

Mary upon her return to Scotland in 1561; see T. Christopher Smout, *A History of the Scottish People, 1560–1830* (London: Collins, 1969), 53.

8. See *The Cambridge Companion to Gothic Fiction*, ed. Jerrold E. Hogle (Cambridge: Cambridge University Press, 2002), 1–20. For a discussion of the gothic in music of the nineteenth century, see Joe Davies, *The Gothic Imagination in the Music of Franz Schubert* (Woodbridge: Boydell Press, 2024) and Francesca Brittan, *Music and Fantasy in the Age of Berlioz* (Cambridge: Cambridge University Press, 2017).

9. See Thomas Grey, 'Music, Theatre and the Gothic Imaginary: Visualizing the "Bleeding Nun"', in *Art, Theatre, and Opera in Paris, 1750–1850: Exchanges and Tensions*, ed. Sarah Hibberd and Richard Wrigley (Burlington, VT: Ashgate, 2014), 77–106.

10. For a comparative study of Lewis and Radcliffe, see Angela Wright, 'Ann Radcliffe and Matthew Lewis', in *The Cambridge History of the Gothic*, I, ed. Angela Wright and Dale Townshend (Cambridge: Cambridge University Press, 2020), 304–22.

11. Fabio Camilletti, 'Gothic Beginnings, 1764–1827', in *Italian Gothic*, ed. Marco Malvestio and Stefano Serafini (Edinburgh: Edinburgh University Press, 2022), 19.

12. Camilletti, 20. Alessandro Manzoni (1785–1873), a poet, philosopher, critic and novelist, is widely considered the father of the Italian romantic tradition in the nineteenth century. His most famous publication is *I promessi sposi* ['The Betrothed'] (1827), a nationalistic work set in the early seventeenth century that captures much of the political and cultural climate in Italy during the time of the *Risorgimento* movement. Manzoni's death was memorialized by Verdi, who composed the *Requiem* in his honour and conducted the premiere at the Church of San Marco (Milan) on 22 May 1874.

13. Massimiliano Demata, 'Italy and the Gothic', *Gothic Studies* 8/1 (2006): 1.

14. See Melina Esse, 'Donizetti's Gothic Resurrections', *19th-Century Music* 33/2 (2009): 81–109 and Sarah Chesney, 'Gothic Imaginations in *Primo Ottocento* Opera', MMus thesis, New Zealand School of Music, Victoria University of Wellington (2010).

15. For description and analysis of the work, see Ashbrook, 297–98 and Esse, 'Donizetti's Gothic Resurrections'. Other gothic-tinged operas that were composed in the 1820s and became widely successful throughout the nineteenth century include Carl Maria von Weber's *Der Freischütz* (1821), François-Adrien Boieldieu's *Le dame blanche* (1825) and Heinrich Marchner's *Der Vampyr* (1828).

16. See Ashbrook, 235–82; Kimbell, *Italian Opera* (Cambridge: Cambridge University Press, 1991), 408–10 and Esse, who argues that the gothic, as exemplified by Donizetti and Cammarano's *Maria de Rudenz* (1838, based on Lewis's gothic novel *The Monk*), had a peculiar legacy in Italy, whereby Donizetti sought to materialize in the opera the terror expressed by the characters rather than the invisible realm of the supernatural. And by so doing, Donizetti was able to accommodate the genre-bending reality of the gothic within the conventions of *bel canto* writing and expand them.

17. Walter Scott, *The Bride of Lammermoor* (Edinburgh: Adam & Charles Black, 1893), ix–xviii.

18. For information about the legendary circumstances of Scott's story, see Coleman O. Parsons, 'The Dalrymple Legend in *The Bride of Lammermoor*', *The Review of English Studies* 19/73 (1943): 51–8.

19. For a comprehensive discussion of the gothic novel throughout the nineteenth century, see *The Cambridge Companion to Gothic Fiction*.

20. 'Parco. Nel fondo della scena un fianco del castello, con picciola porta praticabile. Sul davanti la cosi detta fontana della Sirena, fontana altra volta coperta da un bell' edifizio, ornato di tutti i fregi della gotica architettura, al presente dai rottami di quest' edifizio sol cinta. Caduto n' è il tetto, rovinate le mura, e la sorgente che zampilla di sotterra, si apre il vareo fra le pietre, e le macerie postele intorno, formando indi un ruscello. E sull'imbrunire. Sorge la luna'. Cammarano, 9; compare with Scott, *The Bride of Lammermoor*, 42.

21. Scott, 43.

22. Scott, 43.

23. Regnava nel silenzio alta la notte e bruna . . . Colpìa la fonte un pallido raggio de tetra luna . . . quando sommesso gemito fra l' aure udir si fe', ed ecco su quel margine l'ombra mostrarsi a me! Qual di chi parla muoversi il labbro suo vedea, e con la mano esanime chiamarmi a sè parea. Stette un momento immobile, poi rapida sgombrò, e l' onda pria sì limpida, di sangue rosseggiò!

Cammarano, 9–10.

24. Cammarano based the character of Alisa on Alice in Scott's novel.

25. For a discussion of the ghost in *Lucia* in relation to the ghosts in other nineteenth-century operas, see Charles Jernigan, 'Donizetti's Ghosts', Associate Article of the Donizetti Society, 23 November 2013; www.donizettisociety.com/Articles/articledonizettighosts.htm (accessed 21 July 2024).

26. 'Ne' tempi a rimonta questo avvenimento, fu in Scozia comune credenza, che il violatore di un giuramento fatto con certe cerimonie, soggiacesse in questa terra ad un' esemplare punizione celeste, quasi contemporanea all' atto dello spergiuro. Perciò allora i giuramenti degli amanti, lungi dal riguardarsi come cosa di lieve peso, avevano per lo meno l'importanza di un contratto di nozze. La più usitata di

queste cerimonie era, che i due amanti rompevano, e si partivano una moneta. Si è sostituto il cambio dell' anello, come più adatto alla scena'. Cammarano, 12–13.

27. 'I nuziali voti che il ministro di Dio non benedice nè il ciel, nè il mondo riconosce'. Cammarano, 19.

28. 'Hai tradito il cielo, e amor! Maledetta sia l'istante che di te me rese amante . . .. Ah! di Dio la mano irata ti disperda'! Cammarano, 25. In the duet finale to Act I, 'Heaven' and 'Love' are claimed by Edgardo and Lucia (respectively) as witnesses to their nuptial agreement.

29. 'La seconda sera viddi cosa insolitissima in Napoli cioè, che al finale, dopo grandi evviva all' adagio, Duprez nella maledizione si fece applaudire al sommo prima della stretta. Ogni pezzo fu ascoltato con religioso silenzio e da spontanei evviva festeggiato' ['I saw a thing most uncommon in Naples, namely, at the [Act II] *finale*, after the great cheers for the *adagio* ["Chi me frena in tal momento?"/ "Who stops me at this moment?"], [Gilbert] Duprez in the curse [to Lucia] caused himself to be applauded to the heights [of the theatre] before the *stretta*']. *Le prime rappresentazioni delle opere di Donizetti nella stampa coeva*, ed. Annalisa Bini and Jeremy Commons (Milan: Accademia Nazionale di Santa Cecilia per i testi per le immagini, 1997), III, 518.

30. Emanuele Senici, *Music in the Present Tense: Rossini's Italian Operas in their Time* (Chicago: Chicago University Press, 2019), 131.

31. See Pascal James Imperato, Gavin H. Imperato and Austin C. Imperato. The referenced text is published as 'The Second World Cholera Pandemic (1826–49) in the Kingdom of the Two Sicilies with Special Reference to the Towns of San Prisco and Forio d'Ischia', *Journal of Community Health: The Publication for Health Promotion and Disease Prevention*, 40/6 (2015): 1224.

32. In contrast to the Scott original, which has the mother serve as a powerful force in Lucy Ashton's life, Cammarano has the mother dead and buried before the start of the opera.

33. 'Dolente Vergin, che geme sull' urna recente di cara madre, al talamo potria volger lo sguardo? Ah! rispettiam quel core, che per troppo dolor non sente amore'. Cammarano, 6.

34. 'Deh! t'arrendi, o più sciagure ti sovrastano, infelice . . . per le tenere mie cure, per i' estinta genitrice il periglio d' un fratello ti commova . . . o la madre nell' avello fremerà per te d' orror'. Cammarano, 19.

35. 'Taci . . . taci: tu vincesti . . . Lungo, crudel supplizio la vita a me sarà'! Cammarano, 20.

36. 'Se in lei soverchia è la mestizia, maravigliar non dei. Dal duolo oppressa e vinta piange la madre estinta'. Cammarano, 21.

37. 'Io sperai che a me la vita tronca avesse il mio spavento . . . ma la morte non m' aita . . . vivo ancor per mio tormento! Da' miei lumi

cadde il velo ... mi tradì la terra e il cielo! Vorrei pianger, ma non posso ... Ah! mi manca il pianto ancor'! Cammarano, 23.

38. 'Come rosa inaridita ella sta fra morte e vita'! Cammarano, 22–3.
39. Beyond its use in the comedic film *The Princess Bride* (Rob Reiner, 1987), the term 'mostly dead' is used in mortuary archeology that views dead individuals as having agency in the world despite being deceased; see Tiffiny A. Tung, 'Agency, "Till Death Do Us Part?" Inquiring about the Agency of Dead Bodies from the Ancient Andes', *Cambridge Archaeological Journal* 24/3 (2014): 437–52.
40. 'Lucia è in succinta e bianca veste: ha le chiome scarmigliate, ed il suo volto, coperto da uno squallore di morte, la rende simile ad uno spettro, anzicchè ad una creatura vivente. Il di lei sguardo impietrito, i moti convulsi, e fino un sorriso malaugurato manifestano non solo una spaventevole demenza, ma ben anco i segni di una vita, che già volge al suo termine'. Cammarano, 32.
41. 'Par dalla tomba uscita'! Cammarano, 32.
42. 'Presso alla tombo io sono ... odi una prece ancor ... Deh! tanto almeno t'arresta, Ch'io spiri a te d' appresso ... Già dall' affanno oppresso Gelido langue il cor ... un palpito gli resta ... È un palpito d' amor. Spargi di qualche pianto il mio terrestre velo, mentre lassù nel cielo Io pregherò per te ... Al giunger tuo soltanto Fia bello il ciel per me'! Cammarano, 34.
43. 'M' odi, e trema. Sulla tomba che rinserra il tradito genitore, al tuo sangue eterna guerra io giurai nel mio furore: Ma ti vidi ... in cor mi nacque altro affetto, e l' ira tacque ... pur quel voto non è infranto ... io potrei compirlo ancor'! Cammarano, 12.
44. 'Porrà fine al nostro foco sol di morte il freddo gel'! Cammarano, 13.
45. 'Tu che a Dio spiegasti l' ali, o bell' alma innamorata, ti rivolgi a me placata ... teco ascenda il tuo fedel. Ah! se l' ira de' mortali fece a noi sì lunga guerra; se divisi fummo in terra, ne congiunga il Nume in ciel. Io ti seguo'. Cammarano, 37.
46. To simplify the action, Cammarano conflated Scott's original casting of the Ashton men (father and older brother) into Henry (Enrico), who is in fact the younger brother to Lucy in the novel.
47. Scott, 161.
48. Vijay Mishra, *The Gothic Sublime* (Albany, NY: State University of New York Press, 1994), 1–2.
49. 'Mi tradì la terra e il cielo'! Cammarano, 23. For a discussion of female madness in nineteenth-century society, see Elaine Showalter, *The Female Malady: Women, Madness, and English Culture, 1830–1980* (New York: Penguin Books, 1985) and Michel Foucault, *Madness and Civilization: A History of Insanity in the Age of Reason*, trans. Richard Howard (New York: Vintage, 1973), 38–64. For a discussion of female madness in opera, see (among many)

Sean Parr, *Vocal Virtuosity: The Origins of the Coloratura Soprano in Nineteenth-Century Opera* (New York: Oxford University Press, 2021), 95–140; McClary, *Feminine Endings*, 80–111 and Smart, '"Dalla tomba uscita": Representations of Madness in Nineteenth-Century Italian Opera' (PhD diss., Cornell University, 1994).

50. For a comprehensive social history of the disease, see Ilza Veith, *Hysteria: The History of a Disease* (Chicago: University of Chicago Press, 1965) and Sabine Arnaud, *On Hysteria: The Invention of a Medical Category between 1670 and 1820* (Chicago: University of Chicago Press, 2015).

51. The medical diagnosis of hysteria was taken up by several men of science in the early nineteenth century, most especially in France, the center of medical research in Europe. Along with the work of Dubois d'Amiens, some of the more well-known publications around the time of *Lucia*'s premiere in 1835 include Philippe Pinel, *Nosographie philosophique ou méthode de l'analyse appliquée à la médecine* (Paris: Maradan, 1797 and J. A. Brosson, 1802, 1807, 1810, 1813, 1818); Étienne-Jean Georget, *De la psychologie du système nerveux et spécialement du cerveau: Recherches sur les maladies nerveuses en général, et in particulier sur le siège, la nature et le traitement de l'hystérie, de l'hypochondrie, de l'épilepsie et de l'asthme convulsif* (Paris: J. B. Baillière, 1821); Marshall Hall, *Commentaries on Some of the Most Important of the Diseases of Females* (London: Longman et al., 1827); James Cowles Prichard, *A Treatise on Insanity and Other Disorders Affecting the Mind* (London: Sherwood, Gilbert and Piper, 1835) and Jean Étienne Dominique Esquirol, *Des maladies mentales, considérées sous les rapports médical, hygiénique et médico-légal* (Paris: J. B. Baillière, 1838).

52. Dubois d'Amiens, *Histoire philosophique de l'hypochondrie et de l'hystérie* (Paris: Deville-Cavellin, 1833), 238. For a discussion of the life and work of d'Amiens, see Alexandre Klein, 'Frederic dubois d'Amiens, médecin-philosophe. L'exemple de la question de la Société Royale de Médecine de Bordeaux de 1830', *Histoire des sciences medicales*, 45/2 (2011): 131–45.

53. 'Lucia si arresta presso la soglia: la pallidezza del suo volto, il guardo smarrito, e tutto in lei annunzia i patimenti ch' ella sofferse, ed i primi sintomi d' un' alienazione mentale'. Cammarano, 16.

54. 'La sorpresa, ed il più vivo affanno si dipingano nel suo volto, ed un tremito l' investe dal capo alle piante'. Cammarano, 17.

55. D'Amiens, 176.

56. D'Amiens, 270.

57. Much is written on the connection between female hysteria and sexual stimulation, most especially found in the controversial work

of the French physician Jean-Martin Charcot (1825–93); see Jean-Martin Charcot, *Charcot, the Clinician: The Tuesday Lessons*, trans. Christopher G. Goetz (New York: Raven Press, 1987); Showalter, *The Female Malady*; Rachel P. Maines, *The Technology of Orgasm: Hysteria, the Vibrator, and Women's Sexual Satisfaction* (Baltimore, MD: The John Hopkins University Press, 1999) and Asti Hustvedt, *Medical Muses: Hysteria in Nineteenth-Century Paris* (New York: Norton, 2011).

58. For information about the Aversa asylum, see Carmel Raz, 'Music, Theater, and the Moral Treatment: The Casa dei Matti in Aversa and Palermo', *Laboratoire Italien: Politique et société*, 20 (2017): 1–20.

59. Black, 'Cammarano's Notes for the Staging of *Lucia di Lammermoor*', *Donizetti Society Journal* 4 (1980): 38.

60. See Janet Miron, *Prisons, Asylums, and the Public: Institutional Visiting in the Nineteenth Century* (Toronto: University of Toronto Press, 2011), 34–55 and Jennifer L. Bazar and Jeremy T. Burman, 'Asylum Tourism', *The Monitor on Psychology* 45/2 (2014): 68.

61. In Tuscany, for example, Leopold II's *motu proprio* of 2 August 1838 described the procedures for civil confinement valid for Florence and its nearby asylums; see Giuseppe Pantozzi, *Storia delle Idee e delle Leggi Psichiatriche: 1780–1980* (Trento: Centro Studi Erickson, 1994), 78.

62. Y. Thoret and S. Kantin, 'Historical Development of Legal Protection for the Rights of Mentally Ill Persons in France', *Hospital and Community Psychiatry* 45/12 (1994): 1211–14.

63. See Sander L. Gilman, *Seeing the Insane* (Lincoln, NE: University of Nebraska, 1996), 212; Elizabeth Fee and Theodore M. Brown, 'Freeing the Insane', *American Journal of Publish Health* 96/10 (2006): 1743 and Showalter, 1–4, who argues that the painting presents a particular male gaze in depicting the rationality of men and the madness of women.

64. See Raz, 'Music, Theater, and the Moral Treatment', 2–4.

65. D'Amiens, 516–18.

66. 'T' arresta … la stato suo'! Cammarano, 33.

67. Scott, 303.

68. See Foucault, *Madness and Civilization*, whose compelling text argues that in nineteenth-century society a sense of normality is achieved through the suppression and exclusion of the abnormal, whereby the mentally ill, criminal and the idle poor were placed in houses of confinement.

69. Luigi Cherubini's opera *Médée* (1797) is an early example of a female opera heroine who murders and gets away with it. In the opera, Médée avenges herself against Jason by poisoning his new lover and slaying his two sons before she escapes and leaves the city.

70. See Parsons, 'The Dalrymple Legend in *The Bride of Lammermoor*', 51–8.

71. For a critical discussion of this topic, see Lisa Downing, 'Murder in the Feminine: Marie Lefarge and the Sexualization of the Nineteenth-Century Criminal Woman', *Journal of the History of Sexuality* 18/1 (2009): 121–37; Ruth Harris, *Murders and Madness: Medicine, Law, and Society in the Fin de Siècle* (Oxford: Oxford University Press, 1991) and Ann-Louise Shapiro, *Breaking the Codes: Female Criminality in Fin-de-Siècle Paris* (Stanford, CA: Stanford University Press, 1996).

72. See, for example, the noted work of feminist scholar Catherine Clément, *Opera, or the Undoing of Women*, who argues that when women in opera 'cross over a vigorous, invisible line, the line that makes them unbearable; so they will have to be punished' (59). The opera character Médée appears to be the one exception who is able to escape punishment.

73. 'Tremare, o babaro, tu dêi per la sua vita' … 'Tu del versato sangue, empio, tu sei la ria cagion'! Cammarano, 33, 35.

74. The plot for Shakespeare's play is based on a 1554 Italian *novelle* by Mattelo Bandello (c. 1480–1562), which was a well-known work in Italy before Shakespeare's play found its way back to Italy in translation; see the Introduction to *Romeo and Juliet*, ed. René Weis (London: Bloomsbury Arden Shakespeare, 2014), 44–59.

SPEAKING OF GENRE: *LUCIA* AND THE *BEL CANTO* TRADITION

The sweet sound of his voice struck me! . . .
Ah, that voice resounds here in my heart.

(Act III, Lucia)[1]

Lucia is an Italian *bel canto* opera, which means that this 'beautifully sung' opera contains Italian vocal melodies that require a 'smooth emission of tone, beauty of timbre and elegance of phrasing'.[2] What this literally translates to is a style of singing, whereby the singer, through excellent and sustained breath control and agility, is able to create a mixture of vocal expressions as demanded by the dramatic situation, be they the rhythmic or poetic accents of the Italian text, the varying of the tempo, the dramatic tone of the voice or vocal resonance.[3] Owing to this emphasis on the voice, dramatic situations within a *bel canto* opera are more often than not static to allow the voice to be the singular focus within a particular scene. In fact, the term 'bel canto' came into fashion as Italian composers and critics of the middle to late nineteenth century bemoaned the vocal production in operas of the time as having less rhythmic agility, more speech-like inflection, a lack of vocal embellishments and a loss of legato phrasing throughout the entire vocal range.[4] Thus, in this way, *bel canto* in its modern meaning is a vocal style of the early nineteenth century, whereby Italian operas that implement this vocal style highlight the 'beauty of the voice', rather than the overall sonic and dramatic environment of the work.[5] In *Lucia*, Donizetti challenges the static nature of the voice in *bel canto* and presents a number of opportunities for ensembles and the use of complex musical units that combine both the inner and outer action of the characters on stage, which creates an increase in dramatic motion throughout the work. What follows, therefore, is a discussion of *Lucia* that places the opera in the context of the *bel canto* tradition in the early nineteenth century, highlighting where the opera aligns with other *bel canto* operas of the time but also departs and sets a precedent to be followed later.

Dramaturgy within *Bel Canto* Opera

When a nineteenth-century opera is classified as a *bel canto* opera, the term often refers to an opera, be it comic or tragic, where *coloratura* – that is, 'melismatic singing, ornamentation, and improvisation'[6] – matches the identity and purpose of the characters on stage. Each character's dramatic presence and hence the audience's empathy for that character operates within the parameters of a virtuosic vocal style. The principal characters in these operas are often pathetic individuals who at first glance are powerless to change their situation, but when combined with the vocal stylings of a *bel canto* performer the character is revealed to have a certain heroic potential. Particular character types that are often found in *bel canto* opera include an orphan (e.g., Rosina in Rossini's *Il barbiere di Siviglia*, 1815); a poor peasant (e.g., Nemorino in Donizetti's *L'elisir d'amore*, 1832); a political rival in disguise or exile (e.g., Gualtiero in Bellini's *Il Pirata*, 1827); an individual bound by their political position (e.g., Norma in Bellini's *Norma*, 1831); or a woman who has gone mad or has lost all forms of reason (e.g., Elvira in Bellini's *I Puritani*, 1835). The last of these *bel canto* character types, of course, is presented in *Lucia*, but also in other works of the time, including Bellini's *Il Pirata* (1827) and *La Sonnambula* (1831) as well as in Donizetti's *Anna Bolena* (1830), *Lucrezia Borgia* (1833) and *Maria Stuarda* (1835).

What separates *Lucia* from these other representations of *bel canto* characters and what has perhaps allowed the opera to remain in the repertoire today is Lucia's persistent dynamism throughout the work. Often in nineteenth-century *bel canto* opera, the main character is somewhat static and fixed in their situation while the overall dramatic scene or environment around them changes. Such a structural convention in *bel canto* opera forces a *dénouement* that quickly wraps up the action, such as a last-minute pardon (e.g., *I Puritani*), disclosure of unknown information (e.g., *La Sonnambula*) or a sudden moment of clarity or an act of forgiveness (e.g., *Norma*). For example, in Donizetti's *The Elixir of Love*, a so-called *melodrama giocoso* or 'comic melodrama', the entire opera revolves around a simple peasant who wishes to marry a wealthy woman. The peasant (Nemorino) is constantly being duped and controlled by others, including a ranked officer (Belcore), a wealthy landowner (Adina) and a pharmaceutical doctor (Dr. Dulcamara, peddler of the famous elixir). By the end of the opera, Nemorino has acquired a massive fortune from a dead uncle; Belcore has accepted a long-time peasant as his equal; Adina has fallen in love with our hero and the love potion and the doctor are both viewed as a success. All of this is accomplished not by Nemorino *per se* but by changes to his overall dramatic situation put in motion by others. This is the case even with a more serious *bel canto* opera such as Donizetti's *Anna Bolena*. Although the opera was classified by the librettist Felice Romani as a 'lyric tragedy', the opera is every bit a *bel canto* work filled with flowing legato lines and virtuosic stylings throughout the full vocal range of the principal characters, none more so than Anna Bolena. The score reveals her *bel canto* pedigree by having the *prima donna* conclude the opera with a soaring aria that is in response to her husband Henry VIII taking up a new bride and her courage in the face of certain death. And like the comedic Nemorino, the dramatic situation for Anna at the end of the opera is the result of the mechanizations of others.

In *Lucia*, the action does indeed swirl around our main character but we see that Lucia is the pace maker, forcing others to respond to her. For example, in Act I it is Lucia who opens us up to the gothic world with the introduction of a ghost to our story. Be it the start of a crippling mental derangement or a spectre communicating from beyond (see Chapter 1), it is the world of Lucia we are ushered into near the start of the opera, hearing what she hears and coming to know what she sees. And even before her auspicious entrance on stage, one notes that the music of the orchestral prelude (see Chapter 3) mimics what is heard at the end of the opera as the inhabitants of Lammermoor sorrowfully proclaim: 'Oh, poor one! Oh, sad event!'[7] Thus, from the very first notes of the opera, the world of Lucia is made known.

The other persons of the opera – namely, Enrico, Arturo, Normanno, Raimondo and Alisa – remain fairly static figures who attempt to keep Lucia away from Edgardo. Yet, in the end, all of the characters are changed by Lucia's actions, namely her forbidden love of Edgardo, the murder of Arturo and her final death. In this light, she is not the mere victim of her brother's actions or the actions of others but a woman who dies on her own terms (see Chapter 7).

Lucia's partner in all of this of course is Edgardo. Like Lucia, when Edgardo is not on stage he is referred to by others. For example, in the opening scenes of the opera, as Enrico's soldiers search for an intruder on the castle grounds, the names of Edgardo and Lucia are mentioned in the same breath, two individuals who thwart Enrico's future plans. When Lucia appears in the next scene, singing of the haunted fountain, Edgardo appears directly after, where he speaks of his own spectre of sorts, the loss of his father and his desire for revenge. And then of course in Act II, after Lucia signs the wedding contract, Edgardo bursts onto the stage and disrupts the action. Ironically, the musical number that follows his entrance, the sextet, forces everyone's attention back to Lucia as they all show concern for her well-being. This same back-and-forth pairing between the two lovers finally concludes in Act III. After Lucia sings her 'mad scene' and dies off stage, Edgardo appears for the last time with his own curtain-ending number when he commits suicide.

As we can see, both Lucia and Edgardo are linked throughout the opera – where one goes, the other follows. Different from, say, Bellini's *Norma*, where the main character and her lover both perish together, the deaths of Lucia and Edgardo are staggered, allowing for a separate spotlight to be placed on each of their lives in spite of their shared fate. In fact, this staggered appearance of the two caused some to question who was the true sympathetic figure in the opera. In the reviews that followed the premiere, many critics even preferred the death of Edgardo rather than the death of Lucia, seeing the opera more as a 'tenor opera' than a soprano one (see Chapter 7).[8] Nonetheless, such an ending makes *Lucia* dramatically distinct from other *bel canto* operas of the time, confounding the stereotype of a static main character whose life is simply the sum of the actions of others.

Lucia and the *Bel Canto* Voice

Bel canto opera is nothing without a voice that gives it life, which is characterized by a pitch range (e.g., soprano, alto, tenor, bass) and stylistic expression (e.g., lyric, dramatic, spinto[9]). In *opera buffa*, the Italian 'comic opera' genre that was defined a generation before the romantic operas of Donizetti, the voice of the character was linked directly to their societal position as well as their perceived dramatic function.[10] For example, generally speaking, a lyric soprano was used in *opera buffa* to define the vocal lines of a young woman who was naïve both of the world and the challenges she will face throughout the course of the opera. The same can be said for the lyric tenor, a heroic young man equally untested by the world but anxious nonetheless to define his place in it. Both of these voice types often shared soft legato melodic lines with rhythmic figures in the upper register, which allowed for a certain empathetic tone to be struck in the listener, hence the characterization of these lyric voice types as young and innocent.

A particular character that would often complement these two vocal types in *opera buffa* was the *travesti*, the 'disguised' character or 'trouser' role, who was sung by a female mezzo-soprano dressed as a man (as opposed to the celebrated *castrato* in Italian *opera seria*, who is a man who sounds like a woman). One of the main purposes of such characters was to frame the gender roles or duties of the lead male and female characters and put in general relief the dynamics of their relationship. In such a role, this third-gender character would often serve as a confidant to the lead female character. For example, in Mozart's *Le nozze di Figaro* (1786), the *travesti* character Cherubino, a young male page sung by a female mezzo-soprano, serves as an intimate friend to all the women in the opera. By doing so, Cherubino is a comedic foil to the highly abusive behaviour of the count.[11]

Although exceptions do remain, the *travesti* role fell out of favour by the mid nineteenth century, where female-voiced parts were increasingly sung by women who 'dress' and 'act' as women.[12] In *Lucia*, for example, we see that the mezzo-soprano character Alisa (first sung by Teresa Zappucci) functions as a foil to Lucia, most especially in Act I, when Alisa questions Lucia's desire to see Edgardo who she knows is her brother's enemy. Being the only other female character in the opera, Alisa models for the audience how a dutiful woman should act and yet she continually supports Lucia throughout the opera, not serving as a rival (as seen, for example, with Giovanna Seymour in *Anna Bolena* or Adalgisa in *Norma*) – a possible holdover, once again, of the dramatic role of the *travesti* defined a generation before.

In addition to the lyric soprano and lyric tenor, the other stock characters from *opera buffa* include *basso buffo* or the 'buffoon bass', a low male voice with fast patter and comedic folly, and the serious bass or *basso profondo*, a male voice with a smooth and often imposing low register that commands respect. For example, the first time we see Figaro on stage, the *basso buffo* character from *Le nozze*, he is chattering about how to fit a large bed in his room in preparation for his wedding night. This is contrasted with the *basso profondo* character Dr. Bartolo, who is a serious-minded figure who seeks to punish Figaro for his past slights.

The *bel canto* operas of the nineteenth century use the same voice types as mentioned earlier – namely the lyric soprano, lyric tenor, *basso buffo* and *basso profondo* – but infuse them with vocal activity that moves us away from a fixed character type (e.g., the young lover, the comedic fool) to a more dynamic flesh-and-blood character who often populated the pages of novels, plays and the everyday urban or rural landscape. This change primarily came about through the compositional efforts of Rossini, who loosened the formal conventions surrounding the *opera buffa* voice type by setting serious libretti (e.g., *Otello*, 1815; *La donna del lago*, 1819; *Semiramide*, 1823) that accommodated greater dramatic expressiveness for the voice.[13] In addition, the singers in the early nineteenth century also contributed greatly to this change by developing vocal techniques that facilitated more ornamentation and a much wider range than ever before.[14] For example, as *bel canto* composers sought a more nuanced low male voice for various dramatic situations and as low male singers began to develop the upper area of their voice, the baritone became a much more popular voice to set than the standard *basso buffo* or *basso profondo* (e.g., Rossini's *The Barber of Seville*, 1815 and Donizetti's *Don Pasquale*, 1842). Similar to the use of the *travesti* role in *opera buffa*, the baritone in the nineteenth century unified the vocal ranges surrounding it, which allowed the baritone character to have a more dynamic presence befitting the various dramatic situations that were called for by the work. We see this same setting of the baritone voice in Donizetti's vocal writing for the character Enrico (first sung by Domenico Cosselli), who is consistent in his dark intentions to kill every living Ravenswood and to marry off his sister.[15] Throughout the opera, Enrico has lyrical passages that bring attention to his seriousness of purpose but also his vulnerability in that pursuit. A characteristic example from the opera is the opening scene to Act I where Enrico sings what will be the start of a double aria when he learns that Lucia's secret lover is Edgardo ('Cruda ... funesta smania' ['A cruel and fatal frenzy']). In a vocal line centred around B (just below middle C or C4) with a pitch range from D3 to F4, Enrico details his sheer hatred of Edgardo and his utter disdain for his sister. Set to a passage in G major in a dance-like tempo, the voice here appears gleeful in its cruelty as if this is the natural temperament of our character who takes pleasure in violence (see Example 2.1).

Enrico's baritone voice is contrasted with the bass voice of Raimondo (first sung by Carlo Porto), who presents a similar sense of command but owing to his station as a tutor and, more importantly, as a holy man who advises everyone in the opera, his vocal character reflects a starkness of tone that is not found in Enrico.[16] We see this *basso profondo* figure characteristically defined at the end of Act II, where, in the cacophony of raised voices who oppose the appearance of Edgardo at the signing ceremony, Raimondo takes control of the situation and commands:

All respect the mighty majesty of God. In His name I command you to calm your anger and lay down your weapons. God despises the one who commits murder; for it is written, 'he who lives by the sword, will die by the sword'. Peace, Peace.[17]

Set to a vocal line that ranges from a low F♯2 to a high E4, this powerfully sung passage aided by low brass and winds, strings and timpani is primarily situated around C4, which is usually where the bass voice transitions from a rough sounding chest-resonating voice to a light and airy head voice, the so-called *zona di passaggio*.[18] The fact that Raimondo's melodic line sits primarily

Example 2.1 Gaetano Donizetti, *Lucia di Lammermoor* [Piano-Vocal Score], Act I, scene 2, No. 2: 'Cruda, funesta smania', Recitative and *Cavatina*, bb. 59–73.

in this range throughout this passage heightens the strain in his voice, which by the end of the phrase rises up to a high E4 (the very limit of the *basso profondo* range) before dropping down a full octave (E3), a more comfortable bass register set to the word *pace* or 'peace' (see Example 2.2).

Edgardo and Lucia serve as our young romantic leads and as such are set in a characteristic voice type of the lyric tenor and lyric

Example 2.2 Gaetano Donizetti, *Lucia di Lammermoor* [Piano-Vocal Score], Act II, scene 6, No. 10: 'Tallontana, sciagurato', Last Scene of Finale II, bb. 32–43.

soprano, respectively. But as we have seen in the other voice types inherited from *opera buffa*, these stock characters take on a far more dramatic potential, where their vocal lines are infused with fast runs, trills and wide leaps that denote a particular uneasiness or restlessness but also an inner strength that guides them to their destiny. This is certainly the case with the vocal characterization of both Edgardo and Lucia, who at first glance might appear young and naïve but by the end of the opera have gained a weightier quality to their voice and to their dramatic situation. This is probably the reason why the roles are sometimes sung by larger voice types, such as the so-called 'dramatic tenor' (e.g., Luciano Pavarotti) and the 'dramatic coloratura soprano' (e.g., Joan Sutherland), who both lend a certain degree of fatalism to the characters, where their deaths at the end of the opera are presaged by a heavier vocal colour.[19]

The French dramatic tenor Gilbert Duprez was cast as Edgardo at the premiere, which became one of his most popular roles during his lifetime.[20] In a passage titled 'Tenors as Trumpets', the musicologist

Mary Ann Smart describes Duprez's voice as having a potent 'masculine' sound, whereby he would often sing a high C5 (C above middle C) in full chest voice (not in *falsetto* or the head voice register), so much so that he was often cast as a romantic 'love interest'.[21] Although no sustained high C's are written for Edgardo in *Lucia* (there is a high E♭5 in the Act I duet and a number of high B♭4's), the character maintains nonetheless a high *tessitura* throughout, which allows us to perceive him more as a fully rounded tragic hero and not simply just the lover of Lucia.

Before we move on to discuss the voice type of Lucia, we must also mention the other tenor roles in the opera, namely Normanno and Arturo, who are both cast as lyric tenors. In the case of Normanno (first sung by Teofilo Rossi),[22] the captain of Enrico's troops, we find that he is the first to inform Enrico of Lucia's secret love for Edgardo (Act I, scene 2) and the same one who forges Edgardo's signature in a letter that is used to trick Lucia (Act II, scene 1). Serving as a meddlesome character but one of rank and station, Normanno has a vocal setting that is primarily set in lyrical dialogue (*parlante*) with melodies that give the voice little opportunity to bloom or express a more complex personality. The only extended lyrical moment occurs at the beginning of the opera where he leads Enrico's troops in the search for an intruder on the castle grounds. Intermixed with a male chorus of basses and tenors, Normanno soars above the other voices, highlighting perhaps his candid desire to serve Enrico, unaware of the harm it will cause (see Example 2.3).

Normanno's zeal to help Enrico is the very thing, however, that convicts him in the eyes of Raimondo at the end of the opera:

Raimondo: 'Impious spy, take pleasure in your work!'
Normanno: 'What are you saying?'
Raimondo: 'You are guilty of this family's destruction. You were the one who lit the first flame.'
Normanno: 'I did not think . . .'
Raimondo: 'Wretch, you spilled blood! You are the cause! That same blood accuses you now in Heaven. God's mighty hand has already signed your death warrant. Go and tremble [before God]'. *Normanno departs.*[23]

Example 2.3 Gaetano Donizetti, *Lucia di Lammermoor* [Piano-Vocal Score], Act I, scene 1, No. 1: 'Percorriamo le spiagge vicine', Prelude and Introductory Chorus, bb. 72–9.

This final dialogue appears right after Lucia sings her final *cabaletta* as everyone is left on stage to comprehend the murder of Arturo and the disturbing appearance of Lucia. Normanno's lack of understanding of his part in what just transpired is underlined once again in his vocal characterization as a lyric tenor: a man who is naïve to his own actions.

The other lyric tenor, Lord Arturo Bucklaw (first sung by Achille Balestracci),[24] is the first to die in Act III and like other characterizations of this lyric voice type, he is unaware of his fate.

44

Serving as a rival to Edgardo, both vocally and dramatically, Arturo's only vocal setting occurs in Act II in the *finale*, where he shares lyrical dialogue with Enrico and Lucia before he joins the rest of the principals in the sextet, equally taken aback by Edgardo's appearance at the proceedings. The comparison between Edgardo (dramatic tenor) and Arturo (lyric tenor) in this scene, however, leaves Arturo with little chance to be seen and heard as anything more than what he is: a third wheel.

The final voice type to mention is the *coloratura* soprano, which is set for the title character Lucia.[25] Traditionally, when one heard this voice type in an eighteenth-century *opera buffa*, the character was often a sorceress or a woman of such power and ability that her high soaring and rhythmically agile voice echoed her ability to wage violence (e.g., The Queen of the Night in Mozart's *The Magic Flute*, 1791). In nineteenth-century opera, this powerful female role shares an extreme vocal range with its *opera buffa* cousin, but dramatically speaking, the character is far more varied in her expression, where a level of vulnerability is also mixed with an unrelenting desire to take action. Along with *Lucia*, other *bel canto* operas by Donizetti that use this voice type for its lead female role include *Anna Bolena* (1830), *Lucrezia Borgia* (1833), *Maria Stuarda* (1835) and *Roberto Devereux* (1837). As mentioned in the Introduction, Fanny Tacchinardi-Persiani was the soprano who interpreted the role of Lucia and so she was the first to map out the dramatic potential of this character, namely a woman who can summon the strength to kill a grown man and still suffer such overwhelming heartache that she seeks her own death. Although her voice was often described as 'too soft and gentle to portray violence and extreme feelings', Tacchinardi-Persiani excelled in her technical ability to produce fast runs and trills and the uncanny talent to hit high notes with flawless perfection, including high E6 and F6, two octaves above middle C.[26] Nowhere is this on display more than in the 'mad scene' in Act III (see Example 2.4). Although this infamous scene will be discussed in more detail in Chapter 6, suffice it to say that here in the context of our discussion of *bel canto* voice types, the *coloratura* role that Donizetti composed for Tacchinardi-Persiani served both the drama and the singer, so

45

Example 2.4 Gaetano Donizetti, *Lucia di Lammermoor* [Piano-Vocal Score], Act III, scene 5, No. 14: 'Alfin son tua', Recitative and Aria, bb. 328–46.

much so that every vocal ornament, hair-raising high note and fast melodic run highlight the aural signature of a talented vocal technician as well as a woman who has gone mad.[27]

La Solita Forma in *Lucia*

Beyond the individual voice types and the overall heroic quality of the main characters, *bel canto* opera also contains various set pieces.[28] As we have seen throughout this chapter, the main *raison d'être* of nineteenth-century Italian opera is the voice, but for it to remain so the opera needs to have structural elements that allow the voice to stand out from the surrounding musical texture. In this way, the vocal set piece is the building block for the opera's dramatic expression and solidifies the audience's expectations regarding the overall pacing of the work's narrative flow.[29]

The most prominent of all vocal set pieces in *bel canto* opera is the 'double aria' or what is sometimes referred to in Italian as the *solita forma* or the 'conventional form'. In this formal design for a solo singer, duet or ensemble, made conventional through its invention and continual use by Rossini and its proliferation throughout the *bel canto* era, a varied dramatic characterization is presented, where there is introductory music and/or recitatives (*scena*), followed by a slow section (*cantabile*) and then a fast vocal finale (*cabaletta*) (see Appendix B). A prime example of this form can be found in the aria 'Una voce poco fa' ['A voice I heard a little while ago'] from Rossini's famous *bel canto* opera *The Barber of Seville* (1816). This opening aria or *cavatina* is sung by the character Rosina, a *contralto* (low soprano) with soft legato lines filled with rhythmically accented passages in the opening section and fast flowing *melismas* in the *cabaletta* (see Examples 2.5a and 2.5b).[30] Although this structure became a tried and true formula throughout the *bel canto* era, it was still malleable enough to fit any dramatic situation owing to the forward motion and inner character development that occurs from one section to the other. In addition, it was also a wonderful showpiece for the singer who was expected to improvise throughout the *cabaletta*, which made a fairly static moment in the opera come alive with energy and theatrical excitement.

Example 2.5a Gioachino Rossini, *The Barber of Seville* [Piano-Vocal Score], Act I, No. 7: Rosina's Cavatina [*Cantabile*], bb. 11–20.

Example 2.5b Gioachino Rossini, *The Barber of Seville* [Piano-Vocal Score], Act I, No. 7: Rosina's Cavatina [*Cabaletta*], bb. 56–62.

Rossini, Bellini and Donizetti all added to this basic two-part form by extending it further with lyrical dialogue (*parlante*) as well as a middle section (*tempo di mezzo*) that helped to smooth out the transition from the opening *cantabile* to the concluding *cabaletta* (see Appendix B). In this way, the aria, duet or ensemble presented a stronger sense of realism and dramatic plausibility that could be sustained over an entire scene. We see this done to great effect in *Lucia*. For example, in Lucia's *cavatina*, 'Regnava nel silenzio' ['At dead of night'], the piece opens with an orchestral introduction that moves us into a set of recitatives between Lucia and Alisa (*scena*) as they both search and then wait for Edgardo.[31] Following the word 'Escolta' ['Listen'], Lucia proceeds to tell Alisa about the ghost. Set to a *larghetto* tempo in <6/8>, accompanied by soft string pizzicatos on the beat and a clarinet with rising and falling arpeggios in E♭ minor, the *cantabile* section of the aria contains two stanzas of text treated similarly but with added *melismas*, trills, rhythmic variants, a short vocal cadenza and a modulation to the relative major (G♭ major), all occurring in the second stanza as Lucia becomes more agitated by her ghostly vision.[32] Following the opening slow section, Alisa interrupts Lucia's aria with lyrical dialogue (*tempo di mezzo*), pleading with Lucia to give up her love for Edgardo. In defiance, Lucia responds in E♭ major (a key often used in the nineteenth century to define heroic action) with the words 'a grieving heart has no other existence but hope', punctuated with trills and a lilting *cadenza* on the words 'he brings comfort to my suffering'.[33]

This sets up the final *cabaletta* section of the aria, 'Quando rapito in estasi' ['When he is rapt in ecstasy'], where a moderately paced tempo is presented by strings, harp, woodwinds and horn, all in A♭ major, a key often associated with deep tenderness, such as in the second movement of Beethoven's Fifth Symphony (1808) or Schubert's *Impromptu*, no. 4 (1827). The A♭ major accompaniment serves to characterize Lucia as carefree while she sings of her love for Edgardo: 'When he is rapt in ecstasy of the most burning love ... the heavens open up to me.'[34] As Lucia sings the first verse of the *cabaletta* melody, Alisa once again interrupts her, warning Lucia of dark days ahead. Lucia's aria does not end here, however, as the music once again returns to the start of the *cabaletta* section, which allows Lucia to repeat her words but this time they are filled with *coloratura*, including fast melodic runs,

49

changes of tempo and quick intervallic leaps. Rather than featuring vocal display as mere spectacle, this *coloratura* has a strong dramatic purpose to infuse the words 'heaven' and 'open' with a particular meaning for Lucia, who up to now has had little to no freedom in her life. This repeat leads directly into the final *stretta* or quick-paced conclusion that was broken off before by Alisa but is now able to continue as Lucia gleefully sings in a rapidly paced tempo to end the scene.

Lucia's aria is structured similarly to Rosina's in *The Barber of Seville*, where both arias share a slow section (*cantabile*) and a fast section (*cabaletta*). However, Lucia's aria is far more integrated within the storyline of the drama. Not only does Alisa's commentary help to frame the aria as something more than a simple aside or a stop-action moment for Lucia to share her feelings, but it also provides us with important plot developments, namely a description and history of the ghost. In addition, Donizetti alters the tempo in the middle of the aria (*tempo di mezzo*) to allow for a more even flow between Lucia's two worlds: her fear of the ghost or possibly death itself and her love for Edgardo (see Appendix B).

We see a similar mindfulness of the drama in Donizetti's use of the conventional form in the *finale* to Act II. This final ensemble number is based on an expanded multipart form, which includes an opening chorus, a *tempo d'attacco* or a fast interactive section between voices, a slow *cantabile* for the large ensemble, a *tempo di mezzo* and then a final *cabaletta* for all the voices. This four-part form with an opening chorus or instrumental number was the same structure used by Rossini in his duets (e.g., Cinderella and Ramiro in *La Cenerentola*, 1817 and Isolier and Comte in *Le Comte Ory*, 1828). The form used here by Donizetti still contains slow and fast sections, but one notes that in the Act II *finale* the multipart form allows for a high amount of character integration and audience comprehension in spite of the changes in action and the opposing sentiments expressed.

The *finale* to Act II is laid out over three scenes (scenes 4 through 6). After a simple opening chorus with repeated lines, 'Per te d'immenso' ['All around you is filled with immense joy'], Enrico and Arturo present lyrical dialogue (*scena*) as traces of the happy chorus are still heard in the background (scene 4). Their conversation leads directly into the *tempo d'attacco*, which presents the inner and external dialogue surrounding Lucia who is filled with anxiety (scene 5). After Lucia signs the wedding contract, the mood suddenly switches to terror as timpani, trombones and trumpet herald Edgardo's entrance onto the stage (scene 6). This eventually transitions into the start of the slow *cantabile* section composed as a sextet in D♭ major, beginning with Edgardo and Enrico and then the rest of the principals, all of whom take turns singing the famous melody 'Chi mi frena in tal momento?' ['Who stops me at this moment?'] (see Example 2.6).

Following the conclusion of the *cantabile* section, the tempo and harmony change again as we begin the *tempo di mezzo*. Here in a faster tempo in D major, Enrico and Arturo demand that Edgardo leave, whereupon Raimondo commands everyone to lower their weapons and to renounce violence. After Edgardo explains why he is there, Raimondo tells him that Lucia has already signed the contract, making her previous marriage to Edgardo null. Edgardo of course explodes with anger, taking back the ring he gave to Lucia and stomping on it. All of the action in this *tempo di mezzo* section is sung with lyrical dialogue, interspersed with short expressive melodies (*ariosos*) that highlight the emotional position of each individual. The final *cabaletta* or *stretta* 'Esci, fuggi' ['Leave, depart'] now begins in a quick <6/8> with all the principal voices, chorus and orchestra resounding as the act concludes (see Appendix B).

In over 500 bars of music that contain nearly seventeen minutes of full-throated singing, the Act II *finale* in *Lucia* goes beyond the simple kinetic–static binary of other *bel canto* operas and masterfully creates a work with emotional depth, spectacle, plot development and melody that provides both external and internal commentary (see Chapter 5 for a detailed analysis). From the opening chorus and dialogue between characters to the virtuosic sonic display of internal emotional conflicts, the Act II *finale* challenges the assumption that *solita forma* is artistically stilted and lacks dramatic conviction.[35] Traditionally, the ensemble-finale was one that provided resolution to the various misunderstandings that have previously occurred in the opera, allowing the principals to confront one another and to gain insight on all that was done in secret. However, the 'irresistible effectiveness' of this

Example 2.6 Gaetano Donizetti, *Lucia di Lammermoor* [Piano-Vocal Score], Act II, scene 6, No. 9: 'Chi me frena in tal momento', Recitative and Quartet, bb. 133–35.

finale, as Ashbrook writes, 'is due to Donizetti's skill at transform-
ing the rhetoric of confrontation into melody in such a way that it
expands this moment so that the audience both feels and savors its
pathos'.[36] This development of the traditional set piece was due to
the melodramatic elements found in *Lucia* to be sure, but were part
of a larger trend within Donizetti's compositional style in the
1830s to increase the dramatic potential of the set form, filling it
with a varied set of emotions and actions.[37]

We will continue to discuss the conventional form in the context
of *Lucia* in later chapters (Chapters 4–6) as we examine the
separate vocal numbers of each act and how they come together
to present the musico-dramatic structure of the entire work. In the
next chapter, however, we must go beyond the voice and discuss
Donizetti's use of the orchestra in *Lucia*, namely the opening
orchestral prelude, off-stage band in Act II and the various cli-
matic scenes in the opera that allow for instrumental display. As
we shall see, Donizetti presents a number of interesting orchestral
sounds and sonic gestures throughout the score, which highlight
not only the exotic gothic environment but also the world of
madness, death and love.

Notes

1. 'Il dolce suono mi colpì di sua voce! . . . Ah! quella voce m' è quì nel
   cor discesa'! Cammarano, 32.
2. Osborne, 1. For a detailed discussion of the history of *bel canto*, see
   Rodolfo Celletti, *A History of Bel Canto*, trans. Frederick Fuller
   (Oxford: Clarendon Press, 1991) and Lucie Manén, *Bel Canto:
   The Teaching of the Classic Italian Song-Schools, Its Decline and
   Restoration* (Oxford: Oxford University Press, 1994).
3. Robert Toft, *Bel Canto: A Performer's Guide* (Oxford: Oxford
   University Press, 2013), 4. Toft mentions a number of 'tools of
   expression' not listed here, including vocal emphasis, register,
   phrasing, legato, staccato, *portamento*, *messa da voce*, ornamentation and gesture (4–5).
4. In 1858, while in semi-retirement and living in Paris, Rossini apparently made the comment 'Alas . . . we have lost our native *bel canto*',
   further noting that 'not a single voice of the new generation is capable
   of rendering in *bel canto* the aria "Casta diva" [from Bellini's
   Norma]'; see Owen Jander, 'Bel Canto', in *The New Grove*

Dictionary of Opera, ed. Stanley Sadie, 1 (New York: Macmillan Reference Limited, 1997), 380–1 and Richard Taruskin, *The Oxford History of Western Music*, 3 (Oxford: Oxford University Press, 2005), 37–40.

5. Many authors define different dates to the so-called '*bel canto* era', some even go as far back as the early 1600s. For our purposes, however, the era is defined primarily by the operas of Rossini, Bellini, Donizetti and early Verdi.

6. Parr, *Vocal Virtuosity*, 3. As Parr later explains, 'The tradition of coloratura as an essential part of solo singing was quite prominent during the bel canto period of the early nineteenth century and was used by Rossini, Bellini, and Donizetti, who employed it as part of normal melodic text treatment, rather than necessarily linking it to a particular emotion or dramatic situation' (Parr, 6).

7. 'Oh meschina! Oh caso orrendo'! Cammarano, 36.

8. Black, *The Italian Romantic Libretto*, 30.

9. Throughout this section, I will be defining various voice types via the German *Fach* system, a well-known and convenient way to categorize opera voices by pitch range, vocal weight (e.g., thinness or lightness vs. heaviness in texture) and vocal timbre (e.g., bright, dark, mellow). For more information on the *Fach* system, see Pearl Yeadon McGinnis, *The Opera Singer's Career Guide: Understanding the European 'Fach' System*, ed. Marith McGinnis Willis (Lanham, MD: Scarecrow Press, 2010).

10. Although *opera buffa* literally means 'comic opera', my use of the term here is in reference to the Italian operatic genre that rose in the early eighteenth century in response to the elaborate vocal writing, mythological plots and allegorical displays of power found in *opera seria* of the Baroque era.

11. For an analysis of the character Cherubino and the function of the trouser role in general, see Heather Hadlock, 'The Career of Cherubino, or, the Trouser Role Grows Up', in *Siren Songs: Representations of Gender and Sexuality in Opera* (Princeton: Princeton University Press, 2000), 67–92.

12. Examples of *travesti* roles in early nineteenth-century opera include those by Rossini (*Tancredi*, 1813; *Semiramide*, 1823; and *Le Comte d'Ory*, 1828), Bellini (*I Capuleti e I Montecchi*, 1830) and Donizetti (*Anna Bolena*, 1830 and *L'Assedio di Calais*, 1836). For a history of *travesti* roles and how the female-sounding character type morphs from the male-sung voice of the *castrato* in the seventeenth century to women playing women in the early nineteenth century, see Naomi André, *Voicing Gender, Travesti, and the Second Woman in Early Nineteenth-Century Italian Opera* (Bloomington, IN: Indiana University Press, 2006).

13. See Philip Gossett, 'Rossini, Gioachino', *Grove Music Online* (Oxford: Oxford University Press, 2001); date of access 12 June 2024.

14. This is a massive area of research that places the singers (rather than the composers) of *bel canto* opera at the center of the change in vocal style and technique at the start of the nineteenth century; see Susan Rutherford, *The Prima Donna and Opera, 1815–1930* (Cambridge: Cambridge University Press, 2006); Roger Parker, *Remaking the Song: Operatic Visions and Revisions from Handel to Berio* (Berkeley, CA: University of California Press, 2006); Hilary Poriss, *Changing the Score: Arias, Prima Donnas, and the Authority of Performance* (Oxford: Oxford University Press, 2009); James Q. Davies, *Romantic Anatomies of Performance* (Berkeley, CA: University of California Press, 2014), 13–40, 123–51 and Parr, *Vocal Virtuosity.*

15. See Ashbrook, 98, 376 and Elizabeth Forbes, 'Cosselli, Domenico', in *The New Grove Dictionary of Opera*, ed. Stanley Sadie (London: Macmillan Reference, 1992), I, 968.

16. See Ashbrook, 632 and Forbes, 'Porto, Carlo', in *The New Grove Dictionary of Opera*, ed. Stanley Sadie (London: Macmillan Reference, 1992), III, 1073.

17. 'Rispettate, o voi, di Dio la tremenda maestà. In suo nome io vel comando, deponete l' ira e il brando. Pace, pace . . . Egli abborrisce l' omicida, e scritto sfa: Chi di ferro altrui ferisce, pur di ferro perirà'. Cammarano, 24.

18. Richard Miller, *The Structure of Singing: System and Art in Vocal Technique* (New York: Schirmer Books, 1986), 115–7.

19. Both Pavarotti and Sutherland appear on a 1972 studio recording with Richard Bonygne directing the Choir and Orchestra of the Royal Opera House (Decca Label, UK, Set 528–30, 1972). Today, the roles of Edgardo and Lucia are more often sung by singers who specialize in the lightness of tone, quick rhythmic figures and rich legato styling required of *bel canto* opera, such as Lawrence Brownlee and Pretty Yende.

20. Often understood as the first *tenore di forza*, Duprez (1806–96) had an extremely successful career, which allowed him to sing principal roles in all the leading opera houses in Europe; see John Warrack and Sandro Corti, 'Duprez, Gilbert (-Louis)', in *The New Grove Dictionary of Opera*, ed. Stanley Sadie (London: Macmillan Reference, 1992), I, 1281.

21. Mary Ann Smart, 'Roles, Reputations, Shadows: Singers at the Opéra, 1828–1849', in *The Cambridge Companion to Grand Opera*, ed. David Charlton (Cambridge: Cambridge University Press, 2003), 117–22.

22. Herbert Weinstock, *Donizetti and the World of Opera* (New York: Pantheon Books, 1963), 348.

23. '[R:] Delator! gioisci dell' opra tua. [N:] Che parli! [R:] Sì, dell' incendio che divampa e strugge questa casa infelice hai tu destata la primiera favilla. [N:] Io non credei ... [R:] Tu del versato sangue, empio, tu sei la ria cagion! Quel sangue al ciel t' accusa, e già la man suprema segna la tua sentenza ... or vanne, e trema'. Cammarano, 34–5.

24. Weinstock, 348.

25. The Italian term *coloratura*, as used here, is connected to a particular *fach* or voice type that was codified during the *bel canto* era when such vocal virtuosity was defined in extremes. For more information on this topic, especially *coloratura* singing and its 'gendered providence of female singers' in the nineteenth century, see Parr, *Vocal Virtuosity* and Rutherford, *The Prima Donna and Opera*.

26. For a critical discussion of Tacchinardi-Persiani's career, see Claudio Vellutini, 'Fanny Tacchinardi-Persiani, Carlo Balocchino and Italian Opera Business in Vienna, Paris and London (1837–1845)', *Cambridge Opera Journal* 30/2–3 (2018): 259–304.

27. The interpretation of Lucia's vocal display in the 'mad scene' is a topic of discussion by many scholars who either analyse it as reflective of feminine madness or conventional vocalization typical of the era, see for example Smart, 'The Silencing of Lucia'; McClary, *Feminine Endings*, 80–111 and Naomi Matsumoto, 'Manacled Freedom: Nineteenth-Century Vocal Improvisation and the Flute-Accompanied Cadenza in Donizetti's *Lucia di Lammermoor*', in *Beyond Notes: Improvisation in Western Music of the Eighteenth and Nineteenth Centuries*, ed. Rudolf Rasch (Turnhout: Brepols, 2011), 295–316.

28. The phrase 'solita forma' was first coined by Abramo Basevi (1818–1885) in his *Studio sulle opere di Giuseppe Verdi* (Florence: Tofani, 1859), where he sets out to analyze the operatic style of Verdi. For a critical perspective on the form, see Harold S. Powers, 'La Solita Forma' and 'The Uses of Convention', *Acta Musicologica* 59/1 (1987): 65–90; Roger Parker, *Leonora's Last Act: Essays in Verdian Discourse* (Princeton, NJ: Princeton University Press, 1998), 42–60 and Francesco Izzo, 'Donizetti's *Don Pasquale* and the Conventions of Mid-Nineteenth Century Opera Buffa', *Studi musicali*, 33/2 (2004): 387–431.

29. Although beyond the scope of this study, for a detailed discussion of how Italian opera composers set the meter, tempo and rhyme scheme of the libretto and thus define the dramatic pacing of the text, see Philip Gossett, *Divas and Scholars: Performing Italian Opera* (Chicago: Chicago University Press, 2006), 41–8.

30. The term 'cavatina' can have different meanings, depending on the context. Generally speaking, as defined in the operas of the *bel canto* era and as used here, a *cavatina* is a short introductory aria sung by a principal character, which usually appears as the opening slow section of a more extended aria or duet.

31. This same aria was replaced in one of its first revivals in Venice in 1836 at the Teatro Apollo with 'Perché non ho del vento' from Donizetti's 1834 two-act opera *Rosmonda d'Inghilterra*. The change was instigated by Tacchinardi-Persiani, who wanted a more 'gentile' subject to showcase her voice and one that she was more familiar with to sing (she premiered the role of Rosmonda in Florence at the Teatro della Pergola). For more information on the substitution of this aria in later performances of *Lucia*, see Hilary Poriss, 'A Madwoman's Choice: Aria Substitution in *Lucia di Lammermoor*', *Cambridge Opera Journal* 13/1 (2001): 1–28.

32. For an analysis of the *cavatina* and the unconventional use of strophic form in the setting of the text, see Smart, 'The Silencing of Lucia', 133–7.

33. 'Al cor che geme questo affetto è sola speme … è conforto al mio penar!', Cammarano, 10.

34. 'Quando rapito in estasi del più cocente amore … si schiuda il ciel per me', Cammarano, 10.

35. This was the common complaint levelled at *bel canto* opera by later commentators, most especially Wagner in his *Opera and Drama* (1851); see Jens Malte Fischer, 'Wagner and *Bel Canto*', *The Opera Quarterly* 11/4 (1995): 53–8.

36. Ashbrook, 265.

37. See Ashbrook, 256–82.

3

THE SONIC LANDSCAPE: THE ORCHESTRAL PRELUDE AND SCORE

On the breeze will come to you my ardent sighs,
you will hear in the murmuring sea the echo of my laments.

(Act I, Lucia and Edgardo)[1]

This chapter reflects upon the sonic landscape in *Lucia*. In other words, it defines the orchestral sounds that Donizetti composed alongside his musical writing for the voice (see Chapter 2). These accompanying sounds refer to particular musical instruments heard in the orchestra (instrumentation) and their combination with other instruments (orchestration). In early-nineteenth-century Italy, it was common to compose the orchestral music for an opera when rehearsals began with the singers.[2] As rehearsals for *Lucia* did not begin until a month before the premiere on 26 September 1835, Donizetti had little time to complete the score.[3] Despite the lack of time, which was typical due to the enormous demand for new operatic works, Donizetti was able to create an imaginative combination of unique orchestral timbres that established a sense of realism within the opera, where innocent love, a wedding celebration, mental illness and death are all heard. The instruments Donizetti used to materialize these dramatic ideas include piccolo, 2 flutes, 2 oboes, 2 clarinets, 2 bassoons, 4 horns, 2 trumpets, 3 trombones, bass drum, cymbals, triangle, a stage band (*banda sul palco*), harp, glass harmonica, bell and a full set of strings. And coupled with the unique acoustic dimensions of one of the largest opera houses in Europe, the Teatro di San Carlo, the very theatre where Donizetti served as music director from 1828 to 1838 (see Appendix A), the instrumental music within *Lucia* became a powerhouse of haunting expressiveness, which one can still grasp today by studying the score.[4]

One of the many sources used by musicologists today to understand the dramatic sounds of the orchestra in the first half of the nineteenth century is Hector Berlioz's *Treatise on Modern*

Instrumentation and Orchestration (1844).[5] The author, a French composer well-known for his colourful use of the orchestra in his operas and symphonic works, sought to present in the *Treatise* a composer's guide to the 'character and expressive potential' of each musical instrument commonly found in Europe. Although the *Treatise* reflects more often than not Berlioz's own musical taste, a man who travelled widely in Central Europe as both a music critic and composer and favoured the music of Gluck and various other German composers, the *Treatise* nonetheless enjoyed great circulation throughout the nineteenth century and still remains in publication today. Donizetti died just a few years after the *Treatise* was published, so he would not have known of Berlioz's work.[6] Still, the *Treatise* discusses many of the same instruments used in Donizetti's score, which was written with the orchestra of the Teatro di San Carlo in mind, a modern opera house Donizetti knew very well.[7] And, as Dotto and Parker discuss in the critical edition, *Lucia* was a forward-looking opera that relied upon modern orchestration and instrumentation, including valve horns, a relatively new invention at the time.[8] The *Treatise*, therefore, will be used throughout this chapter to contextualize Donizetti's use of the orchestra in Lucia and how the 'expressive potential' of various instruments in the score matches the dramatic ideas found in the libretto.

The Orchestral Prelude

Donizetti wrote a relatively short orchestral prelude to begin the opera,[9] which consists of only thirty-three bars of music. Albeit brief, the opening sounds of *Lucia* paint an aural picture of the tragic work's physical and emotional setting. Like the orchestral opening of *Lucrezia Borgia* (1833), a sombre mood is established at the start of *Lucia* with slowly paced drum beats and rolls written for both the timpani and bass drum. Both percussion instruments play softly to create a sense of spatial distance for the listener, as if a far-off funeral march was being heard. In addition, as Berlioz remarks in his *Treatise*, the pairing of both the timpani (pitched to B♭) and the bass drum (unpitched) helps to 'give an impression of the strange and terrifying noises that signal great natural catastrophes', so that the hollow sound of the bass drum mingles with the ringing tone of the timpani to create an even more dour and gloomy sound.[10] After three bars of timpani and bass drum alone, Donizetti writes another set of three bars, but for a quartet of horns, who all softly play a choral-like lament in B♭ minor. At this time in the nineteenth century, the horn was often played with open and stopped notes, meaning that the notes were played with either a clear resonant tone or a muffled, flat, raspy tone as the hand lay inside the horn to close a portion of the bell's opening. Donizetti does not seem to distinguish either style of playing in the score but having the four horns in such a soft register with notes that rise and fall chromatically seems to suggest stopped notes on the horn, thus creating a hoarse sound on the instrument that emulates more the sound of soft wailing or whimpering. Throughout the prelude, in fact, the horn, understood by Berlioz as a 'noble, melancholy instrument', maintains the sombre mood established by the timpani and bass drum at the start, serving as a quartet of mourners that accompany the beating of funereal drums.[11]

As the horns move the harmony to the dominant of the key, the drumbeats and rolls begin again, thus reaffirming the march-like rhythm that began at the start of the prelude. When the horns enter a second time, they are joined by a larger ensemble of bassoons, clarinets, oboe, trombones and trumpet. This enlarged ensemble plays a slowly rising and falling chromatic melody for three bars before the drums take up their now familiar march rhythm. Donizetti's choice of instruments here signals his desire to create an orchestral colour that establishes a pitiful and pathetic sound as the instruments present falling half steps, a common musical gesture to denote weeping. Donizetti further enhances this sound of woe by placing this passage (bb. 1–18) in a medium, alto-tenor range that highlights a warm, comfortable sound, one that is more reflective perhaps of the human voice in a sorrowful lament than the high-pitched register of a piccolo or flute. This slow melodic passage is presented twice, eventually modulating to major as if grief has given way to hope or resignation. This, too, changes as the prelude without warning (b. 19) presents an extreme dynamic shift from piano to fortissimo with the entire orchestra now brought into the fray, including flute, piccolo and tremolo strings, which have been completely silent up to this point. In addition, joining the upper strings and upper woodwinds at this moment in the prelude is the crash cymbal, which collectively creates a terrifying shock, as if all of one's senses are suddenly frozen, collapsed into one frightful resounding chord. This is heard three times in succession, with each dissonant chord rising slightly in pitch every time (see Example 3.1). The hearing of three sudden loud chords in the context of a soft, lugubrious funeral march seems to foreshadow the similar shock that occurs at the end of the opera as the bell tolls three times to announce the death of Lucia. The reference here in the prelude to the later tolling of the bell in Act III is a chilling one and takes on an even more frightful sound as Donizetti unleashes every instrument of the orchestra to play what amounts to three strokes of horror.

Following these three loud chords, the quiet, sombre mood of the prelude resumes with drumbeats outlining every pulse with accents on the bar, followed by drum rolls. Our woeful ensemble of horns, bassoons, oboe, trumpet and trombone have also returned following the three chords but now with the addition of pizzicato strings. The prelude ends with the drums ceasing their steady pulse, leaving the quartet of horns to conclude the opera's orchestral opening with an unresolved dominant seventh chord (F–A–C–E♭) in B♭ minor followed by three bars of rest – like a question left unanswered (see Example 3.2).

The unresolved dominant seventh chord of the prelude remains like a fog at the start of the opera, lingering as we await the action of Act I. The music of the opening scene begins with the entire orchestra (strings, woodwinds, brass and timpani) playing a fast *vivace* tempo of repeated F notes in several octaves, a kind of galloping gesture to quicken the dramatic pace as Enrico's soldiers enter the stage. The repeated F's thus allow the ending chord of the prelude to resonate further into the start of the opera, which, when Normanno appears on stage, soon moves the unresolved dominant F harmony of the prelude to its tonic of B♭ major, a chivalric sound of hope and courage that dispels any previous thoughts of death and mourning.

To sum, we hear a foreshadowing of the dark events to come in the prelude. In fact, a similar group of instruments (bass drum, timpani,

Example 3.1 Gaetano Donizetti, *Lucia di Lammermoor* [Orchestral Score], Prelude, bb. 19–26. **Lucia di Lammermoor**. Words and Music by Gaetano Donizetti; Critical Edition by Gabriele Dotto and Roger Parker. Copyright © 2022 Casa Ricordi Srl, part of Universal Music Publishing Classics & Screen. This arrangement Copyright © 2024 Casa Ricordi Srl, part of Universal Music Publishing Classics & Screen All Rights Reserved. Used by Permission. *Reprinted by permission of Hal Leonard LLC.*

Example 3.2 Gaetano Donizetti, *Lucia di Lammermoor* [Piano-Vocal Score], Prelude, bb. 29–33 and Introduction to Act I, bb. 1–19.

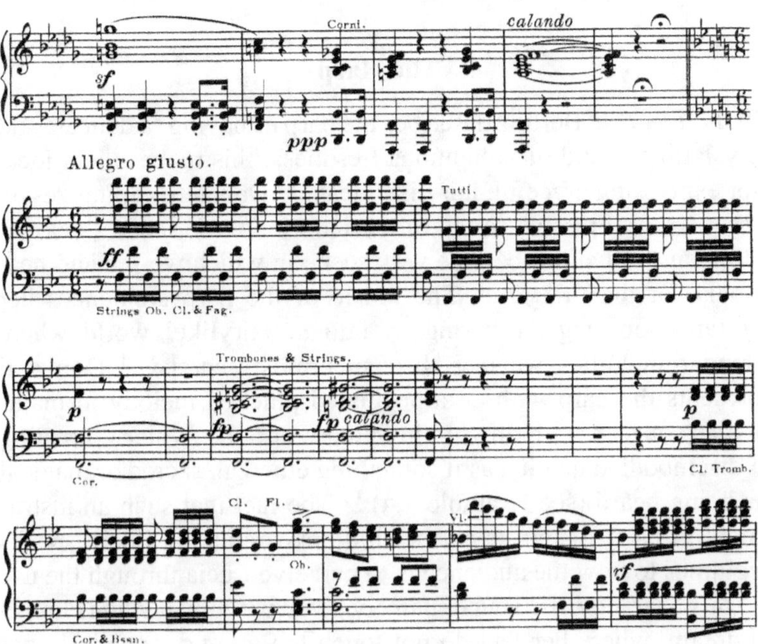

horns, clarinet, oboe, bassoon and trombone) is heard at the end of the opera in Act III as Edgardo stands among the tombs of his forefathers ('Tombe degli avi miei' ['Tombs of my ancestors']) and as the chorus waits to hear news of Lucia's death ('Oh, meschina! Oh, fato orrendo!' ['Oh, poor one! Oh, sad event!']). In addition, the pairing of horns, trombones and bassoon is continually used by Donizetti throughout the opera at times when words sung by the principal characters are filled with anger, as if to strike fear in those who hear them (e.g., Enrico's opening lines in Act I, Enrico in his study at the start of Act II and Raimondo's call for peace at the end of Act II). Thus, the sounds of the prelude – the funeral drum beats, the sudden loud chords that emulate the tolling of a mourning bell and the pitiful sounds of low and medium-ranged instruments – detail to us that *Lucia* is a tragedy filled with death and vengeance. Like dark smoke that bellows into the theatre, the prelude creates a gloomy atmosphere that successfully captures Walter Scott's gothic setting and connects the orchestral opening to death and dying.[12]

The Harp

In the *Treatise*, Berlioz describes the harp as having 'a delicate and crystalline sound of voluptuous freshness; this makes them ideal for expressing graceful, fairylike ideas'.[13] Donizetti capitalizes on this same expressive sound of the harp in Act I, scene 4 (No. 2: 'Regnava nel silenzio'), the very scene in which we see and hear Lucia for the first time. The music of the harp announces her entrance on stage, ushering us into a 'fairylike' world where 'tender melodies whisper their innermost secrets'.[14] Donizetti presents the harp with an arpeggiated plucked melody in major with notes too high to imitate with the voice, creating a disembodied quality, as if something ethereal, sacred or magical is being heard (see Example 3.3).[15] The fact that such an instrument is used to introduce the first appearance of Lucia speaks volumes to how the audience is to perceive Lucia through the use of this characteristic sound, namely a young woman who is lost in a dream, where her feet do not touch the ground, angelic in her wanderings and naïve to her surroundings.[16] In fact, the harp only appears in Act I, which serves to accompany both Lucia's opening aria (in the *tempo di mezzo* and *cabaletta*) and the love duet, though only when Lucia joins Edgardo in singing the final verse of 'Verranno a te sull'aure i miei sospiri ardenti' ['On the breeze will come to you my ardent sighs'] (the *tempo di mezzo* section). By isolating the appearance of the harp to Act I and using it primarily to accompany Lucia's voice, Donizetti further highlights its dramatic association with innocence, a sentiment that we know will soon be eclipsed.

In addition to the unique crystalline timbre of the harp and its dramatic association with innocence, when the harp is first presented in the score it is introduced with sudden *forte* chords played by the orchestra, a kind of Rossinian 'tah-dah' musical gesture that contrasts with the soft sound of the harp. Following this orchestral flourish, the harp presents a series of cascading arpeggios in E♭ major, as if the harp player is warming up the instrument for what

Example 3.3 Gaetano Donizetti, *Lucia di Lammermoor* [Piano-Vocal Score], Act I, scene 4, No. 3: 'Regnava nel silenzio', Recitative and Cavatina [Lucia], bb. 1–15.

we will eventually hear: the melody from 'Tu che a Dio spiegasti l'ali' ['You who have spread your wings to God'], which is Edgardo's final aria, the *cabaletta* section (see Chapter 6). The melody heard here on the harp in Act I is not as sorrowful or resigned as at the opera's end. Rather, it possesses a quiet contentment, highlighting the delicate love between Edgardo and Lucia. Coupled with Donizetti's orchestration – soft pizzicato strings and long-held notes on the horn and clarinet that echo at times the harp's rhythmic flourishes – the melody in hindsight takes on a kind of sonic memoriam, marked by a tenderness that reminds us that the love shared by Lucia and Edgardo was always to be lost in a dream.[17] The fact that the melody of Edgardo's final aria is introduced in this way, even before Lucia sings a single note, is evidence perhaps of Donizetti wanting to memorialize Lucia and her final destiny in Heaven with the dying words of Edgardo:

> You who have spread your wings to God,
> oh, beautiful, beloved soul
> turn towards me serene and calm:
> with you ascends your true love.
> Ah, if on Earth the anger of mortals
> Waged a war against us,
> and kept us divided,
> let God unite us in Heaven.[18]

The Glass Harmonica

The glass harmonica was to make its one and only appearance in Act III, starting in scene 5 to the end of scene 6 (No. 8: Coro e Scena Lucia), during Lucia's so-called 'mad scene'. Donizetti composed the part and even had it rehearsed by Domenico Pezzi, the resident glass harmonica player at the Teatro di San Carlo.[19] However, due to complications that arose over Pezzi's employment at the theatre, Donizetti assigned the glass harmonica part to the flute. Donizetti's music for the harmonica nonetheless appears in the orchestral manuscript, allowing us to view his original intent to use the harmonica at a time in the opera when Lucia is noticeably deranged in voice, mind and appearance: disheveled with convulsive movements, a malevolent smile and wearing a white nightdress scattered with her victim's blood. Because the glass harmonica is often used today in performances of *Lucia* at opera houses around the world, the instrument's history and legacy will be discussed as well as Donizetti's music for the glass harmonica as originally defined in the orchestral score.

Although Berlioz does not mention the instrument in his orchestral treatise, we know that the glass harmonica was invented by the American polymath Benjamin Franklin in 1761.[20] In his invention, Franklin took the earlier-known technique of rubbing glasses filled with different amounts of water and devised an apparatus to fit horizontally glasses of different sizes on a rotating crank, which was operated by a foot pedal. Of the sounds produced on this new musical instrument, Franklin details in a letter of 1762 that the tones 'are incomparably sweet beyond those of any other . . . an instrument that seems peculiarly adapted to Italian music, especially that of the soft and plaintive kind'.[21] Owing to the instrument's sustained vibrato that matched a high female voice in pitch and range, the glass harmonica enjoyed great popularity with musicians and composers in the decades following Franklin's invention, including Mozart, Beethoven and the English musician Marianne Davies (1744–1818), who is considered one of the first virtuosos on the instrument.[22]

The glass harmonica's high ringing tone also became an object of considerable trepidation among many of its early listeners and performers. For example, the eighteenth-century glass harmonica player and composer Karl Leopold Röllig (1754–1804) remarked in his published writings that the instrument could make women faint, send a dog into convulsions, force a sleeping girl to awake screaming and even cause death.[23] The German doctor Franz Anton Mesmer (1734–1815) even went so far as to use the instrument to cause catalepsy in his patients, who would later fall into a deep sleep to bring about healing within the body and the mind.[24]

Putting these two aspects of late eighteenth-century reception together, namely an instrument known to emulate the ethereal sound of the female voice and one that contains the sonic power to unlock the unconscious areas of the mind, one can see why Donizetti was particularly keen on using the instrument to accompany Lucia's 'mad scene' in Act III. He had already used it in an earlier opera, *Elisabetta al castello di Kenilworth* (1829), which he composed for the Teatro di San Carlo, just a year after taking over as musical director.[25] And, according to the 'Historical Introduction' to the critical edition of the score, Donizetti was also already aware of various performance techniques on the instrument as 'the phrasing and expression marks [in the score] are careful and detailed, even down to the indication *ondeggiante* [seesaw] on a long-held note'.[26] For example, in the original score, one notes that the pitches are doubled at the octave with rising arpeggios that create a building-up-of-sound effect. This style of phrasing culminates into rocking figures in the upper register that emulate a trill or the upper and lower troughs of an undulating sound wave (see Example 3.4). Such auspicious writing for an instrument that bore a curious legacy in both the world of music and medicine (albeit spurious) highlights Donizetti's intent to capitalize on its ability to stimulate profound emotions and feelings within the listener.

Originally planned by Donizetti to be heard offstage and thus out of sight of the audience, the music for the glass harmonica begins with the melody from Lucia's *cavatina* from Act I, 'Regnava nel silenzio' ['At dead of night']. The melodic line of this haunting vocal melody, which we recall details the gothic-tinged dream of Lucia as she tells Alisa of the ghost she saw at the fountain, is dramatically timed to begin right before Lucia's opening words in Act III, where she sings in a simple *parlante* or speaking style 'il dolce suono mi colpì di sua voce' ['the sweet sound of his voice struck me']. By presenting these words in a conversational-like manner, following the entrance of the glass harmonica, Lucia acknowledges, on the one hand, the peculiarity of the harmonica's sound, as if Lucia is breaking the fourth wall and becomes a part of the listening audience. On the other hand, her acknowledgment of the glass harmonica's disembodied sound reflects not only what we hear in the audience but what she hears in her own mind, which is Edgardo's voice conflated with her tragic memory of the ghost. The glass harmonica, as used here by Donizetti, therefore, is a sonic signifier of Lucia's confused state, reflected in the harmonica's uncanny sound and the recounting of an earlier traumatic memory. It is as if another Lucia has entered the stage unseen but heard, presenting a schizophrenic reality for both the audience Sond Lucia. In fact, present-day commentators have even viewed this combination of Lucia's voice and appearance with the glass harmonica as one that 'was originally intended to conjure up anxieties about young women's vulnerability to

68

Example 3.4 Gaetano Donizetti, *Lucia di Lammermoor* [Orchestral Score], Act III, scene 5, No. 8: Coro e Scena Lucia, bb. 320–24. **Lucia di Lammermoor**. Words and Music by Gaetano Donizetti; Critical Edition by Gabriele Dotto and Roger Parker. Copyright © 2022 Casa Ricordi Srl, part of Universal Music Publishing Classics & Screen. This arrangement Copyright © 2024 Casa Ricordi Srl, part of Universal Music Publishing Classics & Screen All Rights Reserved. Used by Permission. *Reprinted by permission of Hal Leonard LLC.*

nervous derangement, taboo eroticism, and alienation from healthy, normal society … a genuine invocation of the uncanny.'[27] Others have even viewed the use of the glass harmonica in this scene as one that leads Lucia to a Mesmeric 'crisis', as if the glass harmonica itself was a Mesmeric instrument inducing memories of the past within Lucia, who eventually succumbs to the harmonica's power and collapses at the end of the scene.[28]

Furthermore, one notes in the original score that Donizetti has the glass harmonica play melodies that mirror Lucia's vocal lines. We see this occurring throughout Lucia's final aria, nowhere more explicitly than in the vocal cadenza at the end of the *cantabile* section (before the arrival of Enrico on stage). Although Donizetti composed a short vocal cadenza for this section, it was still expected for the singer to improvise the cadenza in order to impress audiences with their musical ability and, in a sense, to make it their own. However, starting in the late nineteenth century, in an effort to extend the vocal cadenza even further beyond Donizetti's score, it became customary to add a flute melody to the vocal accompaniment (see Chapter 7 for more information on this modern performance practice). This new version of the cadenza has been performed by singers ever since, and more recently, it has been performed with the glass harmonica (e.g., Diana Damrau's concert performance of the vocal cadenza with glass harmonica in 2014).[29] In this modern interpretation of the cadenza, one notes that the performer becomes enthralled with the sound of the glass harmonica as it mimics the vocal line, first with interplay between the melodic phrases and then simultaneously with the voice. The performer and the audience are thus paired as spectators to the combined sound of the voice and the glass harmonica: an aural showcase of two instruments whose sonic reality highlights the world of the unconscious.[30]

Mourning Bell ('*Campana Di Moribondi*')

Donizetti's music for the bell or the 'campana di moribondi' [mourning bell] is only nine measures long. The brevity of its appearance (Act III, Final Scene, No. 9: Ultima Scena, bb. 151–59), however, does not match its importance to the opera as we hear it just as Edgardo resolves to visit Lucia on her deathbed. The bell tolls the death of Lucia to all those on stage, serving as a diegetic sound or music from within the opera. This accords with what Berlioz mentions about bells in his *Treatise*, where he argues that the instrument is to be used for dramatic rather than musical purposes, 'appropriate for solemn or tragic scenes'.[31] Berlioz in fact used the bell to great effect in the fifth movement ('Dream of a Witches' Sabbath') of his *Symphonie fantastique* (1830), where he stationed offstage two large bells tuned to C and G (respectively) that resound just as the notes of the medieval chant *Dies irae* are played by bassoon, ophicleide (an early tuba) and trombone. The heavy low brass orchestration joins the metal 'clang' of the two bells, which alternate between C and G (tonic and dominant) to create a diabolical sound of horror. Donizetti orchestrates his tolling of the bell in *Lucia* in a similar manner by having a single bell tuned to G (the central note of the harmony) toll for two beats as the rest of the orchestra is silent for a brief time before trombones and horns in G, accompanied by timpani rolls in D and tremolo strings, respond with a dotted rhythm followed by long held notes (G's in octaves) that slowly dissipate in volume (see Example 3.5). This is repeated twice with the second and third bell toll joined by bassoons, which fill out the G harmony with shifting chords, like a kaleidoscope creating new colour combinations with every turn. Donizetti thus orchestrates around the bell and its tolling to enhance its dramatic weight as a sound that heralds the death of Lucia and Edgardo's worst fear.

Stage Band ('*Banda Sul Palco*')

It was customary in Italian opera in the first half of the nineteenth century to have a local wind ensemble perform on stage ('sul palco'), either literally on stage or offstage in the wings. This practice helped provide a sense of realism to the production and perhaps present a tinge of local pride for the audience. According to Philip Gossett, these wind ensembles were supplied by musicians from the local military garrison with approval coming from the city municipal authority.[32] Rossini was, in fact, the one who began the trend by including a stage band in his *Ricciardo e Zoraide* (Teatro di San Carlo, 1818), a serious opera set during the Crusades and filled throughout with military conflict.

When writing for a stage band, 'normally a composer would prepare a short score of the music to be played by the *banda* . . . whereby a local bandmaster would arrange this music for whatever contingent of band instruments could be made available'.[33] In *Lucia*, Donizetti presents his short score for a stage band in Act II, appearing right as Lucia asks her brother 'what's that?' ('che fia!'), to which he responds rather haughtily, 'So you hear the festive sounds coming from the shore?'. Similar to the use of the bell in Act III, the use of the *banda* here in Act II highlights music heard

Example 3.5 Gaetano Donizetti, *Lucia di Lammermoor* [Orchestral Score], Act III, scene 9, No. 9: Ultima Scena, bb. 151–56. **Lucia di Lammermoor**. Words and Music by Gaetano Donizetti; Critical Edition by Gabriele Dotto and Roger Parker. Copyright © 2022 Casa Ricordi Srl, part of Universal Music Publishing Classics & Screen. This arrangement Copyright © 2024 Casa Ricordi Srl, part of Universal Music Publishing Classics & Screen All Rights Reserved. Used by Permission. *Reprinted by permission of Hal Leonard LLC.*

from within the work. And in the context of the audience hearing a local military ensemble in the middle of an opera, it helps to put in relief the true reality of Lucia's desperation.[34]

The stage band music in *Lucia* is rather simple, with fast repetitive notes in a dance-like meter in F major, a relatively straightforward key for any military wind ensemble, which was most likely made up of brass, woodwinds and percussion. In the critical edition to the score, the editors produced a contemporary instrumentation of the stage band, found in a Milanese manuscript that accompanied the first performance of *Lucia* at La Scala in 1839.[35] Here we see a rather large ensemble of piccolo, four clarinets, two bassoons, two contrabassoons (or ophicleide), four horns, six trumpets, three trombones, a side drum and a bass drum. In both the original score of 1835 and in this later manuscript, the passage is thirty-two bars long, presenting music as for a parade that alternates between the tonic (F major) and dominant (C major). All the instruments of the stage band play as one ensemble, sounding together on each note, rhythm and chord. One notes that this passage is similar to the start of Act I with its rousing F major chords in a fast <6/8> meter, detailing a sound of pomp and military action. In a crucial dramatic twist here, however, Donizetti integrates the sound of the stage band with the pleas of Lucia and Enrico, who argue while the instruments play off-stage (see Example 3.6). In fact, the libretto indicates that 'festive sounds are heard in the distance', which is further evidence that Donizetti (and Cammarano) wanted the sound of the band to have more of a psychological effect than anything else.[36]

Conclusion

Despite its importance, as argued here, it must be remembered that orchestral music was not often heard as a featured element in Italian *bel canto*. As William Ashbrook reminds us:

In the musical world that Donizetti entered as an opera composer in 1817, new works were designed to produce, hopefully, an immediate success. The ready assimilability of opera in Italy at this time was assured by the composer's general adherence to a number of conventions of musical forms and procedures; and it follows that a work's success was measured by the composer's skill, or want of it,

Example 3.6 Gaetano Donizetti, *Lucia di Lammermoor* [Orchestral Score], Act II, scene 2, No. 4: Duetta Enrico e Lucia, bb. 224–37. **Lucia di Lammermoor**. Words and Music by Gaetano Donizetti; Critical Edition by Gabriele Dotto and Roger Parker. Copyright © 2022 Casa Ricordi Srl, part of Universal Music Publishing Classics & Screen. This arrangement Copyright © 2024 Casa Ricordi Srl, part of Universal Music Publishing Classics & Screen All Rights Reserved. Used by Permission. *Reprinted by permission of Hal Leonard LLC.*

in filling these forms with music that struck an audience as fresh and dramatically appropriate, rather than as novel or innovative.[37]

The result was that orchestral parts of an Italian opera were composed quickly and conformed to the musical forces at hand. In comparison to French or German opera at the time, we know that Italian opera put a far greater emphasis on the beauty of the voice ('bel canto') than on the sound of the orchestra, which was further compromised by the brief amount of time allowed between the commission of an operatic work and its premiere. We see in Donizetti's score, however, a bucking of the trend, whereby the orchestration and instrumentation capture much of the shifting emotions, character development and overall dramatic pacing of the work. And in an opera set in a gothic environment with murder, suicide, death and the world of madness and the unconscious, the orchestra had a mighty role to play. This very point was picked up by the reviewers at the premiere. For example, the reviewer for the Napoli newspaper *L'omnibus*, when comparing the score of *Lucia* to Donizetti's previous operas, such as *Anna Bolena* (1830) and *Persiani* (1833), wrote that the 'dramatic effect and richness in instrumentation' was as great as anything heard by the composer.[38]

It is no wonder that *bel canto* opera, with its emphasis on vocal style and expression, gave way to a greater use of the orchestra in the 1840s and beyond (e.g., Donizetti's *Maria di Rohan*, 1843 and Verdi's *Ernani*, 1844) as Italian composers sought to attract a larger international audience whose tastes lay in a more hybrid mix of theatre (note from Appendix A that soon after the premiere of *Lucia*, Donizetti left Italy for France in 1838 and then later for Austria in 1842, which once again highlights the composer's desire to grow beyond the Italian *bel canto* tradition).[39] Indeed, scholars have argued that around the time of the premiere of *Lucia* is when *bel canto* opera began to show the influence of more 'romantic' source texts (the works of Victor Hugo, for example) that demanded 'single words and phrases [to be] communicated to the listener in a far more direct manner' than the Rossinian penchant for 'vocal expression' alone.[40] In this transition to a mixed (and international) style of opera, the orchestra in Italian opera became a far more useful tool than earlier in the century in detailing the subtle emotions of the principal characters and the overall setting. Perhaps again, this is one of the reasons why *Lucia* remains a mainstay in opera houses today – effectively revealing a violent and complex narrative in a rich sonic landscape similar to that found in the more naturalistic works of Verdi and his contemporaries.

3 Sonic Landscape: Prelude and Score

Notes

1. 'Verranno a te sull' aura i miei sospiri ardenti, udrai nel mar che mormora l' eco de' miei lamenti'. Cammarano, 13.
2. Gossett, *Divas and Scholars*, 63.
3. If the vocal music was already prepared, then the orchestration and instrumentation, whose primary function was to accompany the voice, could be written rather quickly by the composer. This is corroborated in the 'Sources' section of the critical edition of the score for *Lucia*, where the editors state that Donizetti completed the orchestration after rehearsals began and that it was not done in a linear fashion; see Dotto and Parker, II, 618.
4. The Teatro di San Carlo was first built by King Charles VII of Spain, Naples and Sicily in 1737 as a home for *opera seria*. After a ballet rehearsal on 12 February 1816, in which an oil lamp was knocked over and ignited a fire on stage, the 3,300-seat opera house was destroyed. The hall was soon rebuilt by King Charles's son Ferdinand IV; it reopened on 12 January 1817 with an enlarged stage, improved acoustics and an impressive painted dome ceiling depicting Apollo and the goddess Minerva. For more information about the history of the hall and its unique acoustic environment, see Karyl Charna Lynn, *Italian Opera Houses and Festivals* (Lanham, MD: Scarecrow Press, 2005), 277–89; G. Innace, C. Ianniello, L. Maffei and R. Romano, 'Objective Measurement of the Listening Condition in the Old Italian Opera House "Teatro di San Carlo"', *Journal of Sound and Vibration* 232/1 (2000): 239–49 and Franco Mancini, *Il Teatro di San Carlo, 1737–1987*, 3 vols. (Naples: Electa, 1987).
5. Hector Berlioz, *Grand traité d'instrumentation et d'orchestration modernes* (Paris: Schonenberger, 1844). For an English translation of the treatise with critical annotations and remarks, see Hugh Macdonald, *Berlioz's Orchestration Treatise: A Translation and Commentary* (Cambridge: Cambridge University Press, 2002).
6. Berlioz was not a great fan of Italian opera but he did find *Lucia* – albeit in French translation (*Lucie de Lammermoor*) and performed by a less than adequate orchestra (9 August 1839, Théâtre de la Renaissance) – an admirable work with 'some very beautiful pieces, which in their dramatic expression is generally much more plentiful than in a great number of serious operas by the modern Italians' ['Disons seulement qu'elle contient de fort beaux morceaux, que l'expression dramatique y est généralement beaucoup plus respectée que dans le grand nombre des opéras sérieux des Italiens modernes']. Hector Berlioz, 'Feuilleton du *Journal des débats*: Première representation de *Lucie de Lammermoor*', *Journal des débats politiques et littéraires*, 9 August 1839.

7. For a discussion of the opera orchestra in Italy in the *primo otto-cento*, especially the size and balance of the instruments used to accompany singers, see Gregory W. Harwood, 'Verdi's Reform of the Italian Opera Orchestra', *19th-Century Music*, 10/2 (1986), 109–12.

8. Dotto and Parker, I, xxii.

9. According to Ashbrook, the difference between an orchestral prelude and an overture is that 'a prelude is short, ranging from five measures (*Elvida*) to fifty-two (*La Zingara* and *Dom Sébastien*) ... [while] overtures are longer and usually follow the basic Rossinian pattern – first movement form without development ... [and] end with a coda and a full set of cadential figures' (Ashbrook, 235).

10. Macdonald, 281.

11. Macdonald, 176.

12. The preludes to *Lucrezia Borgia* (1833) and *Maria de Rudenz* (1838), Donizetti's other gothic-tinged works, are composed with similar orchestral openings that vacillate between the sombre sound of a lone timpani to sudden *forte* diminished chords played by a full orchestra. These works also contain murderous acts of revenge, suicide and sudden twists of fate that are presaged in their separate preludes, which appear to be more atmospheric than declamatory; see Ashbrook, 237–40.

13. Macdonald, 74. Berlioz is apparently describing the sound of the double-action pedal harp, which was the most common type of European harp in use in the 1830s. The instrument was invented by the French instrument maker Sébastien Erard in 1810 to replace the single-action pedal harp. Erard's invention allowed the harp to play a full range of chromatic notes no matter the key in order to 'pluck or arpeggiate all chords' (Macdonald, 67).

14. Macdonald, 74.

15. According to Berlioz, the Italian name for harp ('arpa') is due to its natural ability to present an 'arpeggio', which is how it is presented here in *Lucia*; see Macdonald, 70.

16. Donizetti also composed a similar part for the harp in *L'elisir d'amore* (1832), which accompanies the tenor Nemorino as he laments his unrequited love for Adina ('Una furtiva lagrima', Act I). As in *Lucia*, the arpeggiated music for the harp characterizes Nemorino's love as beyond compare and one that reflects a sacred pining of the soul.

17. The famous harp virtuoso Elias Parish-Alvars (1808–49) used the harp music from Act I as the basis of his *Grand fantasie sur des motifs de l'opéra 'Lucia di Lammermoor* (Vienna: Artaria & Co., 1845), which also contains harp arrangements of the love duet

between Edgardo and Lucia at the end of Act I and Edgardo's final aria from Act III.

18. 'Tu che a Dio spiegasti l'ali, o bell'alma innamorata, ti rivolgi a me placata, teco ascenda il tuo fedel. Ah! se l' ira de' mortali fece a noi sì lunga guerra; se divisi fummo in terra, ne congiunga il Nume in ciel'. Cammarano, 37.

19. Dotto and Parker, I, xxvii.

20. Peter Pesic, 'Composing the Crisis: From Mesmer's Harmonica to Charcot's Tam-tam', *Nineteenth-Century Music Review* 19/1 (2022): 9.

21. Benjamin Franklin, Personal Letter to Giambattista Beccaria, 13 July 1762; see *The Papers of Benjamin Franklin*, 10, ed. Leonard W. Labaree (New Haven, CT: Yale University Press, 1959), 127.

22. Rebecca Wolf, 'The Sound of Glass: Transparency and Danger', *Performing Knowledge, 1750–1850*, eds. Mary Helen Dupree and Sean B. Franzel (Berlin: De Gruyter, 2015), 113–36.

23. Karl Leopold Röllig, *Über die Harmonika, ein Fragment* (Berlin, 1787). For a discussion of Röllig's views on both the virtues and hazards of the glass harmonica, see Hadlock, 'Sonorous Bodies'.

24. See Pesic, 'Composing the Crisis', 7–30.

25. The glass harmonica appears in Act III, scene 2, as Amelia, the wife of Leicester (who also happens to be Queen Elizabeth's favourite), laments her imprisonment and recalls the joy of past romantic love; see William Ashbrook, 'Elisabetta al castello di Kenilworth (1829)', *The Opera Quarterly* 14/3 (1998): 116–9.

26. Dotto and Parker, I, xxvi.

27. Hadlock, 534; see also Emilio Sala, 'Women Crazed by Love: An Aspect of Romantic Opera' (Eng. trans. William Ashbrook), *The Opera Quarterly* 10/3 (1994): 19–41.

28. See Pesic, 18–20. Hadlock also shares this same impression of the instrument in the 'mad scene', especially in the vocal cadenza; see Hadlock, 534–35.

29. Warner Classics, 'Diana Damrau sings *Lucia di Lammermoor* Mad Scene Live', 7 November 2014 (https://youtu.be/BEM3bvdNS_g?si=luk1Yv7jSAdh7Xr7; accessed 6 April 2023).

30. The sonic legacy of the glass harmonica to represent the uncanny can be found in film scores of the twentieth century, such as in *The War of the Worlds* (Leith Stevens, 1953); *Glass Harmonica* (Alfred Schnittke, 1968); *Fellini's Casanova* (Nino Rota, 1976); *The Tenant* (Philippe Sarde, 1976); and *Star Trek II: The Wrath of Khan* (James Horner, 1982).

31. Macdonald, 274.

32. Gossett, 64.

33. Gossett, 64.

34. For a discussion of the dramaturgical use of stage bands in Italian opera, see Luca Zoppelli, '"Stage Music" in Early Nineteenth-Century Italian Opera', trans. Arthur Groos and Roger Parker, *Cambridge Opera Journal* 2/1 (1990): 29–39.
35. Dotto and Parker, II, 581–4.
36. 'Si ascoltano echeggiare in lontananza festivi suoni, e clamorose grida'. Cammarano, 17.
37. Ashbrook, 235.
38. 'E l' augurio non sembri sconsigliato se diremo che questa *Lucia* sarà tutta sorella della ... *Parisini* per l' effetto drammatico e la ricchezza di strumentale'. *L'Omnibus*, 3 October 1835.
39. See Roger Parker, 'The Opera Industry', in *The Cambridge History of Nineteenth-Century Music*, ed. Jim Samson (Cambridge: Cambridge University Press, 2001), 104–17.
40. Parker, 'The Opera Industry', 110–1.

4

ACT I: THE DEPARTURE

The star that guides my fortunes has waned, while
Edgardo – that mortal enemy of my family – from his
ruined tower, shows his bold face and mocks me.

(Act I, Enrico)[1]

In the next three chapters we will use the source texts
(Chapter 1), the *bel canto* genre (Chapter 2) and the orchestral
score (Chapter 3) to analyse the musico-dramatic narratives set
forth in each of the three acts of *Lucia di Lammermoor*. This
chapter focuses on the opera's first act, which takes place
entirely out in the open, just outside the Ravenswood Castle,
an area where individuals roam beyond the protection of the
castle walls. In nineteenth-century opera, an 'open space' such
as a forest glen or a city square is one where a character's
intimate thoughts are often revealed to others on stage. From
this perspective, we see that the 'open space' that begins the
opera literally opens us up to the inner world of the characters,
so much so that we soon learn that the Ashton family is in dire
straits, Lucia has a secret lover and Edgardo is that lover. In
addition, we also find out that this open space is wild and
dangerous, where intruders traipse the land, where Lucia was
nearly killed by a raging bull, where her mother is buried, where
oaths of revenge are made and where the ghost of a dead woman
appeared at the mouth of a fountain. All of this we learn from
the first four scenes of the opera.[2] As the opera historian Hervé
Lacombe writes, in Romantic librettos there always remained
a 'close link between nature and drama ... the setting for the
action mirrored the forces working upon the hearts and minds of
the characters'.[3] If this is indeed the case, then we see that the
'open space' of Act I is linked to the very forces that are acting
upon Lucia, namely death in all its guises.

Introduzione

As dictated by the libretto, Act I is set in a park near the shoreline at dusk with the remains of a gothic fountain scattered nearby.[4] The act begins as Enrico's soldiers enter the scene attempting to discover the identity of an intruder. Their need to find out the name of this individual is also demanded by the dictates of an 'open space', where 'truth may flash like a lightning bolt in a grey clouded sky'.[5] With hunting horns, trumpets, trombones, drums, woodwinds and strings, their chivalric call to action, where 'honour demands and honour requires it',[6] rings out in B♭ major as the wildness of the setting matches the intensity of Enrico's men (see Appendix B for a mapping of the compositional structure of this scene).

Such bravado is also found within Enrico, who along with Raimondo now enters and joins Normanno on stage. Upon his entrance, Enrico describes to both men his frustration with his rival Edgardo and his sister Lucia. Seeking their advice, Edgardo first hears from Raimondo, who tells him that Lucia needs time to grieve before she can begin to love someone, while Normanno counters with a rumour that Lucia has already found a lover – Edgardo, the man who saved her from the bull.

Donizetti sets their exchange in a simple *parlante*-style, which helps not only to clarify the words being sung but also what each man desires. But more so than the vocal style of their exchange, Donizetti accompanies the words of these men with particular phrase structures and rhythmic patterns that help to solidify their position. For example, when Enrico begins his recitative, Donizetti composes a sudden *forte-piano* dynamic to be heard on the trombones and bassoons, which present a stepwise descending phrase that starts on D♭ and then descends an interval of a fourth to A♭, which is soon repeated on E♭, which descends an interval of a fifth to A♭ (see Example 4.1). This phrase structure heard in the accompaniment repeats with a B natural (C♭) descending an interval of a tritone (F), then an A♭ descending an interval of a seventh (B♭). In addition, Donizetti gives the stepwise utterances in the brass and bassoons a martial-like feel that is punctuated with

Example 4.1 Gaetano Donizetti, *Lucia di Lammermoor* [Orchestral Score], Act I, scene 2, No. 1: Introduzione, bb. 135–43. **Lucia di Lammermoor**. Words and Music by Gaetano Donizetti; Critical Edition by Gabriele Dotto and Roger Parker. Copyright © 2022 Casa Ricordi Srl, part of Universal Music Publishing Classics & Screen. This arrangement Copyright © 2024 Casa Ricordi Srl, part of Universal Music Publishing Classics & Screen All Rights Reserved. Used by Permission. *Reprinted by permission of Hal Leonard LLC.*

a long-short-short-long-long rhythm, which helps to emphasize the conviction of Enrico's lines. This melodic and rhythmic sequence in the accompaniment is not significant on its own but when compared to the accompaniment supporting the recitatives of Raimondo and Normanno, the dramatic effect becomes clear.

The vocal line of Raimondo is supported by a dry accompaniment with little to no melodic activity in the orchestra. The strings present long-held chords that slowly descend stepwise on changing harmonies (D, C♯, B♮), a stern and somewhat pallid complement to Raimondo's counsel, which appears to have little effect upon Enrico. Normanno's recitative by contrast shares much of the same phrase structure found in Enrico's recitative but accompanied primarily on the first violin, which Donizetti also presents with a stepwise melody set to a martial-like rhythm. Here, we have opening notes played with the same *forte-piano* dynamic that descend an interval of a fourth (C–G), then a fifth (D–G), followed by an interval of a fourth (A–E) and then an interval of a fifth (B–E). By sharing a similar accompaniment and phrase structure, both Enrico and Normanno appear to share the same opinion, namely that Edgardo cannot be trusted and that Lucia is a problem.

Convinced now more than ever of Edgardo's treachery and Lucia's deceit, Enrico swears vengeance in a double aria. As mentioned in Chapter 2, Donizetti composes a two-stanza *cavatina* in G major with a slow <3/4> tempo accompanied by strings, trombones, bassoons, horns and upper woodwinds, which all bring about a stately dance-like feel to Enrico's aria that is tinged with a bit of horror:

> A cruel and fatal frenzy
> hast thou given birth to in my heart –
> So horrid and so terrible
> is this suspicion that I
> shudder and tremble now;
> my hair stands up on my head.
>
> Full of so much dishonour
> has my 'nun'[-like sister] been born to!
> If lightning should strike you [Lucia]
> before I prove your guilt of this deceitful love,
> the worse off my fate would be.[7]

On the second stanza listed above, both Normanno and Raimondo join Enrico, where Normanno confesses he only told him the truth to protect his honour while Raimondo resigns himself to sighs and a prayer of hope that Normanno's words are not true. As the *cantabile* section comes to an end, the soldiers return to report that Edgardo was indeed the intruder, set to a similar bravura accompaniment and melody as the B♭ major chorus that began the act. Raimondo, fearing the worst, immediately jumps in and tells Enrico not to believe their report ['non crudere ... sospendi ...']. Without skipping a beat, Enrico silences Raimondo and swears to all: 'I will not listen [to you Raimondo]. Your pity for her dictates you in vain ... none shall speak but the voice of vengeance'.[8] This outburst, which is the close of the middle part of Enrico's aria, the *tempo di mezzo*, soon transitions to a faster dance-like <12/8> section accompanied by full orchestra. Donizetti composes this final section of Enrico's aria in G major, the same key as the *cavatina* and thus a continuation of the same gleeful violence and hate expressed earlier. Enrico's words in this *cabaletta* section become embittered and enflamed as the tempo quickens and Normanno and the rest of the soldiers join in and ensure Enrico that 'the guilty one will not escape thy fury' ['Quell' indegno al nuovo albore l' ira tua fuggir non può']. To such unfiltered rage, Raimondo can only muster a pitiful aside: 'Ah, what a terrible [dark] cloud now hangs over this house.'[9]

The dramatic purpose of the *introduzione* is to set the drama in motion and to articulate the main conflict that will ensue. Beginning with the soldier's chorus, a heavy masculine presence is defined from the start of the opera, which fills the hall with sounds of bravura, hunting and violence. This male-driven enterprise continues throughout the *introduzione* as Enrico sings his *cavatina/cabaletta* aria, interspersed with the voices of the soldiers and his head council, an army captain (Normanno) and a man of God (Raimondo). Primarily set in G major and spanning two scenes of dialogue in the libretto, Enrico's aria (scenes 2 and 3) of gleeful hate captures much of the negative energy that will follow Lucia and Edgardo throughout the opera, driving them both to their grave.

The Departure

Following the *introduzione*, Lucia and Alisa arrive on stage to the accompaniment of a harp. (The significance of the harp is discussed in Chapter 3.) Serving as both a signifier of angelic innocence as well as a theatrical sonic trope of transition from one scene to another, the harp helps to direct the listener's attention away from the world of men and towards an intimate feminine setting, where both Lucia and Alisa talk of love, hope and gothic visions under a rising moon. Similar to the exchange that occurred between Enrico and his men, Lucia and Alisa are in conversation at the start of this scene (scene 4) right before Lucia begins her famous *cavatina*, 'Regnava nel silenzio' ['At dead of night'] (see Chapters 1 and 2 for a discussion of the *cavatina* in relation to the opera's gothic narrative and the conventional form in *bel canto*, respectively).

The *cavatina* opens in the key of E♭ minor, a key often used in the nineteenth century to depict an austere but emotionally reflective sound (e.g., Beethoven's orchestral opening to the oratorio *Christ on the Mount of Olives*; Chopin's Étude No. 6, Op. 10 and Prélude No. 14, Op. 28 or Clara Schumann's Romance, No. 1, Op. 11). This, in conjunction with the *larghetto* tempo, the ballad-like <6/8> meter, and sparse orchestration (clarinet, horns, bassoon and pizzicato strings) creates a dreamy sonic landscape for Lucia's legato line, which is shaped by a rising interval of a minor sixth (B♭4 – G♭5) before descending stepwise back to the starting note. Donizetti's music here is aligned with the libretto, which presents a retelling of a past vivid experience tinged with fear. The harmony, however, soon modulates from E♭ minor to the relative major (G♭ major), creating a change in mood as Lucia becomes more excited by her vision of the ghost. This same major key persists in the second stanza of the *cavatina* ('I saw her lips move as if she were speaking, and with her lifeless hand she seemed to beckon me to come')[10] and combined with the increase in *coloratura* in the voice and a thicker orchestral texture, including the added use of the harp and timpani, the change to the relative major suggests that Lucia is somehow removed from the reality of this horror-filled tale and is now consumed with the possibility of

Example 4.2 Gaetano Donizetti, *Lucia di Lammermoor* [Orchestral Score], Act I, scene 4, No. 2: Cavatina Lucia, bb. 93–6. **Lucia di Lammermoor**. Words and Music by Gaetano Donizetti; Critical Edition by Gabriele Dotto and Roger Parker. Copyright © 2022 Casa Ricordi Srl, part of Universal Music Publishing Classics & Screen. This arrangement Copyright © 2024 Casa Ricordi Srl, part of Universal Music Publishing Classics & Screen All Rights Reserved. Used by Permission. *Reprinted by permission of Hal Leonard LLC.*

hope – help from beyond the grave. The sense of joy that now consumes Lucia in the *cavatina* is capped with a vocal cadenza, which appears to transform the *cavatina* from a ballad aria of grisly horror to one of hope and resistance (see Example 4.2).[11] This change from death to hope continues into the *cabaletta* ('Quando rapito in estasi del più cocente amore' ['When he is rapt in ecstasy of the most burning love']), where Lucia speaks of her love for Edgardo and how his love for her 'opens up the heavens'.[12]

In sum, Lucia's opening aria presents her as a complex character. Her *coloratura*, the modal mixture and the surrounding musical environment all suggest a woman who is strong and has an inner drive that even the fear of death cannot fade. Her aria leads directly to the final scene of Act I (scene 5), which gives the act its name: 'The Departure' ['*La partenza*'].[13] When Edgardo finally arrives, the orchestra heralds his entrance with a fast short-long repeated rhythmic pattern played on the strings. This two-bar phrase, which is introduced by Alise's words, 'I hear him coming', gives way to a set of noble-sounding chords in C major, each one attacked with a strong accent that rises in pitch for two bars before settling on a series of held notes for another two bars. The wood-winds, brass and strings all play this chordal passage, which, when added to the initial dotted rhythm heard in the strings, suggest that the hero has arrived on a horse that soon slows before ending its gait. Although Edgardo's entrance music presents sounds of heroic promise and hope, the mood soon changes to regret as Edgardo tells Lucia he has to leave. But before he departs, Donizetti presents us with an act-ending duet that reveals not only the depth of the couple's love but also the significance of this vocal number to the entire work.

As mentioned in the Introduction, the duet finale between Edgardo Ravenswood and Lucia Ashton presents the promise of eternal love, which is affirmed out in the open in front of the very fountain where the ghost appeared to Lucia. The duet thus aligns the betrayal of the ghost by her Ravenswood lover with Lucia's later betrayal of Edgardo in Act II. Although it could be argued that Lucia only betrayed Edgardo owing to Edgardo's seeming betrayal of her as presented in the false letter, the two are never able to reconcile with the truth as both die with the knowledge of the other's betrayal.

Beginning with the *scena*, the opening dialogue indicates that Edgardo wants to make peace with Enrico before he leaves but Lucia pleads with him to keep their love a secret. To such words, Edgardo responds with bitter contempt: 'I understand your intentions!' ['Intendo!']. Just as he sings this line, bassoons and trombones, a usual pairing in the score when something has gone awry, pronounce ominous chords on the dominant harmony, which begins a dramatic passage in A minor (the start of the *tempo d'attacco*), matching Edgardo's growing indigitation:

> I understand your intentions! The guilty persecutor of my house
> is not yet satisfied; he robbed me of my father,
> usurped the inheritance of my family – is this not enough?
> What else does he want?
> What does that base and ferocious heart now want?
> My blood? . . . My utter ruin? . . . He abhors me![14]

Example 4.3 Gaetano Donizetti, *Lucia di Lammermoor* [Orchestral Score], Act I, scene 5, No. 3: Scena e Duetto Finale, bb. 36–40. **Lucia di Lammermoor**. Words and Music by Gaetano Donizetti; Critical Edition by Gabriele Dotto and Roger Parker. Copyright © 2022 Casa Ricordi Srl, part of Universal Music Publishing Classics & Screen. This arrangement Copyright © 2024 Casa Ricordi Srl, part of Universal Music Publishing Classics & Screen All Rights Reserved. Used by Permission. *Reprinted by permission of Hal Leonard LLC.*

The notes set to the words above sit in a relatively comfortable but powerful range for the tenor (A3 to G4), as if Edgardo is saying something that he knows all too well and sings rather easily. In support of Edgardo's words, the double basses and second violins play four short notes that rise an interval of a third and then descend back to the starting note as the rest of the strings play tremolos (see Example 4.3). A similar rhythmic motive is heard earlier in the *scena* as Edgardo tells Lucia of his plans to depart but here in the *tempo d'attacco* they become more pronounced as his anger continues to build. Further adding to the tension, the trombones, an instrument heard here as one that portends doom, play long chords at the end of Edgardo's phrases, revealing a menacing power that fuels his words. The tempo also quickens, bringing in the entire orchestra as Edgardo starts to list all that Enrico has taken away from him. Here, the strings present a Rossini-like crescendo with fast-moving semiquavers and held notes in the woodwinds and brass that drown out Lucia's cries for Edgardo to remain calm. The tension in the music continues to build until Edgardo sings the phrase 'M'odi, e trema' ['Hear me and tremble'], with a long-held G4 on the word 'tremble', accompanied by bassoons, horns, trumpets, trombones and drum rolls on the timpani. This climax of the *tempo d'attacco* leads to a *larghetto* passage sung by Edgardo, which becomes the start of the *cantabile* section of the conventional form of a *bel canto* duet. Donizetti composes this opening part of the duet in G minor as pizzicato strings present a version of the four-note motive heard earlier in his anger-filled dialogue, reiterating Edgardo's demand for justice but now tinged with a precarious sound as the strings pluck softly underneath the voice (see Example 4.4).

Donizetti shortens the vocal phrases to less than two bars at the start, suggesting that Edgardo's opening lines ('On the grave, which encloses the betrayed ashes of my father, I, in my fury, swore an eternal war against thy blood') have such emotional weight that it is difficult for him to get out the words, forcing him to take a brief pause after every two words.[15] But when Edgardo's thoughts turn to Lucia ('But then I saw you' ['ma ti vida']), the vocal phrasing becomes longer, filled with held legato notes that appear as if Edgardo is stating in one breath all that Lucia means to him (see Example 4.4). Accompanied now by flutes, clarinets, horns and strings, this passage marked *dolce* in the score reveals a softness to Edgardo that we have not yet heard. As his vocal line later ends and cadences on the G tonic, Lucia picks up that same note and continues where Edgardo left off but now the harmony modulates to G major – a sleight of hand that trades Edgardo's vengeful anger for Lucia's loving calm.

To highlight the change in the overall mood and a coming together between the two, bowed strings (in the second violin part) are intermixed with pizzicato strings, as well as melodic phrases in the upper woodwinds and horns, which echo Lucia's vocal line. This section (marked *con affetto* in the score) is evenly paced with melodic phrases that contain repeated rhythmic group-ings. All of which create a calming effect and drive the duet to our first vocal pairing, allowing both Lucia and Edgardo to sing in harmony at an interval of a third/sixth, a sure sign of agreement owing to the interval's structural importance to the underlining harmony (more on the importance of this interval in Chapters 5 and 6). In spite of what now appears to be a coming together of

Example 4.4 Gaetano Donizetti, *Lucia di Lammermoor* [Piano-Vocal Score], Act I, scene 5, No. 4: 'Sulla tomba che rinserra', Recitative and Duet Finale I, bb. 60–78.

emotions, Edgardo clings to his words 'Still, my vow is not broken! I may yet fulfil it!' ['Io potrei compirlo ancor!'], while Lucia pleads with Edgardo: 'Love only should invade thy heart. Ah, the noblest, the holiest of all thy vows is a chaste and pure love'.[16] Accompanied only with a cello, Edgardo presents a crescendo to these words,

Example 4.5 Gaetano Donizetti, *Lucia di Lammermoor* [Piano-Vocal Score], Act I, scene 5, No. 4: 'Sulla tomba che rinserra', Recitative and Duet Finale I, bb. 115–23.

raising the pitch with each syllable, from B3 to G4, to eventually end on a F♯4, sounding as a dissonance against the G in the bass. Lucia responds to Edgardo with the words 'give in, give in to me' ['cedi, cedi a me'], which are sung on a cadential passage that moves from E♭ to G in order to return Edgardo to G major by means of the flat sixth. Lucia's words and simple descending line help to diffuse the harshness of Edgardo's F♯, essentially relaxing the dissonant harmony to allow Edgardo's line to conform to G major as muted horns and woodwinds slowly draw the *larghetto* section of the duet to a close (see Example 4.5).

The duet now moves to the *tempo di mezzo* ('Qui, di sposa eterna fede' ['Swear here your eternal faith to me']), which is marked by a change in tempo (from *larghetto* to *allegro*), harmony (from G major to B♭ major) and overall mood, which at this point in the duet is one of haste and increased excitement. Edgardo proposes to Lucia by removing a ring from his finger and placing it on Lucia's, whereupon Lucia does the same. Precipitated by fast triplets played by the entire orchestra, which seem to get louder and higher at every turn, increasing the overall intensity of the moment, Edgardo's proposal is first presented in lyrical dialogue. As the couple exchange rings, however, they come together once again at an interval of a third/sixth to sing the words 'Only the icy hand of death will end our love'.[17] At first glance it seems that these words should be sounded with much more dramatic weight in both the accompaniment and the voices but the passage goes by so quickly (a possible result of the kinetic nature of the *tempo di mezzo*) that it leaves one wondering if the couple even know what they are saying. Indeed, soon after this four-bar phrase, Lucia names 'love' as her witness, while Edgardo counters with 'Heaven' as his, thus indicating that love and faith are all they need to stay true to one another.

As they conclude their vows, the music returns to the busy and frenetic sound of the woodwinds and strings that began this section of the duet as Edgardo reiterates to Lucia that he must leave. Lucia responds with a tearful plea (*piagendo* or crying is written in the score): 'Ah, at least send me letters, companions to your thoughts, so that hope may grow in a life not my own'.[18] Soft pizzicatos accompany Lucia's words at every two-bar phrase, as if the plucking strings mimic the sound of tears that fall at every pause in the vocal line. The absence of the full orchestra at this point in the duet highlights not only Lucia's painful words but also the importance that Edgardo's letters will have for Lucia moving forward, a vital plot element that is exploited by Enrico in Act II.

The most memorable part of the duet (if not the entire opera) follows this brief exchange with the words 'Verranno a te sull' aura' ['On the breeze will come to you my ardent sighs']. This is the start of the *cabaletta* section of the duet, which ends the act (see Example 4.6). The affective power of this phrase is defined in its shape, which opens with an octave leap that appears to float effortlessly above, where it is sustained before falling and then rising again to a set of slurred notes.[19] Like a delicate feather that blows in the wind, the melody successfully 'paints' the words:

Example 4.6 Gaetano Donizetti, *Lucia di Lammermoor* [Piano-Vocal Score], Act I, scene 5, No. 4: 'Sulla tomba che rinserra', Recitative and Duet Finale I, bb. 189–203.

On the breeze will come to you my ardent sighs,
you will hear in the murmuring sea
the echo of my laments:
know that I survive on pain and grief alone.
And on this pledge shed a mournful tear.[20]

Lucia and Edgardo share both the same melody and words, which are accompanied by light accents in the strings that fall on every beat of this <3/4> section. The accompaniment helps to provide a rhythmic lilt to the passage in order to keep the melody line pressing forward in spite of its drawn-out lyrical phrasing. Joining the strings are the woodwinds and horns that mimic the vocal melody with legato phrases and soft chords. After Lucia and Edgardo present the melody separately, they join together to sing it a third time, but instead of singing at an interval of a third/sixth, they sing now in unison, signifying a full coming together, no longer simply in harmony or in agreement but as one voice. To anticipate the dramatic importance of this final phrase, Lucia and Edgardo sing 'Ah' on a single note (F) for four bars (bb. 288–91), as if drawing a massive breath before approaching the octave leap that will start the melody line all over again.

Set to an even more expanded accompaniment than before with harp and second clarinet presenting arpeggios up and down the octave as the flute, upper strings and first clarinet play in unison with the voices, the duet takes on a strong magical feel in this final reprise (bb. 292–342). And in a gothic setting – the open night air under the light of the moon – the duet presents a special theatrical moment that fixates the audience's attention on the couple's love as one that is absolute.

The *cabaletta* ends with a final *stretta* that allows both Edgardo and Lucia to say their goodbyes. Instead of simply ending the duet here, Edgardo interrupts the rapid pace of this final section with a lasting reminder: 'Rammentati! Ne stringe il Ciel!' ['Remember, we are united by Heaven!'] (see Example 4.7). Accompanied only by trombones, horns and bassoons, sounding a fully diminished-seventh chord (C#-E-G-B♭) for four bars, Edgardo's fateful reminder is sung to a high $G4$, which in combination with the diminished chord clashes with both the loving sentiment of the duet and the B♭ major harmony. This sudden change in the overall dramatic feel of the duet, serves to foreshadow the tragedy to come and presents a possible pronouncement of the curse as witnessed by the fountain, ghost and the exchange of rings (see Chapter 1 for a discussion of the curse).

The act thus ends as Lucia and Edgardo sing in unison a set of long held notes from $F4/F5$ to $B♭4/B♭5$ with no accompaniment – Edgardo's line is set to the words 'Addio!', while Lucia simply sings 'Edgardo!'. As Edgardo exits, Lucia sings alone on stage the high $B♭5$ for another two bars before (according to the MS score) falling unconscious ['cade svenuta'] as the full orchestra plays on for another 22 bars with tremolo strings, timpani rolls and B♭ major chords in the brass and woodwinds.[21] This same key triumphantly presented here was of course heard at the start of the act associated with the bravura actions of Enrico's men but now the B♭ major harmony supports the couple's courageous act of love declared in this wild and open space. The high $B♭5$ held alone by Lucia thus frames her as an unrelenting hero amongst the sounds of the full orchestra and reaffirms that Lucia is desperate for Edgardo to return.

Example 4.7 Gaetano Donizetti, *Lucia di Lammermoor* [Piano-Vocal Score], Act I, scene 5, No. 4: 'Sulla tomba che rinserra', Recitative and Duet Finale I, bb. 351–82.

Conclusion

The 'open space' of Act I details the forces that motivate the actions of all the principal characters in *Lucia*. This is an outdoor area that

is full of wild beasts, spectres and furious tempers and yet it remains
the setting of a bold and daring act of love between two people
whose families are at war. The melodies sung in this act, such as
Lucia's *cavatina* ('Regnava nel silenzio' ['At dead of night']) and
the *cabaletta* from the love duet ('Verranno a te' ['On the breeze
will come to you my ardent sighs']), come back in Act III to haunt
Lucia and remind her of what once was. In addition, various plot
points are planted here in Act I that have drastic consequences later
in the opera, such as Enrico's bloodthirst, the curse that surrounds
the gothic fountain, Lucia's desperate hope to receive letters from
Edgardo and Edgardo's own desire to avenge his father. Act
I therefore sets the stage for the tragedy that ensues, defining not
only realistic characters within a historic backdrop but also a highly
emotional environment that is methodically constructed with
orchestra, voice and libretto. The structure of this opening act is
fairly conventional, where a male chorus (scene 1) leads into an aria
(scenes 2 and 3), followed by a second aria (scene 4) and then the
duet finale (scene 5). The harmonic language, however, is anything
but conventional as the B♭ minor of the orchestral prelude (see
Chapter 3) transitions to B♭ major (scene 1) and then G major
(scenes 2 and 3), E♭ major-E♭ minor-G♭ major-E♭ major-A♭ major
(scene 4) and then finally C major-A minor-G minor-G major-B♭
major (scene 5); see Appendix B.[22] Beginning and ending the act in
the same key provides symmetry to the opening and closing of the
act but nonetheless obscures the emotional journey that was tra-
versed by the characters, from anger and hate to hope and love. As
we now turn to Act II, an act that takes place entirely within the
walls of the castle, we will see that this supposed place of protection
is not a place of love but of fear, death and betrayal.

Notes

1. 'Del mio destin si ottenebrò la stella ... intanto Edgardo ... quel
   mortal nemico di mia prosapia, dalle sue rovine erge la fronte
   baldanzosa e ride'! Cammarano, 6–7.
2. The wild bull that attacked Lucia is mentioned by Normanno in Act
   I, scene 2 (Cammarano, 6). He explains to Enrico that Lucia was on
   her way to visit her mother's grave when she was attacked by the

bull. The bull was shot and killed by Edgardo as it charged. The story of the ghost is mentioned in Act I, scene 4 (Cammarano, 10).

3. Hervé Lacombe, *Les voies de l'opéra français au XIXe siècle*, Eng. trans. Edward Schneider, *The Keys to French Opera in the Nineteenth Century* (Berkeley: University of California Press, 2001), 87.

4. The *introduzione* refers to the 'piece or pieces that follow the rise of the curtain[,] launch[ing] the exposition of the plot', see Ashbrook, 243–44.

5. 'Fia che splenda il terribile vero come lampo fra nubi d' orror'! Cammarano, 5.

6. 'Lo domanda … lo impone l' onor'. Cammarano, 5.

7. 'Cruda … funesta smania tu m' hai destata in petto! È' troppo, è troppo orribile questo fatal sospetto! Mi fa gelare e fremere! Mi drizza in fronte il crin! Colma di tanto obbrobrio chi suora mia nascea! Pria che d' amor sì perfido a me svelarti rea, se ti colpisse un fulmine, fora men rio destin'. Cammarano, 7.

8. 'Udir non vo'. La pietade in suo favore miti sensi invan ti detta … se mi parli di vendetta solo intender ti potrò'. Cammarano, 6–7.

9. 'Ahi, qual nembo di terrore questa casa circondò'. Cammarano, 8.

10. 'Qual di chi parla muoversi il labbro suo vedea, e con la mano esanime chiamarmi a sè parea'. Cammarano, 10.

11. Smart in fact sees the *cavatina* as an example of Lucia's 'resistance to formal convention', a characteristic example of the female voice breaking free from order and control as defined by 'her elaborate and formally anomalous musical expression'; Smart, 'The Silencing of Lucia', 133, 137.

12. 'Parmi che a lui d'accanto si schiuda il ciel per me'! Cammarano, 10.

13. Cammarano, 5.

14. 'Intendo! Di mia stirpe il reo persecutore ancor pago non è! Me tolse il padre … il mio retaggio avito con trame inique m' usurpò … nè basta? Che brama ancor! Chi chiede quel cor feroce, e rio? La mia perdita intera, il sangue mio? Ei mi abborre'! Cammarano, 11.

15. 'Sulla tomba che rinserra il tradito genitore, al tuo sangue eterna guerra io giurai nel mio furore'. Cammarano, 12.

16. 'Solo amor t' infiammi il petto … Ah! il più nobile il più santo de' tuoi voti è un puro amor'! Cammarano, 12.

17. 'Porrà fine al nostro foco sol di morte il freddo gel'. Cammarano, 13.

18. 'Ah! Talor del tuo pensiero venga un foglio messaggiero, e la vita fuggitiva di speranza nudrirò'. Cammarano, 13.

19. The MGM film *Gaslight* (1944) used this melody to invoke a feeling of nostalgia and lost dreams. The film centers around the death of a female opera singer, whose niece (played by Ingrid Bergman)

inherits her fortune but also the evil intentions of her murderer (played by Charles Boyer); see Appendix C.

20. 'Verranno a te sull' aura i miei sospiri ardenti, udrai nel mar che mormora l' eco de' miei lamenti … pensando ch' io di gemiti mi pasco, e di dolor. Spargi una mesta lagrima su questo pegno allor'. Cammarano, 13.

21. In contrast to Lucia 'falling unconscious' in Donizetti's MS score, the published 1835 libretto (and indeed in the Schirmer 1898 piano-vocal score) indicates that 'Lucia returns to the castle' ['Lucia si ritira nel castello'] (Cammarano, 14).

22. Soon after the premiere, piano and voice reductions of the main numbers in *Lucia* appeared (*pezzi staccati* or 'detached scores' and full piano-vocal scores for the amateur public), which transposed Lucia's *cavatina* from Act I down a semitone (from E♭ minor to D minor) in order to make it easier to sing. This is indeed the case with the Schirmer piano-vocal score (1898) and the Ricordi piano-vocal score (1973) referenced in this handbook; see Dotto and Parker, I, xxviii.

ACT II: THE NUPTIAL AGREEMENT

You have betrayed Heaven and love!
Cursed be that moment when I became your lover!

(Act II, Edgardo)[1]

In contrast to the 'open space' of Act I, Act II is set entirely inside the castle, a place seemingly of comfort and protection. But as we know, it is a 'closed space' full of deception, betrayal and murder. At least in the environs outside the castle, one can see the enemy from a distance. Here, dangers are near and unsuspected, ripe for secrets, shock and torment. Act II begins in Enrico's living quarters and so it reflects the domestic affairs of the head of the Ashton family. The curtain opens on Enrico who sits alone in his study, burdened by the thought of losing his entire family fortune as well as his life. The music abruptly begins with a fortissimo descending arpeggio in D major, played in unison by the entire orchestra with a sustained A followed by F#-E-D in a dotted, march-like rhythm. The timpani roll that underpins this bar of music imbues it with an immediacy that grabs our attention. We might well hear this in the context of the sense of determination within Enrico and the fear that now grips him. This dramatic opening gesture soon gives way to a quiet, contemplative passage presented by a chorus of horns and bassoons set a third/sixth apart. The mellow sound of this soft chordal phrase is in direct contrast to the opening unison, which is further distinguished by a light accompaniment of pizzicato strings on the weak beats of the bar. This contrasting phrase is in fact a version of what Lucia later sings in the next scene after she reads the forged letter given to her by Enrico. After being introduced separately in this way, the two opening motifs, one triadic and brash and the other soft and mixed in tone, intermingle in the D major harmony to highlight the conflict that exists between brother and sister. Thus, the clash between these two sonic worlds at the start of Act II – one that is loud, short and abrupt presented by the entire orchestra and the other, soft and legato and defined by a unique set of instruments – reflects both the dry and straightforward world of Enrico and the heartfelt, complex concerns of Lucia, respectively.

Family Feud

Normanno arrives on the scene and is the first to speak, breaking the tension already established by the orchestra. Avoiding any formal greeting, Normanno, always the good soldier, tells Enrico that 'Lucia will be here soon' ['Lucia fra poco a te verrà']. Enrico immediately replies: 'Trembling, I await her' ['Tremante l' aspetto']. As if echoing the sentiment of his words back to him, the orchestra now responds with the same music that began the act, thus ratcheting up the tension of what we know will be a contentious meeting between brother and sister.

After Normanno gives Enrico the forged letter and departs, the orchestra focuses our attention on Lucia, who, according to the libretto, now appears at the threshold of Enrico's study, pale and wearing a 'bewildered expression [that] all point to her suffering and the beginning of a mental derangement'.[2] At her entrance, the orchestra, now in B minor and set to a *larghetto* tempo, presents a solo melody played by a clarinet in the *clarion* register, a relatively high intermediate range that Berlioz characterized as 'the voice of heroic love . . . [filled with] delicacy, elusive nuance and mysterious sensibilities'.[3] The loneliness of Lucia's situation is highlighted by this lone clarinet, which is accompanied lightly by the strings so as not to disturb the precariousness of the sound, as if one false accent would extinguish it entirely. This fragility in the texture appears to mimic the position of Enrico, who, when he sees Lucia standing in his doorway exhibiting signs of mental distress, sings in *parlante* style carefully chosen words that are set to a short range of pitches, all of which are broken up in simple one-bar phrases that help to present both calmly and systematically his concerns:

> Come closer, Lucia.
> I hoped to see you happy and smiling today.
> On this day, when Hymen's torch is lit for you,
> why do you stare at me and remain silent?[4]

Example 5.1 Gaetano Donizetti, *Lucia di Lammermoor* [Piano-Vocal Score], Act II, scene 2, No. 6: 'Il pallor funesto, orrendo', Recitative and Duet, bb. 43–50.

To such words, Lucia immediately breaks from her apparent stupor, which is signalled by the orchestra's sudden move to a martial-like tempo in A major. This is the start of the duet proper (the *tempo d'attacco* section) between Enrico and Lucia, which has Lucia present the first of many angry words to her brother: 'This mortal paleness that is horribly spread o'er my face, silently blames you for my grief and my pain. May God forgive you for your inhuman cruelty.'[5] Her words are sung with increasing rhythmic energy and vocal range, as if Lucia is slowly gaining the strength to stand up to her brother. Set to a ternary form (a b a'), her simple melody concludes with a several-note coloratura passage that rises and falls on the word 'cruelty' (*rigor*) (see Example 5.1). This sets up the final phrase, which has Lucia present a vocal cadenza on the words 'my pain' (*mio dolor*).

Not to be outdone by his younger sister, Enrico presents Lucia's melody back to her but now in the dominant (E major), which immediately strikes one as having a different feel altogether, as if Enrico was mocking Lucia using her same accompaniment, phrase structure and tempo. The melody sung by Enrico has little vocal display and is presented rather matter-of-factly, with words set to each note to re-emphasize the importance of his counter to Lucia: 'I was right for being cruel with you owing to your shameful actions; but enough of the past, I am still your brother'. Similar to Lucia's vocal melody, Enrico's melody line increasingly rises in pitch, reaching the very height of his baritone range (F♯4) on the final phrase: 'My anger [for you] has left me, now may you also leave this baseless love'.[6]

Following their angry exchange, Enrico thrusts the false letter into Lucia's hand and demands that she read it. Having done so, a 'shiver shakes Lucia from head to toe'.[7] This tremor is reflected in the orchestra with fast ascending notes in the upper woodwinds and tremolos in the strings, as Lucia cries out: 'Ah, my heart falters' ['core mi balzò']. Enrico, who now sees how much Lucia is suffering, rushes to her side, which prompts Lucia to sing softly and slowly in short phrases, 'Ah, how wretched I am. I have been struck by a lightning bolt'.[8] This F#-minor passage serves as the transition to the *cantabile* section of the duet. Set to a slow *larghetto* tempo and introduced with horns as well as a solo oboe, bassoons and strings in C major (a key often designating purity and innocence owing to its lack of flats or sharps), Lucia sings a version of the same soft motif that began the act, which is characterized by a rising interval of a sixth that gently falls and rises again to eventually return to the opening note (see Example 5.2b).[9] The melody ('Soffriva nel pianto' ['I suffered in tears']) contains a melodic contour similar to that of 'Verranno a te' ['On the breeze will come to you my ardent sighs'], the *cabaletta* of the love duet from Act I (see Example 4.6). This pairing makes sense dramatically since the sentiment behind 'Verranno a te' is about sending and receiving letters from Edgardo. However, a far more analogous melody to the one presented here in Act II is Lucia's Act I *cavatina* 'Regnava nel silenzio' ['At dead of night'] (see Example 5.2a). The two vocal melodies begin with the same rise of a sixth (albeit a major sixth here in Act II as compared to

Example 5.2a Gaetano Donizetti, *Lucia di Lammermoor* [Piano-Vocal Score], Act I, Scene 3, No. 3: 'Regnava nel silenzio', Recitative and Cavatina, bb. 55–63.

Example 5.2b Gaetano Donizetti, *Lucia di Lammermoor* [Piano-Vocal Score], Act II, Scene 2, No. 6: 'Il pallor funesto, orrendo', Recitative and Duet, bb. 120–32.

a minor sixth in Act I), a similar descending line, the same *larghetto* tempo and a similar rolling-arpeggio accompaniment figure. This comparison between the *cantabile* section and Lucia's *cavatina* also makes dramatic sense given that the latter presents Lucia's vision of the ghost, a woman killed by her Ravenswood lover, while here in Act II, the music presents Lucia's heartache owing to her own apparent betrayal by a Ravenswood:

> I suffered in tears, I languished with grief,
> my hopes, my life, I pledged to one heart,
> now that faithless heart is given to another!
> The hour of my death is upon me![10]

A third more interesting melodic and dramatic pairing is the final *cabaletta* section of Edgardo's aria ('Tu che a Dio spiegasti l'ali' ['You, who have spread your wings to God']), which shares a similar *larghetto* tempo, orchestration, phrase structure, mixed-major mode (D major vs. C major) and melodic contour (see Chapter 6 for an analysis of Edgardo's final aria). In addition, both arias speak of death owing to the loss of the other, which further emphasizes the strong emotional bond between Edgardo and Lucia in life and in death.

Whatever previous or later melody Lucia's aria might reference in the score (perhaps all), her vocal response after reading the false letter is a heart-wrenching one.[11] As if lost in a dream, Lucia sings her vocal line in long drawn-out, two-bar phrases, whose angelic character is further highlighted in its simple harmonic movement in C major with slight chromatic touches to the parallel minor, while pizzicato strings and a harp-like arpeggio on the second violin accompany the voice.

Enrico's response to his sister who is obviously crestfallen with the news of Edgardo's infidelity is close to cruel as he immediately takes her words and replaces them with a new, more rhythmically active melody line. Here, off-beat syncopations in the bassoons, horns and upper strings are combined with Enrico's moderately paced legato melody that appears more carnivalesque than serious. Similar to what occurs in the *cantabile* section of the duet finale in Act I between Lucia and Edgardo, Enrico's response to Lucia here twists her words to reflect a different sentiment, one of resilience and resolve, rather than one of defeat and sorrow:

> A mad, evil love consumed you,
> you betrayed your kin for a vile seducer.
> But heaven has given you a just reward:
> that faithless heart is now given to another.[12]

As if 'gaslighting' her, forcing Lucia to accept a lie for a truth, Enrico successfully manipulates her, whereupon Lucia begins to replace her own words with his. Both brother and sister now sing together in harmonic agreement (at the interval of a third) as they share florid *coloratura* passages to close out the *cantabile* section of the duet (see Example 5.3).

This happy detente is soon broken by festive sounds heard in the distance. Here, at the start of the *tempo di mezzo* section, Donizetti composes several lines for a *banda sul palco* in F major (see Chapter 3 for a discussion of the stage band). Upon hearing the wind band, as if suddenly awoke from a dream, Lucia asks 'what's that?' ['che fia!'], to which Enrico responds coldly that the festive music she hears signals the arrival of her new husband, forcing sister and brother to argue once again. As if the forged letter never existed, Enrico now tries to persuade her of the merits of the marriage he arranged for her with news that his political situation is under threat, whereby her marriage to Arturo is the only thing that will save him. Set amongst increasing dynamics and a fast-moving tempo in the strings and bassoons, Enrico's vocal line becomes more and more rhythmically intense as the orchestral texture begins to thicken around him with full brass, strings, woodwinds and timpani, leaving Lucia barely any time or space to respond. With cut-off phrases such as 'and I . . .', 'Enrico . . .', '. . . to another I swore . . . .', '. . . but', Lucia simply cannot get a full sentence in. When Enrico does finish his salvo of words, Lucia's only response is a cathartic one, so much so that the entire orchestra is silent as she proclaims: 'Oh, heaven! Oh, heaven!' ['Oh ciel! Oh ciel!']. Lucia's pitiful emotional state is further highlighted with a grand pause in the score, making her lone voice all the more resonant in the hall. Set to the notes of a G#-fully diminished seventh chord (D – B, F# – G#), Lucia's tearful exasperation is answered by three bars of soft chords on the bassoons and a solo horn as they echo her voice in the quiet (see Example 5.4).

Example 5.3 Gaetano Donizetti, *Lucia di Lammermoor* [Piano-Vocal Score], Act II, scene 2, No. 6: 'Il pallor funesto, orrendo', Recitative and Duet, bb. 157–68.

Example 5.4 Gaetano Donizetti, *Lucia di Lammermoor* [Orchestral Score], Act II, scene 2, No. 4: Duetto Enrico e Lucia, bb. 275–82. **Lucia di Lammermoor**. Words and Music by Gaetano Donizetti; Critical Edition by Gabriele Dotto and Roger Parker. Copyright © 2022 Casa Ricordi Srl, part of Universal Music Publishing Classics & Screen. This arrangement Copyright © 2024 Casa Ricordi Srl, part of Universal Music Publishing Classics & Screen All Rights Reserved. Used by Permission. *Reprinted by permission of Hal Leonard LLC.*

Now that Enrico has effectively squashed any further dissent from Lucia, he becomes markedly impatient and threatens her with a gruesome description of the blood-stained axe of the executioner that awaits him if she does not marry Arturo and that his dead body will haunt her in her dreams. Set as the start of the *cabaletta* section of the duet, Enrico's words move along at a fast *vivace* tempo, all in A major (prepared by the G# of Lucia's last words) with an ever-expansive group of instruments joining in at the start of each new phrase (see Example 5.5). If it were not for the grisly words that Enrico invokes to shock and terrorize Lucia, one would think that the music in this passage celebrates a joyful victory or a triumph of some sort. Perhaps this is exactly the point, for we have seen (and heard) that Enrico is a man who takes pleasure in violence, even when it is used to scare Lucia into submission. And in the context of the conventional form of a duet, the quick tempo, the lyrical form (a-a'-b-a") and the change of mood all successfully communicate to the audience the start of the *cabaletta*.

Following the conclusion of Enrico's vocal line, Lucia takes up this same fast lyrical melody but fills it with words that indicate a prayer for mercy:

> You [oh God] who sees my tears,
> you who reads what is in my heart,
> if my grief is not ignored in Heaven,
> as it is here on Earth,
> take, eternal God,
> this hopeless life of mine.
> I am so wretched that death
> will be a boon for me.[13]

With her head tilted towards the top of the stage [*volgendo al cielo gli occhi gonfi di lagrime*], indicating a desperate plea for God's mercy, Lucia both slows and quickens the pace of the *cabaletta* to enhance the sincerity of her words. Enrico, who is more determined than ever, starts the melody again, reasserting his control over Lucia as he sings the opening two phrases (a-a') in A major, while leaving the middle phrase to be sung by Lucia (b) in C# minor. Both brother and sister now conclude the duet by singing the final phrase (a") in A major with their vocal pairing

Example 5.5 Gaetano Donizetti, *Lucia di Lammermoor* [Piano-Vocal Score], Act II, scene 2, No. 6: 'Il pallor funesto, orrendo', Recitative and Duet, bb. 228–41.

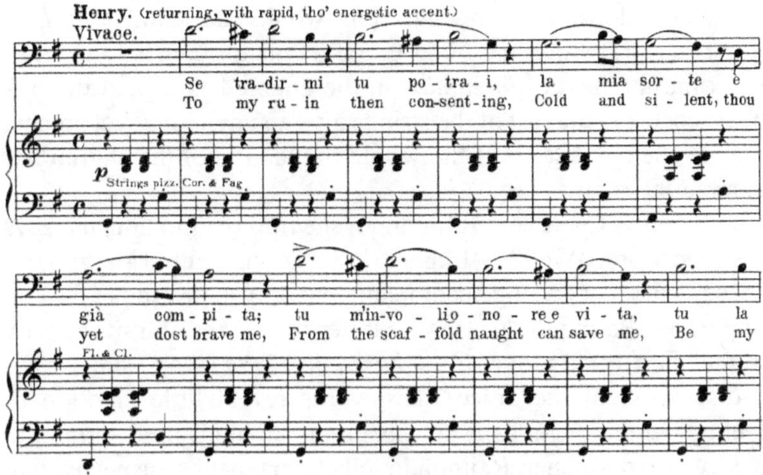

locked in at the interval of a third on every downbeat as heard earlier in the *cantabile* section and the love duet in Act I. This interval of a third is significant here as it is used throughout the score to highlight a shared understanding or agreement between two voices. However, although brother and sister conclude the final phrase of the duet at this 'interval of agreement' and cadence together on the A tonic, their words could not be further apart. Lucia continues to ask God for mercy, while Enrico insists that his death will be on her hands. In contrast to the duet finale of Act I, the duet here in Act II has the 'appearance' of agreement but remains nonetheless at odds internally. Seeing no point in arguing further, Enrico departs the stage hastily [*affrettata-mente*], leaving Lucia alone as she falls despondently into a nearby chair [*si abbandona su d'una seggiola*].

Religious Counsel

The mood of the music in scene 3 reflects a dark but mysterious tone, which is highlighted by bowed *sforzandos* in A minor played by the double basses on the downbeat of the bar as the rest of the strings complement the phrase with trills and soft legato lines that rise and fall on the offbeat.[14] This eleven-bar phrase serves as the introduction to Raimondo, who has come to counsel Lucia on what she should do. Similar to what Verdi would later emulate in *Don Carlos* (1867) when the blind grand inquisitor comes to counsel the king, the heavy *sforzandos* in the double basses and the off-beat accents in the rest of the strings give an unyielding yet archaic tone to the passage, as if the whole foundation of the church has entered the room.

As soon as Lucia sees Raimondo, she runs over to him and says just one word, 'Well?' ['Ebben?']. Set to the natural rhythms of speech with a dry string accompaniment only appearing at the end of phrases, Raimondo's response is very measured and sits heavily in the chest-filled range of the *basso profondo* (see Chapter 2 for a discussion of the voice). His words reveal little emotion or feeling behind them, as if he was giving an uninspired sermon to a drowsy parishioner. Raimondo tells Lucia that he suspected that her brother would block all forms of communication, so he took it upon himself to send Edgardo a letter in secret, but he too did not receive a response. Raimondo thus concludes that when it comes to lovers, correspondence 'never remains silent ... in silence only infidelity speaks!'[15]

Believing his words to be true, Lucia asks Raimondo for his advice. Raimondo, who apparently can only think as a minister, responds simply: 'bend to fate' ['Di piegarti al destino']. He then proceeds to dictate biblical law (now accompanied by tremolo strings): 'neither Heaven nor the world recognizes wedding vows that God's minister does not bless.'[16] Lucia responds in kind, saying 'the mind is in agreement ... but the heart resists' ['Persuasa la mente ... ma sordo alla ragion resiste il core'], or essentially, 'the spirit is willing, but the flesh is weak'.[17] Upon such words, Raimondo gives Lucia further religious advice by simply stating 'conquer your heart' and then proceeds to sing the aria 'Ah, cedi, cedi' ['Ah, surrender, surrender'].

The opening *cantabile* section of Raimondo's bass aria is slow with pizzicato strings presented as triplets on beats 1 and 3 of the bar in common time. This *obbligato* passage highlights a stern quality to Raimondo's vocal line, which when sung by a steady low bass in

F major resounds as words of instruction tinged with a sense of religious duty. Like other arias in the score, Raimondo's vocal line begins with a rising sixth before settling on a set of dotted rhythmic figures that rise and fall within the range of an octave and a half (A2–E4). The wave-like contour of the melody is placed in an extended lyric form structure (a a' b a'' c a''') that initially projects a child-like sentiment, one that is filled with soft words of fear and death, which later intensify as chromaticism is added to the phrase:

> Ah, surrender, surrender
> or more misfortunes will come to you.
> Be moved by my tender care, for the sake of a dead parent
> and the peril facing your brother,
> or your mother will turn over in her grave.[18]

When Raimondo sings his final line, 'or your mother will turn over in her grave', there is an increase in tension in the slow and steady orchestral accompaniment, which quickens to *allegro* (the *tempo di mezzo*) with Raimondo repeating his words more emphatically. Employing a similar tactic to that of Enrico in the previous scene, Raimondo presents a message of guilt and horror, which forces Lucia to cry out in protest: 'Taci, taci' ['Enough, enough']. This prompts Raimondo to press upon Lucia the fact that the peaceful rest of her dead mother and the life of her brother are now in her hands. Lucia has no words to offer a man of God, especially one who speaks of guilt, eternal damnation and death. With a mixture of both exasperation and resignation, Lucia's voice ascends to A♭5 on the word 'Ah', where it remains for three intense beats before descending nearly an octave below as she proclaims, 'you won' ['tu vincesti'].

Raimondo rejoices with a 'song of praise' as his aria enters the *cabaletta* section, 'Al ben de' tuoi qual vittima offri' ['For the greater good, Lucia, you offer yourself as a sacrifice']. Perhaps in an effort to offer Carlo Porto, the bass who premiered the role of Raimondo, a vocal number to showcase his rich bass voice, Donizetti writes here a jubilant and celebratory conclusion to the F-major aria with bass drum, cymbals, brass and woodwinds. Although it is one of the last numbers added to the autograph score (presumably added during rehearsals), the *cabaletta* to

Example 5.6 Gaetano Donizetti, *Lucia di Lammermoor* [Piano-Vocal Score], Act II, scene 3, No. 7: 'Ah, cedi, cedi', Recitative and Aria, bb. 87–96.

Raimondo's aria presents in lyric form (a a' b a") a vocal character that sounds more like a *basso buffo* with its rhythmically accented phrases that rise up and down the bar, mimicking a man who is laughing and skipping as he sings, a facet of the writing that has yet to be exploited in performance (see Example 5.6):[19]

> For the greater good, Lucia, you offer yourself as a sacrifice,
> and this costly offering will be marked in Heaven.
> If the mercy of men is not granted to you,
> there is a God, there is a God who will hold back your tears.[20]

Lucia is swept up in Raimondo's singing as she joins him in the *cabaletta*'s reprise. Although their vocal melodies are rarely synchronized, Lucia and Raimondo appear to agree as they echo one another and remain mostly at an interval of a third. This distance however is exaggerated by the vocal separation between a low bass and a high soprano (at least two octaves) but also by their separate rhythmic treatment of the melodies, so much so that when Raimondo has a rhythmically active passage Lucia's rhythms remain steady and square.

As the *cabaletta* enters the final *stretta*, the apparent joy Lucia shows in hearing Raimondo's words – 'this costly offering will be marked in Heaven' – seems odd, especially given her earlier protests with Enrico. Her reaction may simply be because she is moved by her Christian faith and is willing to sacrifice her desires to do what is right for the family. As Raimondo continues to sing, Lucia thanks him for his guidance, repeating his words 'will be marked in Heaven'. The possibility that Lucia is hatching a different plan, perhaps to take her own life, is completely lost on Raimondo, who is caught up in his celebratory vocal line. As he concludes the aria, Lucia, now weeping, cries out 'I am out of my mind' ['son fuor di me'] and 'that ungrateful Edgardo' ['Edgardo ingrato'] (see Example 5.7). These two short statements go unnoticed by Raimondo (and possibly, because of the thickness of the texture, by the audience as well) but reveal a certain ambiguity nonetheless in their meaning. Indeed, in a number of productions of this scene, Lucia either serendipitously takes up a dagger from Enrico's desk at these words (as in the Mary Zimmerman production at The Metropolitan Opera in 2007) or simply remains limp in expression as she is led out of the room to join her new husband (as in the David Alden production at the ENO in 2008). Whether she is moved to marry Arturo out of devotion to her family, on account of a letter detailing Edgardo's infidelity or owing to the new-found knowledge that her sacrifice will be 'marked in Heaven', Lucia has decidedly chosen a different path for her life and one that does not include Edgardo.

The Nuptial Agreement

The *finale* of Act II is set in a glittering grand hall in the Ravenswood castle. All the inhabitants of Lammermoor, including members of the Ashton family, knights, squires, ladies in waiting and numerous guests arrive to receive Lord Arturo Bucklaw. The music of Raimondo's aria (as well as the off-stage band music from earlier in the act) prepare us for this lavish celebration, which shares the same dotted-rhythm figure of Raimondo's *cabaletta*. Apart from a full ensemble of strings, woodwinds and brass, this festive opening in G major boasts a huge battery of percussion, including timpani, bass drum, crash cymbals as well as a triangle, which adds a characteristic shimmering effect to the whole. The

5 Act II: The Nuptial Agreement

Example 5.7 Gaetano Donizetti, *Lucia di Lammermoor* [Piano-Vocal Score], Act II, scene 3, No. 7: 'Ah, cedi, cedi', Recitative and Aria, bb. 154–68.

luxuriance of this orchestral opening allows the audience to absorb the splendour of the scene as the music bathes the listener with pomp and ceremony, which is complemented by a thrusting melodic line that rises and falls as if fireworks were bursting off and then settling back down to the ground only to be launched again.

After several bars, a full chorus (including Enrico and Normanno) joins in with words of love and friendship to Arturo ('Per te d'immenso giubilo'). This chorus is in fact the first of two mixed choral numbers (for both men and women) in the opera and thus presents a wonderful opportunity to showcase a realistic *tableau* that centres our attention once again on the Scottish setting (e.g., as seen in Franco Zeffirelli's famous production at the Royal Opera House, Covent Garden in 1959). In addition, in relationship to the overall drama, the chorus helps to relieve the tension found in the private intimate setting of the first three scenes, so that all things of the past are now cast aside, swept under the rug as it were, as the men and women of the castle sing a simple welcoming chorus (a b a'), which grounds the formality of this important occasion and conceals any equivocation:

> For you, all who are here
> join in a rousing celebration,
> because of you, we see
> reborn a day of hope;
>
> Here friendship guides you,
> here love leads you,
> like a star on a cloudy night,
> like a smile amidst tears.[21]

Following the opening chorus in G major, Arturo, whom the audience has never seen or heard, reveals himself for the first time. Similar to Normanno's aria from Act I, Arturo's opening aria is set in the midst of a chorus, now paused to allow Arturo to express thanks to his host in the form of a toast:

> For a brief time your star
> had fallen into darkness,
> I shall see it rise again,
> brighter and more splendid.

5 Act II: The Nuptial Agreement

Give me your hand, Enrico,
and accept my cordial greeting,
I come to you as a friend,
a brother and a defender.[22]

Arturo's *cavatina* is slow but deliberate in D major, containing two-bar phrases filled with slurs and legato lines set to a lilting dotted rhythm that adds a certain degree of weight or heaviness to the flow of the simple vocal melody (a a' b a"). And when accompanied by light-sounding upper woodwinds, horns and strings, which present staccato triplets on the strong beats of the bar, the aria retains a stiff and pompous feel throughout. This of course helps to define the character of Lord Arturo Bucklaw as one who is frivolously bourgeois, especially when sung by a lyric tenor who shines on soaring high notes that are approached from below, producing the sound of an individual who is perhaps consumed with his own voice and position (e.g., see José Carreras's 1970 recorded performance of Arturo).[23] The chorus immediately responds to Arturo's words with the same G-major melody (a b a') as before but now with the inclusion of Arturo's final lines ('I come to you as a friend, a brother and a defender'), thus resolving his dominant harmony to their G major tonic.

Following the opening chorus, the *finale* to Act II transitions to the *tempo d'attacco* section, which highlights the dialogue between Enrico and Arturo, who asks Enrico, 'where's Lucia?' ['Dov' è Lucia?']. Enrico, who is forced to answer Arturo's question quickly, responds: 'We will see her now' ['Qui giungere or al vedrem']. After these lightly sung words, Donizetti presents in the orchestra a set of descending chords in the strings, which are played in rapid tremolo, highlighting a sense of fear growing within Enrico. The music of the *finale* appears to centre in on Enrico at this point as the accompaniment presents *fp* appoggiaturas that slide from one wind instrument to the next, from the flute to the oboe, to the clarinet to the bassoon, reflecting a kind of twisted, silken melody that effectively substantiates the web of lies that Enrico has spun for Arturo (see Example 5.8). Although structured in a simple lyric form (a a' b a") in A major, Enrico's response appears to meander as his highly angular melody jumps from one interval to the next, causing Arturo to question Enrico further on the rumors he has heard about Edgardo and

Example 5.8 Gaetano Donizetti, *Lucia di Lammermoor* [Orchestral Score], Act II, scene 4, No. 6: Finale Atto Secondo, bb. 113–17. **Lucia di Lammermoor**. Words and Music by Gaetano Donizetti; Critical Edition by Gabriele Dotto and Roger Parker. Copyright © 2022 Casa Ricordi Srl, part of Universal Music Publishing Classics & Screen. This arrangement Copyright © 2024 Casa Ricordi Srl, part of Universal Music Publishing Classics & Screen All Rights Reserved. Used by Permission. *Reprinted by permission of Hal Leonard LLC.*

Lucia. Just as Enrico is about to answer, the chorus signals that Lucia has arrived, much to the relief of Enrico. The orchestra now shifts our attention to Lucia, who appears with Raimondo and Alisa by her side.

Scene 5 presents the signing of the nuptial agreement and so the music marks Lucia's internal struggle. The double basses present a heaviness to her steps with soft plucked notes in C minor, a sort of walking bass line that slowly creeps along as the high woodwinds and strings trade 'weeping' or 'sighing' figures with their descending slurred notes and light crescendos. Amid this gloomy atmosphere, the voices of the principals, namely Lucia, Enrico, Raimondo and Arturo, are interspersed within the score, providing commentary to all that they see and feel. It is a striking bit of writing that Donizetti presents here in the midst of the *tempo d'attacco*, which usually functions within the conventional form as a simple transition from one section to another, but here it presents a powerful reflective moment as both the internal and external worlds of Lucia collide. By presenting the signing of the nuptial agreement in this way, Donizetti draws us into the intimacy of this emotional moment: 'will she, or won't she?' becomes not only the questions of Enrico and Arturo but of the audience as well.

As Lucia approaches the wedding contract, she is constantly being prompted by Enrico with words such as 'be careful', 'do you want to ruin me?' and finally, 'sign it', which raises questions about Lucia's consent to marry Arturo. If there are doubts within Lucia, what drives them? Is it a struggle of faith (as we learned from the previous scene with Raimondo) or is she still harboring feelings for Edgardo? Lucia's words in this scene give us a clue for despite Enrico's urgings, Lucia presents asides, namely 'Oh, God! I must go to the sacrifice' ['Gran Dio … io vado al sacrifizio'] and 'I have signed my death warrant' ['La mia condanna ho scritta']. This final statement is a curious one for it implies several ways in which Lucia's current state can be read: Is she referring to the curse pronounced by Edgardo at the end of Act I? Is her mental instability taking over, causing her to perceive her own death? Or even still, does Lucia see herself as a martyr, who sacrifices herself for the greater good – a righteous act proclaimed by Raimondo earlier as one that 'will be marked in Heaven'?

Although her motivations and doubts are ripe for interpretation, Lucia, who has now signed the nuptial agreement, starts to feel weak as she says to herself 'I freeze and I burn! I faint' ['Io gelo e ardo! Io manco! … ']. Just as she completes the word 'ardo' ['I burn'], Donizetti presents drum rolls on the timpani that introduce a set of loud thumps on the bass drum and accented notes in the full orchestra. These percussive sounds imitate the loud knocking on a heavy door, which is located at the back of the stage. According to the libretto, as the door swings open, an unknown figure appears dressed in a heavy travelling cloak and a large brim hat pulled over his face.[24] All those at the ceremony suddenly question, 'Who goes there?' ['Chi giunge?'], prompting the unknown individual to come forward to reveal his identity. In a highly dramatic moment, as the orchestra continues to pound away, the mysterious individual removes his cloak and proclaims on a high $Gb4$: 'Edgardo!' Like a lightning bolt, everyone in the hall is now shocked and repeats his name, including Lucia who suddenly falls unconscious ('cade svenuta') into the arms of Raimondo and Alisa. The fainting of Lucia is a highly important moment in the action for when Lucia loses consciousness, everyone in the hall now suddenly becomes quiet, which is a quick reversal from the earlier shock of Edgardo's appearance here in the castle. After Alisa and the other ladies of the court place Lucia in a nearby chair, the orchestra slowly awakens with pizzicato strings, which is followed by a mournful chorus of soft horns that present a sound reminiscent of the orchestral prelude (see Chapter 3). This muted response by the orchestra serves as the transition (harmonically, A♭ minor to D♭ major) from the *tempo d'attacco* to the celebrated *cantabile*, 'Chi me frena in tal momento?' ['Who stops me at this moment?'].

As previously discussed in Chapter 2, the *cantabile* section of the Act II *finale* is one of the more memorable melodies from the opera (see Chapter 7 and Appendix C for a discussion of its popularity in the press and in movies, respectively). Similar to what we observed with 'Verranno e te' ['On the breeze will come to you my ardent sighs'] in Act I, the main appeal of this D♭-major melody is its shape, especially as heard in the tenor voice (Edgardo) with its delayed leap of a sixth that descends back to its original note. But unlike 'Verranno a te', the melody here with its unique sixteen-bar phrase structure (a b c d) is introduced with a counter melody in the lower baritone voice (Enrico), which does not simply mirror the upper melody but presents slight rhythmic variations that wonderfully balance the whole. Like the independent strands of a two-part invention, the two vocal melodies of 'Chi me frena' rhythmically, textually and harmonically (set once again at the now familiar 'interval of agreement') complement one another as they present a similar sentiment of shock at seeing Lucia in her unconscious state:

> EDGARDO: Who stops me at this moment?
> Who stemmed the flood of my anger?
> Her grief, her terror are the proof,
> the proof of her remorse!
> But like a withered rose,
> she hovers between life and death!
> I surrender, I am touched,
> I love you, heartless girl, I love you still!

5 Act II: The Nuptial Agreement

ENRICO: Who stops my fury
and the hand which darted to my sword?
I heard within me a plea
for the unhappy girl!
She is my kin! I have betrayed her!
She hovers between life and death!
Ah, I cannot quell
the remorse in my soul![25]

Although set to different text, the vocal lines of Edgardo and Enrico work well together owing to their shared poetic setting (e.g., eight-line stanza, fixed meter, similar syllabic structure), which as we know are focused on Lucia, who eventually awakes to join in the singing (see Example 5.9). Here, as the voices of Lucia and Raimondo (and eventually Arturo and Alisa) are added to what was once a duet, we see that Donizetti composes a set of variations with each entrance of the vocal pairing, which further highlights the sextet (the only time in the opera all six principals sing together on stage) in the midst of both the conventional form and the opera as a whole (see the Introduction and Chapter 2 for a discussion of both the dramatic and conventional structure of the Act II *finale*).

Act II thus ends with Enrico and Arturo drawing swords as they threaten to kill Edgardo (sung together in D major at the 'interval of agreement'); Raimondo attempting to quiet the anger of everyone (D minor); Enrico and Edgardo exchanging angry but measured words set to the same A-major melody (a a' b a'') heard earlier in the *tempo d'attacco* section; and Edgardo finally cursing Lucia for betraying him (A minor). All this back and forth constitutes the entire *tempo di mezzo* section of the finale, which, following the words of Edgardo, leads quickly into the *stretta* as Edgardo is chased out of the castle. As he departs, Lucia falls to her knees and prays for Edgardo's protection, while a double chorus – one led by Arturo, Enrico, Normanno and his men and the other led by Alisa, Raimondo and the ladies of the court – tell him to flee, all set to a fast *vivace* tempo in D major:

CHORUS OF MEN: Begone! Go, or the stain
of your outrage will be cleansed by your blood!
Leave now as [our] burning fury

Example 5.9 Gaetano Donizetti, *Lucia di Lammermoor* [Piano-Vocal Score], Act II, scene 6, No. 9: 'Chi me frena in tal momento', Recitative and Quartet, bb. 115–20.

still refrains from striking you down.
Before long, however, stronger and fiercer,
it shall fall on all those it abhors.

CHORUS OF LADIES AND RAIMONDO:
Ah! Save yourself! Flee. Make haste.
Respect your own well-being as well as hers.
Live on … may your grief one day pass,
the mercy of God lightens all burdens.
How often does one single torment
become replaced by a thousand joys.[26]

Conclusion

The dramatic function of the middle act of an opera is to create anticipation for the final act to come, where questions remain to be answered: Is Lucia well? Will she go through with the wedding? What will Edgardo do now? Act II begins with Lucia experiencing heartache due to Edgardo's departure, the introduction of the false letter by Enrico and the guilt placed upon her by Enrico and Raimondo. This all comes full circle when Edgardo appears before Lucia, who realizes that she is the one who betrayed him. The real tragedy here is that despite their professed love, Lucia and Edgardo are never able to make amends nor understand why they were betrayed by the other. The false letter is key to their downfall, which makes the words and music of 'Verranno a te' ['On the breeze will come to you my ardent sighs'] (the *cabaletta* of the love duet) as well as Edgardo's final warning ('Remember, we are now bound by Heaven') at the end of Act I reverberate even further at the close of Act II.

Musically speaking (see Appendix B for the compositional structure), this central act begins and ends in D major. In a sense, the harmonic motion (primarily among parallel, dominant and mediant harmonies) mirrors the actions of Enrico, who began the act determined to see Lucia marry Arturo and does indeed achieve this in the end but not without a high level of scheming, manipulation and threats of violence. If the main purpose of Act I is to set the action of the opera in motion and to define the main conflict that our hero will face, then the main purpose of Act II is to reveal the power of Enrico and how his castle domain serves to blind Lucia from the truth and deny Edgardo his bride.

Notes

1. 'Hai tradito il cielo, e amor! Maledetto sia l' istante che di te mi rese amante'! Cammarano, 25.
2. 'La pallidezza del suo volto, il guardo smarrito, e tutto in lei annunzia i patimenti ch' ella sofferse, ed i primi sintomi d' un' alienazione mentale'. Cammarano, 16.
3. Macdonald, 125.
4. 'Appressati, Lucia. Sperai più lieta in questo dì vederti, in questo dì, che d' imeneo le faci si accendono per te. Mi guardi, e taci'? Cammarano, 16.
5. 'Il pallor funesto, orrendo che ricopre il volto mio, ti rimprovera tacendo il mio strazio ... il mio dolor. Perdonar ti possa Iddio l' inumano tuo rigor'. Cammarano, 16.
6. 'A ragion mi fe' spietato quel che t' arse indegno affetto ... ma si taccia del passato ... tuo fratello io sono ancor. Spenta è l' ira nel mio petto, spegni tu l' insano amor'. Cammarano, 16.
7. 'Un tremito l' investe dal capo alle piante'. Cammarano, 17.
8. 'Me infelice! Ahi! la folgore piombò'! Cammarano, 17.
9. In the piano-vocal score published by Schirmer (1898) the key is B♭ major.
10. 'Soffriva nel pianto ... languia nel dolore ... la speme ... la vita riposi in un core ... quel core infedele ad altra si diè! L' istante di morte è giunto per me'. Cammarano, 17.
11. Throughout *Lucia*, we see many vocal melodies begin with a rising open interval, especially ones that speak of loss, heartache, sacrifice or regret. The melodies are defined either with a rising interval of a direct sixth (as in the case of 'Regnava nel silenzio', 'Soffriva nel pianto', 'Spargi d'amore pianto' and 'Fra poco a me ricovero'), an interval of a sixth via an interval of a fourth (as in the case of 'Ah, cedi, cedi', 'Chi me frena in tal momento' and 'Tu che a Dio spiegasti l'ali') or an interval of an octave (as in 'Verranno e te'). The fact that the contours, rhythms and tempos of all these vocal melodies appear to be similar highlights not only dramatic ties and connections to the plot structure but also, and more importantly, a certain stylistic tendency within Donizetti when presenting painful emotions that affect the character's development.
12. 'Un folie ti accese, un perfido amore: tradisti il tuo sangue per vil seduttore ... ma degna dal cielo ne avesti mercè: quel core infedele ad altra si diè'. Cammarano, 17.

13. 'Tu che vedi il pianto mio . . . tu che leggi in questo core, se respinto il mio dolore come in terra in ciel non è. Tu mi togli, eterno Iddio questa vita disperata . . . io son tanto sventurata, che la morte è un ben per me'. Cammarano, 18.

14. Following the premiere, this scene was often skipped to focus the audience's attention on the Act II *finale*.

15. 'Taci mai sempre . . . Quel silenzio assai d'infedeltà ti parla'! Cammarano, 19.

16. 'I nuziali voti che il ministro di Dio non benedice nè il ciel, nè il mondo riconosce'. Cammarano, 19.

17. Matthew 26:41 (NIV). On the night he was arrested, Jesus spoke these words when he found his disciples sleeping instead of joining him in prayer.

18. 'Ah! cedi, cedi, o più sciagure ti sovrastano, infelice . . . per le tenere mie cure, per l' estinta genitrice il periglio d' un fratello deh, ti mova; e cangi il cor . . . o la madre nell' avello fremerà per te d' orror'. Cammarano, 19. Cammarno originally wrote 'Deh! t'arrendi' [Ah, give up] for the start of the aria but in the first vocal score published by Girard (October 1835), the aria begins as shown here.

19. See Dotto and Parker, I, xxix and II, 618 and 631. Porto premiered the bass roles of three Donizetti operas prior to *Lucia*, including Ernesto in *Parisina* (1833), Clifford in *Rosmonda d'Inghilterra* (1834) and Talbot in *Maria Stuarda* (1834). All three roles present serious characters, so the comic-like quality here in the *cabaletta* section appears to reflect Donizetti's wanting to feature a different side of Porto's rich bass timbre; see Elizabeth Forbes, 'Porto, Carlo (Ottolini)', *The Grove Book of Opera Singers*, ed. Laura Macy (Oxford: Oxford University Press, 2008), 389.

20. 'Oh! qual gioia in me tu desti! Oh, qual nube hai disgombrata! Al ben de' tuoi qual vittima offri, Lucia, te stessa; e tanto sacrifizio scritto nel ciel sarà. Se la pietà degli uomini a te non fia concessa, v' è un Dio, v' è un Dio, che tergete il pianto tuo saprà'. Cammarano, 20.

21. 'Per te d' immenso giubbilo tutto s' avviva intorno, per te veggiam rinascere della speranza il giorno. Quì l' amistà ti guida, quì ti conduce amore, qual astro in notte infida, qual riso nel dolor'. Cammarano, 20.

22. 'Per poco fra le tenebre sparì la vostra stella; io la farò risorgere più fulgida, e più bella. La man mi porgi Enrico . . . ti stringi a questo cor. A te ne vengo; amico, fratello, e difensor'. Cammarano, 20–1.

23. Jose Carreras, 'Per poco fra le tenebre', *Lucia di Lammermoor*, Conductor Rafael Frühbeck de Burgos, San Sebastian Opera Orchestra and Chorus (19 Aug. 1970); see https://youtu.be/tjCQL1bGPP4?si=k-uqXREnRBfPtEDA; accessed 13 Nov. 2023.

24. 'Egli è ravvolto in gran mantello da viaggio, un cappello con l' ala tirata giù, rende più fosche le di lui sembianze estenuate dal dolore'. Cammarano, 22.

25. '[Edgardo] Chi mi frena in tal momento? Chi troncò dell' ire il corso? Il suo duolo, il suo spavento son la prova d' un rimorso! Ma, qual rosa inaridita, ella sta fra morte e vita! Io son vinto . . . son commosso . . . t' amo, ingrata, t' amo ancor! [Enrico:] Chi rattiene il mio furore, e la man che al brando corse? Della misera in favore nel mio petto un grido sorse! È mio sangue! Io l' ho tradita! Ella sta fra morte e vita'! Cammarano, 22–3.

26. '[Enrico and Men's chorus:] Insano ardir! Esci, fuggi il furor che mi/ ne accende solo un punto i suoi colpi sospende . . . ma fra poco più atroce, più fiero sul tuo capo abborrita cadrà . . . sì, la macchia d' oltraggio sì nero col tuo sangue lavata sarà! [Raimondo and Women's chorus:] Infelice, t' invola . . . t' affretta. I tuoi giorni . . . il suo stato rispetta. Vivi . . . e forse il tuo duolo fia spento: tutto è lieve all' eterna pietà. Quante volte ad un solo tormento mille gioie succedar non fa'. Cammarano, 25–6.

ACT III: THE WEDDING NIGHT
AND THE GRAVEYARD AT DAWN

From the room where I left Lucia with her husband,
a wail, a cry rang out, like a man near death.

(Act III, Raimondo)[1]

Act III returns us once again to the world outside the castle. The curtain rises on Edgardo, who sits alone among the vestiges of his ruined estate: a table, an old high chair and a simple lamp.[2] He lives far from the castle grounds in a broken-down tower, which sits upon the Wolf's Crag, a high cliff on the edge of the sea – a menacing landscape evocatively portrayed by the illustrator Henry Melville in Walter Scott's *The Bride of Lammermoor* (see Figure 6.1). In keeping with the gothic atmosphere, two large glass-stained windows stand near the back of the stage and appear to be broken, letting in flashes of lightning, rain and the sound of wind and thunder from the storm that rages outside. The impression created on the stage – as dictated by the libretto – is one of poverty and loss, coldness and death. With timpani and bass drum rolls, tremolos in the strings, percussive D minor chords in the brass and rolling melodic figures in the piccolo and flute that swell and abate, Donizetti composes a terrifying array of sounds at the start of this final act, which reflects both the external storm as well as the metaphorical one brewing within Edgardo:

This night is gloomy like my fate.
Yes, thunder away, O heaven!
Rage, O lightning! May the universe
be overthrown, and the world perish.[3]

The Act II *finale* left us wondering what will become of Edgardo. It appears he has lost hope and seeks to see the world end and perhaps himself along with it. Within such a depressed state, Edgardo is interrupted by a distant sound amidst the thunderclaps and lightning flashes. Serving as one of several diegetic sounds in the score, horse's

Figure 6.1 Henry Melville, 'The Tower of Wolf's Crag', illus., in Walter Scott, *The Bride of Lammermoor* (London: George Routledge & Sons, 1875), 72–3.

hoofs are portrayed in the orchestra with quick-paced phrasing (three demisemiquavers tied to a quaver) in the first and second violins:[4]

> Am I not deceived but is that the distant sound
> of a galloping steed I hear?
> He stops – who can brave the fury
> of this storm and still come here to find me?[5]

In keeping with the final chapter of Scott's novel, Enrico enters, mocks Edgardo's simple surroundings and challenges him to a duel with polite entreaties that bely the brutality of their deadly meeting. Donizetti reflects the civility of this exchange at the start of the *tempo d'attacco* with a harmonic shift to D major and a paring down of the orchestral accompaniment to a small set of strings that play a simple *maestoso*-paced accompaniment with pizzicatos on the strong beats of the bar. This sudden change in texture, rhythm and harmony provides an air of aloofness at the start of the duet and captures much of the pent-up tension that led to this meeting following Edgardo's sudden appearance at the end of Act II.

The politeness of their opening exchange soon changes as Edgardo tells Enrico, albeit calmly and rationally, that he is not welcome in his

Example 6.1 Gaetano Donizetti, *Lucia di Lammermoor* [Orchestral Score], Act III, scene 2, No. 7: Scena e Duetto Edgardo ed Enrico, bb. 83–5. **Lucia di Lammermoor**. Words and Music by Gaetano Donizetti; Critical Edition by Gabriele Dotto and Roger Parker. Copyright © 2022 Casa Ricordi Srl, part of Universal Music Publishing Classics & Screen. This arrangement Copyright © 2024 Casa Ricordi Srl, part of Universal Music Publishing Classics & Screen All Rights Reserved. Used by Permission. *Reprinted by permission of Hal Leonard LLC.*

home. The rhythm and tempo, now marked *moderato*, project a sound of military action as brass, horns, trumpets, trombones, bassoons, timpani and strings present a persistent rhythmic figure (long, short, short), which creates a possible sonic reference to taps on a military side drum (see Example 6.1). Although the text is filled with spiteful anger, the rhythmic energy upon which it is set is characterized by the orchestra as one of precision and restraint as each voice presents four-bar phrases set to a simple lyrical form with coda (a a' b a" c c'). This *cantabile* section of the duet is further defined by a melody line that is shaped by intervallic leaps of major thirds, perfect fourths and fifths, which are redolent of the intervals played by bugles and horns on the battlefield, as if two noble heads of opposing forces were meeting one another in combat to decide the terms of engagement:

> EDGARDO: In this place still wanders
> the unavenged Spirit of my father . . .
> And it seems death now breathes here for you.
> The ground shakes for you here!
> In crossing this horror-filled threshold,
> Your heart should have stopped.
> You are like a living man
> who has descended into his grave.
>
> ENRICO: Although my dwellings resound
> with festive peals of joy,
> revenge spoke more loudly in my heart –
> I came here nonetheless . . .
> In the midst of the wind and the rain
> could I still hear this voice [of revenge]?
> The fury of the storm
> is in response to my rage.[6]

Following an exchange of insults, Enrico presents a third verse of the *cantabile* melody that is far more direct in revealing his intentions: 'My family's vengeful sword hangs over your head . . . you will not fall by another's hand . . . you know all too well who will take your life!'[7] In this third iteration of the *cantabile* melody in F major, the orchestra presents the lyrical form of the melody (a a' b a" coda) underneath the voice as Enrico sings along with far less elaboration but with enhanced syncopation, as if he is becoming less restrained in his anger towards Edgardo.

Enrico's demand for a duel comes in the *tempo di mezzo* section of the duet, a relatively short section, where they both agree upon the time and location of when and where they will fight to the death: tomorrow morning, before sunrise, at the Ravenswood graveyard. As Enrico is the one who challenges Edgardo to the duel, it is Enrico's vocal line that is primarily accompanied by bassoons and tremolo low strings that slowly modulate the harmony from F major to A minor. Set once again to a martial rhythm but now in a quickened pace (*più allegro*) and with the entire orchestra reinforcing the syncopated passage, the demand for the duel by Enrico reveals a potent quality that soon infects Edgardo with the same blood lust for revenge. This gleeful desire for the other's death spills out into the *cabaletta/ stretta*, which ends the duet in D major as both baritone and tenor

Example 6.2 Gaetano Donizetti, *Lucia di Lammermoor* [Piano-Vocal Score], Act III, scene 2, No. 11: 'Qui del padre ancor respira', Storm, Recitative and Duet, bb. 198–205.

sing the same words an interval of a third apart, thus further underlining their agreement to fight:

> O sun! Hasten thy rising . . .
> Shine bright with a menacing garland
> to illuminate this odious contest
> of blind fury and mortal hate.
> [It's rays] will make our souls a wicked institution,
> Crying out for vengeance . . . the spirit of Avernus –
> Of bellowing thunder, of roaring cloud –
> More terrible is the anger that burns in my heart![8]

If the consonance of the harmony reflects their agreement to fight, the orchestra adumbrates the violence that will ensue by presenting the sound of a victory march with dotted figures, arpeggiations, rising legato lines and quick crescendos, now enhanced with piccolo, bass drum, crash cymbals and trumpet flares – a distinctly rich sound of pageantry not found earlier in the duet (see Example 6.2).

The 'Mad Scene'

The main purpose of the duet between Edgardo and Enrico is to prepare us for the opera's final scene as Edgardo waits for Enrico at the tomb of his ancestors. In between these two scenes is one of the most storied and memorable numbers in *Lucia*, if not in all of *bel canto* opera. Much has been written on the 'mad scene', viewed often as the climax of Lucia's journey from the status of dependency (whether as daughter or sister) to a fully independent woman. (That trajectory is described in full in the Introduction, and the Bibliography provides several sources that deal with it in depth.)[9] The 'mad scene', in fact, comprises the final two scenes of a *scène complexe* or a set of several scenes (scenes 3–6) that flow from one into the other with particular dramatic focus and energy. Such a structure (similar to what we saw for the Act II *finale*) presents a whirlwind of emotion for the characters on stage as well as the audience: joy (scene 3), terror (scene 4), shock (scene 5) and finally regret (scene 6).

Scene 3 is ostensibly concerned with the celebrations surrounding Lucia's wedding. The significance of marriage to the nineteenth century is intertwined in powerful ways in the plot of this opera and in these final scenes in particular, reflecting the onerous social obligations marriage acquired at the time. In fact, marriage was enshrined within the legal codes of many European countries at the start of the nineteenth century owing to the importance of marriage to the future of the democratic state, most notably the Code Napoléon of 1804.[10] This legal system 'assumed that marriage was one of the primary responsibilities of citizens and one of the primary means through which individuals contributed to the well-being of the state'.[11] And combined with the point of view of the Church, which saw in marriage a reflection of the relationship between God and the soul, we find that something abstract and metaphysical is also formed around the concept of marriage, so much so that it defines the principal actions and motivations within the opera, including the actions of Lucia. The chorus number that begins scene 3 cements the importance of Lucia's wedding to the future of the Ashton family:

> Let our joyful cries arise and echo
> across Scotland's shores,
> warning our perfidious enemies that [no matter] the atrocity,
> happier is our reward from above;
> for the stars shine upon us once more.[12]

This chorus of men and women is accompanied in a similar manner to the mixed chorus in Act II with every instrument of the orchestra resounding. Here, the instruments accompanying the chorus present in E major a fast *galop*, a quick-moving lively dance in <2/4> that 'was one of the most popular ballroom dances of the 19th century'.[13] The dance helps to create a bevy of kinetic energy on stage as the castle appears to be full of life as opposed to the previous scene on the Wolf's Crag. Knowing what awaits us for the rest of the act, however, this choral number is both literally and figuratively the calm amidst the storm, as it not only presents evidence of Enrico's words from Scene 2 ('although my dwellings resound with festive peals of joy . . . In the midst of the wind and the rain') but it also dramatically sits between vows of revenge (scenes 1 and 2) and the horror that will follow (scene 4 to the end of the act). Furthermore, the pomp and festive atmosphere of this scene successfully prepares us for a *coup de théâtre*, a sudden turn of events that draws us more directly into the action, allowing us to see, hear and feel what the characters experience at the same time it is revealed on stage.

Just as the chorus completes its *stretta* on the words 'the stars once more' ['le stelle ancor'], Raimondo enters the stage (scene 4) 'breathless and with faltering steps' ['trafelato, ed avanzandosi a passi vacillanti']. Emerging from the crowd, as if he too shared in the dance, Raimondo's entrance quiets the entire chorus and orchestra, bringing everything to a standstill with the words: 'Cease, oh cease this joy' ['Cessi . . . ah! cessi quel contento']. We soon learn of course that it was not the exhaustion of the dance that Raimondo is reacting to but the memory of seeing Arturo's lifeless body and Lucia's quizzical smile as she stood over the body, blood-stained dagger in hand, staring at Raimondo and asking: 'Where is my husband?' All of this is sung by Raimondo as a short aria in four-bar phrases (a a' b a'' c a''') while accented notes in the strings and *maestoso* chords in the brass and woodwinds ring out in B major (see Example 6.3). Raimondo's words

Example 6.3 Gaetano Donizetti, *Lucia di Lammermoor* [Orchestral Score], Act III, scene 4, No. 8: Coro e Scena Lucia, bb. 122–25. **Lucia di Lammermoor**. Words and Music by Gaetano Donizetti; Critical Edition by Gabriele Dotto and Roger Parker. Copyright © 2022 Casa Ricordi Srl, part of Universal Music Publishing Classics & Screen. This arrangement Copyright © 2024 Casa Ricordi Srl, part of Universal Music Publishing Classics & Screen All Rights Reserved. Used by Permission. *Reprinted by permission of Hal Leonard LLC.*

are set in a fashion that is similar to the *cantabile* section of his aria from Act II, as if, once again, he is evoking words of religious instruction as directed to a child. In both cases, he sings a legato melody in the major mode with minor harmonic reflections and subtle intervallic movements that gently rise and fall. Beyond the fact that they are both sung by Raimondo, these two bass arias are connected dramatically: Raimondo's odious warning to Lucia in Act II ('Ah, surrender, surrender, or more misfortunes will come to you') and its fulfillment in Act III ('A wail, a cry rang out, like a man near death … oh, sad misfortune!'). Putting them together, it would seem that Raimondo, a Presbyterian minister, has some level of foresight even though no one appears to follow his advice.[14] This same resignation to fate amid horror carries over to the chorus. They join Raimondo in singing the final lines of his vocal melody but now back in the original key of E major with full orchestra, sharing the same *maestoso* tempo of Raimondo but now with a less pronounced sense of energy that began the act:

> Oh, what a sad event!
> A gloomy terror pervades us all.
> Oh, night, cover this terrible misfortune
> with your dark veil;
> Ah! Let not that blood-stained hand
> draw Heaven's anger upon us.[15]

Lucia's ensuing aria is split between two scenes: the slow *cantabile* section (scene 5) and the fast *cabaletta* section (scene 6). As dictated by the libretto, Lucia appears on stage wearing a night dress, spattered with her victim's blood:

Lucia is in a simple white dress: her disheveled hair and the look of death on her face give her more the appearance of a ghost than of a living creature. Her fixed gaze, her convulsive movements and her malevolent smile disclose not only a frightening insanity but also the signs of a life that is drawing to a close.[16]

To highlight Lucia's confused mental state, Donizetti composed a conventional aria in D minor interspersed with choruses that begin with Lucia's memory of Edgardo's voice ('The sweet sound of his voice'). Somewhere between *coloratura* singing, lyrical dialogue and pathos-filled utterances, the opening section of Lucia's aria (the *scena*) is indeed conventional but given the several tempo changes, the varying lengths of the melodic phrases as well as the spasmodic vocal flourishes that appear throughout, one quickly learns that the voice of Lucia is not steady or assured but searching and lost.

The orchestral accompaniment to this opening section is also given a 'voice' as it brings back the music from Lucia's *cavatina* of Act I ('Regnava nel silenzio' ['At dead of night']), where Lucia tells Alisa of the ghost. As mentioned in Chapter 3, Donizetti wanted this melody to be performed on the glass harmonica, an instrument understood to have connections to hypnosis and the subconscious owing to its disorienting high resonance. Although the instrument was eventually replaced by a solo flute at the premiere and in the published score, the high accompaniment nonetheless remains isolated in pitch range and timbre from the rest of the orchestra, signaling to the listener the lonely and delicate position in which Lucia now finds herself. When placed in the context of her dilapidated appearance – blood spattered in a white night dress with convulsive movements and a stone-filled gaze – the combination of Lucia's voice with the 'voice' of the accompaniment produces a particularly chilling effect, one that highlights the irrational and the uncanny.

In fact, throughout the aria, Donizetti continually presents incongruities between what Lucia sings (the external or diegetic reality of her state of mind) and what we the audience and Lucia both hear (the internal or non-diegetic reality). Note that the reference here is from the chorus's point of view, who does not hear the actual music that Lucia hears in her mind as performed by the orchestra, only we in the audience hear it. It is as if Donizetti wishes a disembodied reality for Lucia: the chorus on stage sees her body and hears her voice but the audience hears her inner thoughts and the reasons why she sings what she sings. Thus, the reactions of the chorus, frozen on stage, who cannot look away, help to frame Lucia as an irrational individual, who appears as a ghost to them – 'Oh, righteous Heaven! She appears as if risen from the grave' – physically present but not all there.[17]

As the *scena* for Lucia's aria continues, which is unusually long (119 bars) as compared to the length of the lyrical dialogue that proceeds other arias and duets in the opera, Lucia appears physically shaking as she urges Edgardo, who appears only in her mind, to let her rest by the Ravenswood fountain: 'Come to the fountain and sit with me'. On cue, just as she sings these words, the flute and clarinet present the same B♭ major melody 'Verranno a te' ['On the breeze will come to you my ardent sighs'], the *cabaletta* from the love duet that was originally sung at the same fountain in Act I. Once again, by placing the love duet melody in the orchestra and not in her voice, to allow the audience to hear what she hears, Donizetti further clarifies Lucia's mental separation from the current environment (see Example 6.4). This happy memory, however, is followed quickly with horrified visions of the ghost, a symbol of death that in Lucia's mind now separates her from Edgardo: 'Oh, no! The terrible ghost now rises and separates us!' ['Ahimè! Sorge il tremendo fantasma e ne separa!']. It is as if her memory of the ghost breaks her imagined revery and she is lucid again, albeit to a horror that only she sees.

Example 6.4 Gaetano Donizetti, *Lucia di Lammermoor* [Piano-Vocal Score], Act III, scene 5, No. 14: 'Alfin son tua', Recitative and Aria, bb. 41–67.

Imagining she is now kneeling at the wedding altar, Lucia hears a hymn, sees the wedding ceremony taking place and speaks to an unnamed individual: 'a celestial harmony, do you not hear it?' ['un' armonia celeste di', non ascolti?']. The music of this final section of the *scena* is a variation on the music for the nuptial agreement from Act II.[18] Here, the music that originally accompanied Lucia's entrance into the meeting hall is cast in a distorted form. As if in a carnivalesque hall of mirrors, where images are familiar but grotesquely exaggerated from the original, the music is transformed to F minor (as opposed to C minor in Act II) with a similar set of instruments that play a jumbled rhythmic and melodic creation from the original that has more in common with a mournful waltz than a wedding march (see Example 6.5).

Example 6.5 Gaetano Donizetti, *Lucia di Lammermoor* [Piano-Vocal Score], Act III, scene 5, No. 14: 'Alfin son tua', Recitative and Aria, bb. 107–19.

This wedding music from Act II, now transformed by the orchestra, is interrupted by vocal cadenzas by Lucia, whose utterances are quieted by a change in tempo and a shift in mood to a *maestoso* section with punctuated *forte* chords, which effectively announce to the audience Lucia's words: 'Oh, this joy that is felt . . . it cannot be expressed!' ['Oh gioia che si sente, e non si dice!'].

Although the orchestra in this section has now moved on to the music of the *cantabile section*, which harkens the sound of a lullaby, Lucia continues as before, lost in an imagined reality singing seemingly unconnected thoughts: 'The burning incense ... the lights of sacred torches all around! ... Here is the minister! Give me your right hand ... Oh, happy day!'.[19] This divide between what the orchestra plays and what Lucia actually sings eventually comes together as the harmony settles on F major, allowing Lucia to proclaim Edgardo as her husband ('At last, I am yours'), which in this context sounds both naively simple and yet fantastically envisioned given her ghostly appearance. This literal coupling of the 'voice' of the orchestra with the voice of Lucia in the *cantabile* section creates a highly textured sound that invites trill-like accents in the upper winds and the flute/harmonica. After witnessing all of this in awe-filled silence, it also encourages a wary chorus to finally respond, 'Lord, have pity on her', before Lucia repeats her original melody with added *coloratura* elements.

As the *cantabile* section comes to a close, Donizetti composes one of the more unique moments in the 'mad aria' as Lucia sings a set of vocal flourishes that are imitated by the flute/harmonica.[20] Appearing as if Lucia has fallen in love with her own voice, the flute/harmonica mimics Lucia's vocal line, first as an interplay between her vocal phrases and then simultaneously with the voice (see Example 6.6). Lucia and the audience are thus paired as spectators to the sounds heard in the orchestra – a sonic showcase of a myopic vision of a diseased mind. (See Chapters 1 and 3 for a discussion of female madness in the nineteenth century and the sound of 'madness' in the orchestra, respectively.)

The middle or the *tempo di mezzo* section of the aria begins with the arrival of Enrico (scene 6), who has just returned from the Wolf's Crag. His entrance here is heralded with a key change to D♭ major as he bursts onto the stage to confront Lucia for spoiling his plans. Raimondo and the chorus stop him by informing him that Lucia has gone 'mad'. Looking now at Enrico, Lucia deliriously asks him 'what are you asking of me?', which forces Enrico to respond, 'Oh, the paleness of her face!' ['Oh, qual pallor!']. What follows is extended lyrical dialogue that starts in G minor before moving to A♭ major and then F minor as all those on stage,

Example 6.6 Gaetano Donizetti, *Lucia di Lammermoor* [Piano-Vocal Score], Act III, scene 5, No. 14: 'Alfin son tua', Recitative and Aria, bb. 160–65.

including Enrico, Raimondo, the chorus and Lucia all remark upon the tragic events of the day. Lucia, for her part, sings of regret for signing the marriage contract as she attempts to assure the missing Edgardo not to leave her ('Ah, no, do not leave, Edgardo!') and that even near death she loves him still.[21]

Lucia's pleading finally ends with an extended *moderato* section ('Spargi d'amaro pianto' ['Shed bitter tears']), which begins the *cabaletta*. As the harmony returns to F major, the same key as the *cantabile* section, Lucia steadily raises the tempo and pitch range to a climactic conclusion, all in a simple four-bar phrase structure with a lilting triple meter that once again invites the flute/ harmonica to mimic and to respond to every vocal flourish, trill and scalar ascent (see Example 6.7). At the conclusion of the aria, serving as a kind of postscript to the entire 'mad scene', Enrico

Example 6.7 Gaetano Donizetti, *Lucia di Lammermoor* [Piano-Vocal Score], Act III, scene 6, No. 14: 'Alfin son tua', Recitative and Aria, bb. 278–96.

asks Alisa to take Lucia away and to watch over her. As Alisa and the other ladies exit with Lucia, Raimondo, accompanied only with strings and a voice filled with religious 'fire and brimstone', curses Normanno for stirring Enrico's anger and commands him to go and repent before God (see Chapter 2 for a discussion of this exchange between bass and lyric tenor).

The spectacular 'mad scene' of Lucia contains over twenty minutes of music (431 bars), where Donizetti presents the listener with changes in meter, harmony, instrumentation, rhythmic pace, cadenzas, sudden silences and re-compositions of earlier music that recall different moments in Lucia's life.[22] It is the climax of a handful of scenes that flow directly from one into the other, helping to propel the emotional energy that began with a chorus of dancing revelers and ends with Lucia being taken off stage. At first glance, this might seem like the perfect place to end the opera – the lead singer Tacchinari-Persiani thought so. The lead soprano apparently disapproved of not being the one who closed the opera. So much so that Donizetti in a private letter to an Italian impresario accused Tacchinardi-Persiani of 'holding back' when performing the role.[23] Bad feelings aside, she had a point. It was common and almost expected that the *prima donna* would sing an aria-*finale*. The fact that Donizetti departed from convention at this crucial moment highlights perhaps the composer's 'quest for greater dramatic power and impetus' in *Lucia*,[24] whereby the audience is given the opportunity to witness our hero's painful reaction to the news of his lover's death – a familiar dramatic trope dating back to the very origins of opera (e.g., Monteverdi's *Orfeo*).

The Graveyard at Dawn

The final three scenes of the opera (scenes 7, 8 and 9) work as a unit to conclude the opera. All three scenes are centered on Edgardo, whom we now encounter in the Ravenswood graveyard at dawn, waiting for Enrico to arrive. The libretto describes a desolate outdoor setting near the back of the castle, where a single room now remains lit. This room is presumably Lucia's, which is visually placed within the setting for Edgardo to remark upon its brightness in the early hours of the morning:

> Tombs of my ancestors,
> the last remnant of an unhappy ancestral line . . .
> The castle still shines with festive lights!
> Ah! [It would seem that] the night was too short for rejoicing!
> Ungrateful woman! While I languish in a desperate plan,
> you laugh and celebrate with your happy husband!
> You are amidst pleasure, while I among the dead![25]

Donizetti composes the opening of this scene with dueling orchestral sounds that present both loss and hope, fear and courage. Powerful percussive chords are presented at the start in E♭ major, which are played by the entire orchestra but are then soon followed by a quartet of mellow soft horns on the dominant. Similar to the beginning of Act II, when Enrico is alone in his study, this orchestral opening depicts Edgardo battling with himself. As his recitative makes clear, Edgardo is a heartbroken man who is intent on dying in the sight of his former lover. It is a sad juxtaposition and one that suggests that Edgardo's desire for death is heroic. In *Lucia*, to die for love is a sacred act and so Edgardo (and Lucia before him) takes on the role of a martyr who would rather give up his life than live without the one he loves. (Traces of *Romeo and Juliet* and *Orfeo* abound here.) This is exactly the sentiment expressed in the vocal setting with notes that are naturally set to the rhythm of a calm and measured speech, which is reflected in the legato notes that soar in the tenor voice like a lone trumpet within the dark (see Example 6.8). This vocal setting is further highlighted with sighing figures in the horns and woodwinds and soft arpeggiated accents in the first violins, which collectively and effectively paint Edgardo as a man trying to fight back the tears.

With a switch to a *larghetto* tempo, a change in meter and a harmonic modulation to D major, the *cantabile* section of Edgardo's aria 'Fra poco a me ricovero' begins:

> I'll be placed soon in a neglected tomb . . .
> And not a remorseful tear will fall on it;
> Among the dead and absent of any comfort!
> You too shall forget this cursed marble:
> Never, oh cruel one, pass by my grave
> with your husband by your side . . .
> At the very least, respect the remains
> of the one who died for you.[26]

The same quartet of horns we heard at the start of this scene (and elsewhere in the opera) now returns to accompany Edgardo's legato melody, which is shaped by a rising interval of a sixth before beginning a scalar descent back to the original note (similar to other melodies we have encountered throughout the opera that speak of love and loss). The simple structure of this lyrical melody in major (a b a' coda), expressed with rising and falling notes in the upper range of the tenor voice, projects an earnest sincerity onto Edgardo's words. Combined with the soft sound of horns, which serenade Edgardo with light chords in a <6/8> metric rhythm, one

Example 6.8 Gaetano Donizetti, *Lucia di Lammermoor* [Piano-Vocal Score], Act III, scene 7, No. 16: 'Fra poco a me ricovero', Final Aria, bb. 21–36.

cannot help but feel for Edgardo at this moment, who is ready to die in a duel for a woman who has married another.

Scene 8 is dominated by a chorus of men (tenors and basses) who stroll from the castle towards Edgardo, heads cast down, expressing words of regret and pity as they attempt to comprehend all that took place within the castle the night before. This *tempo di mezzo* section ('Oh meschina') of Edgardo's aria brings back traces of the orchestral prelude with its funeral-paced music of mournful horns and drum. As in an ancient Greek chorus, the men's voices are set in a simple homophonic texture with recitation tones that rise and fall in the minor mode. Questioning the chorus's words and demeanor in lyrical dialogue, Edgardo soon ascertains that they refer to Lucia's failing health. The chorus's response to Edgardo is presented in B major with *moderato* accents on each beat of the bar to emphasize the emotional weight of the words. Despite the rhythmic accents, the chorus's melody is presented softly with legato styling and set in a simple lyrical form structure (a a b a b' a'), which appears to be an attempt to soften the emotional blow on Edgardo. Doubled in the first violins and flutes, this lyrical melody takes on a shimmering tender quality that invites even Edgardo to join in, further electrifying the whole, rendering it both heartwarming and pitifully woeful (see Example 6.9).

The striking of the mourning bell breaks this tender moment and compounds the tragedy (see Chapter 3 for a discussion of the bell), which effectively indicates that Lucia has passed. Raimondo enters (scene 9) and later confirms her passing. Edgardo's immediate response is a desperate plea – 'Lucia is no longer here?' ['Lucia più non è?'] – ringing out as a solo cry, without accompaniment, and set to the natural rhythm of speech. The final notes of his impassioned question, E natural to G natural, outline a minor third, a conspicuous deviation from the major thirds designated as the 'interval of agreement' throughout the opera (see Chapter 5). Grating against the A major harmony heard in the orchestra, both before and after Edgardo's cry, the minor third sounds all the more harrowing and desperate, especially as it is sung in the *passaggio* range of the tenor, where the voice has a tendency to crack, shifting as it does between the chest voice to the head voice (see Example 6.10). The libretto

Example 6.9 Gaetano Donizetti, *Lucia di Lammermoor* [Piano-Vocal Score], Act III, scene 8, No. 16: 'Fra poco a me ricovero', Final Aria, bb. 134–43.

6 Act III: Wedding Night and Graveyard at Dawn

Example 6.10 Gaetano Donizetti, *Lucia di Lammermoor* [Piano-Vocal Score], Act III, scene 9, No. 16: 'Fra poco a me ricovero', Final Aria, bb. 186–207.

describes Edgardo 'thrusting his hands into his hair, remaining motionless . . . [as one] struck by that immense pain that has no words'.[27] In the orchestral score, a solo horn echoes Edgardo's final notes (E and G), which is followed by a long, extended silence (written 'lungo silenzio' in the libretto). This 'moment of silence' is perhaps out of respect for Lucia's passing as well as Edgardo's loss of his one-time bride (more on this in the conclusion).

As mentioned in Chapter 3, the melody of the *cabaletta*, which closes the opera, is first introduced by the harp in Act I as Lucia enters the stage. There, in Act I, scene 4, amidst an E♭ major harmony, accompanied with soft chords in the horns and clarinets, *pizzicati* in the strings and chordal arpeggiations in the harpist's left hand, the *cabaletta* melody (played by the right hand of the harp) takes on a simple bucolic timbre with no hint of the emotional loss that Edgardo would later express here in Act III (see Chapter 1). Edgardo's melody ('Tu che a Dio spiegasti l'ali') is sung twice in D major (a a' b a" coda) to an accompaniment of horns, oboes, clarinets and plucked strings. According to the memoirs of Duprez (the tenor who premiered the role), he suggested to Donizetti that Edgardo should stab himself in between the two verses and have the melody be taken up by the cello on the repeat.[28] Apparently inspired by the dramatic potential of Duprez's suggestion, Donizetti composed isolated vocal phrases between the cello's melody, as if Edgardo was gasping for air as his lungs fail to operate.

More than a simple concluding number, the *cabaletta* melody of Edgardo's final aria is referenced at key moments in the opera when its sentiments provide lasting commentary upon the whole affair:

> Ah, if on Earth the anger of mortals waged a war against us,
> and kept us divided, let God unite us in Heaven.[29]

It is heard when we see Lucia for the first time ('Ancor non giunse!') and also in a slight variation in Act II, when Lucia receives the forged letter from Enrico ('Soffirva nel pianto'). The melody, with its characteristic dotted pick-up note, which rises an interval of a sixth (via a fourth) before descending back to the starting note, mirrors many of the melodies heard throughout the opera at times of dramatic importance to the overall narrative. In fact, Edgardo's *cabaletta* melody would later be used by Liszt to reference the opera as a whole, as in his 1836 virtuosic piano piece *Marche funèbre et Cavatine de 'Lucie de Lammermoor'* (see Chapter 7 for a discussion of the opera's reception in the nineteenth century).[30]

Conclusion

As we come to the end of our analysis of the musico-dramatic narrative found in each of the three acts, we are left with a dizzying array of notes, melodies, forms, timbres, tempos, rhythms, chords, dynamics, text and voices that collectively resound to reflect a sympathetic tale filled with love, loss, revenge, religious guilt, murder and suicide. Beginning with the orchestral prelude in B♭ minor and its reference to the tragic events in Act III, Donizetti moves the listener through each act using lyrical forms (e.g., a a b a), unique instrumentation and orchestration (e.g., the harp in Act I and the use of horns and trombones throughout the score), the standard conventional form (*cantabile – cabaletta*) and various select harmonies (B♭ major [Act I], D major and F major [Acts II and III]) that serve to anchor the main dramatic moments of the opera to a central key, namely B♭ major (see Appendix B).

B♭ major is first introduced at the start of Act I, but the harmony soon modulates when Enrico enters and sings of revenge and hate. The key, however, returns powerfully near the end of the act as Edgardo and Lucia sing the famous love duet *finale*, 'Qui, di sposa eterna fede' ['Swear here your eternal faith to me'], its arrival pronounced with *forte* brass and woodwinds (see Example 6.11). The same occurs in the *cabaletta* ('Verrano a te sull'aure' ['On the breeze will come to you my ardent sighs']) as Edgardo and Lucia sing unaccompanied a stepwise resolution (F-G-A-B♭) of the dominant chord – similar to the dominant chord at the end of the prelude – while the orchestra presents *forte* chords on the B♭ major tonic to close out the act (see Example 4.7). By using B♭ major in this way to define the courage and strength of the couple's love in Act I and then later reaffirming this same tonal association in the subsequent acts (e.g., the use of D major and F major in Acts II and III whenever the couple's love is declared or their sacrifice is

Example 6.11 Gaetano Donizetti, *Lucia di Lammermoor* [Orchestral Score], Act I, scene 5, No. 3: Scena e Duetto Finale, bb. 121–25. **Lucia di Lammermoor**. Words and Music by Gaetano Donizetti; Critical Edition by Gabriele Dotto and Roger Parker. Copyright © 2022 Casa Ricordi Srl, part of Universal Music Publishing Classics & Screen. This arrangement Copyright © 2024 Casa Ricordi Srl, part of Universal Music Publishing Classics & Screen All Rights Reserved. Used by Permission. *Reprinted by permission of Hal Leonard LLC.*

defined), one could argue that Donizetti provides a 'happy ending' to the opera. That is to say, a classic *Picardy third* relationship is formed between the orchestral prelude and the opera. The raising of the third in minor (e.g., from D♭ to D natural) was used by opera composers since the seventeenth century to right the wrongs of grief and tragedy heard earlier in the work.[31] The use of this compositional device, as suggested here in Donizetti's score, underlines the importance of the B♭ major love duet to the B♭ minor prelude and the opera's overall B♭ major harmonic structure. With the opera ending in D major, Donizetti solidifies the importance of the major third, which, as we have seen throughout the opera, highlights an agreement or union between two individuals. This interval is given more dramatic importance here at the end of the opera when Edgardo cries out with a minor third that remains unanswered in the harmony (E natural to G natural), as if Edgardo has given into the despair of death, where there is no hope of a reunion with Lucia. This, of course, prompts Edgardo to take his own life in the next scene, which would surely be a tragic ending if it was not for the D major harmonic setting that bathes Edgardo's final moments with hope ('let God unite us in Heaven'). In this way, we can hear *Lucia* as a work that proclaims the power of love (B♭ major) over death (B♭ minor).

In addition, we have seen in *Lucia* how Donizetti composes the vocal numbers as self-contained entities and yet each aria and duet retains a melodic shape (e.g., the rise of a sixth) and a rhythmic vitality that is shared throughout the score. Perhaps to create variety among the vocal numbers, the sextet from the Act II *finale* is the one number that is unlike any other, distinct in both harmony (D♭ major) and structure (e.g., the use of a theme and variations form in the midst of the conventional form), which contains two contrapuntal melodies that evolve from a tenor-baritone duet to a massive six-voice ensemble number with chorus and full orchestra.

The only other time D♭ major is heard in the opera is in the 'mad scene', when Enrico approaches Lucia and confronts her. Perhaps the brief appearance of D♭ major here in this scene links the sentiments of 'Chi mi frena in tal momento?' ['What stops me at this moment?'] to Enrico's shock when he sees his sister in her madness-induced state. Whatever the case, according to Ashbrook, this ensemble number 'is far and away the best-known page from any of Donizetti's scores' and 'helped to establish his pre-eminence as a master of ensemble writing'.[32] The number stands out among the ensemble finales of Donizetti's other operas and within *Lucia* itself, for the Act II *finale* is the one and only time the principal characters see and interact with one another on stage, and as such, it is characteristically poised for a violent confrontation. Donizetti, however, switches the dramatic tension of this moment from anger to one of relaxed contemplation, disarming the audience with a set of *larghetto*-paced *pizzicato* strings in major, which emulate the tranquil if not antique sound of mandolins or lutes, as the voices present asides that enumerate their inner feelings rather than angry words to be exchanged.

From the reoccurrence of earlier melodies (e.g., the music of the harp in Act I recalled in Edgardo's final aria in Act III) to impassioned ensembles, from coloristic orchestration to conventional forms, Donizetti continually excites the listener with both familiar and fresh ideas that force one to recognize the characters in *Lucia* as real individuals, who are fleshed out with true human impulses and emotions. Mixed with an inspiring libretto (and Scott's original text), it is remarkable that a work that was composed in a relatively short amount of time should prove to be so complete in its execution of such a varied tragic drama.[33] This is a point we shall explore in the final chapter as we discuss the reception of the opera in the press, music salons and literature following the premiere. What were the initial impressions of nineteenth-century audiences? What musical numbers did they prefer and why? These questions and more will be addressed in Chapter 7, revealing the lasting legacy of a *bel canto* opera that remains fixed in the repertoire today.

Notes

1. 'Dalle stanze ove Lucia trassi già col suo consorte, un lamento . . . un grido uscia, come d' uom vicino a morte'! Cammarano, 31.
2. Soon after the 1835 premiere, this opening scene and the one that followed, namely the duet between Edgardo and Enrico, were often

omitted to allow for the entire last act to be defined by the 'mad scene'; see Dotto and Parker, I, xxix–xxx.

3. 'Orrida è questa notte come il destino mio! Sì, tuona, o cielo … imperversate o turbini, sconvolto sia l' ordine delle cose, e pera il mondo'. Cammarano, 27.

4. Sounds that are heard and responded to by the characters in *Lucia* include distant music to welcome Arturo (Act II, off-stage wind band) and Arturo's welcoming chorus (Act II *finale*); Edgardo knocking on the castle door (Act II *finale*, bass drum and timpani); a thunderstorm (Act III, bass drum rolls and string tremolos); a galloping horse (Act III, triplet figures in the strings); a ball scene (full orchestra with percussion); Lucia's hallucinations (Act III, glass harmonica/flute); and tolls of a mourning bell (Act III, bell).

5. 'Io non m' inganno! Scalpitar d' appresso odo un destrier! S' arresta! Chi mai della tempesta fra le minacce e l' ire chi puote a me venirne'? Cammarano, 27.

6. '[Edgardo:] Qui del padre ancor s' aggira l' ombra inulta … e par che frema! Morte ogn' aura a te qui spira! Il terren per te qui trema! Nel varcar la soglia orrenda ben dovesti palpitar. Come un uom che vivo scenda la sua tomba ad albergar! [Enrico:] Di letizia il mio soggriono, e di plausi rimbombava; ma più forte al cor d' intorno la vendetta a me parlava! Qui mi trassi … in mezzo ai venti la sua voce udia tuttor; e il furor degli elementi rispondeva al mio furor'. Cammarano, 28.

7. 'Onde punir l' offesa, de' miei la spada vindice pende su te sospesa … ch' altri ti spenga? Ah! mai … chi dee svenarti il sai'. Cammarano, 29.

8. 'O sole, più rapido a sorger t' appresta … ti cinga di sangue ghirlanda funesta … così tu rischiara … l' orribile gara d' un odio mortale, d' un cieco furor. Farà di nostr' alme atroce governo Gridando vendetta, lo spirto d' Averno … del tuono che mugge … del nembo che rugge più l' ira è tremenda, che m' arde nel cor'. Cammarano, 29. Avernus is an ancient lake located west of Naples in the volcanic region of the Phlegraean Fields. Owing to its sulfuric gasses and toxic fumes, Avernus was thought to be the entrance to the underworld in the writings of Virgil and Dante. The inclusion of this well-known Italian location in Cammarano's libretto must have resonated well with Napoli audiences.

9. Some authors that explore the emotional and psychological journey of Lucia within the opera include Clément, Hadlock, Pugliese, McClary, Smart, Newark and Poriss.

10. See Isabel V. Hull, *Sexuality, State, and Civil Society in Germany, 1700–1815* (Ithaca, NY: Cornell University Press, 1996) and Jennifer Heuer, *The Family and the Nation: Gender and Citizenship in Revolutionary France, 1789–1830* (Ithaca, NY: Cornell University Press, 2005).

11. Jordan Pascoe, 'A Universal Estate: On Kant and Marriage Equality', in *Kant's 'Doctrine of Right' in the 21st Century*, ed. Larry Krasnoff, Nuran Sánchez Madrid and Paula Satne (Cardiff: University of Wales Press, 2018), 221. The Napoleonic code significantly limited the legal rights of women within marriage, reinforcing the husband's authority over nearly every aspect of life within the home; see Stephanie Coontz, *Marriage, A History: From Obedience to Intimacy, How Love Conquered Marriage* (New York: Penguin, 2005).

12. 'D' immenso giublio s' innalzi un grido: corra la Scozia per ogni lido; e avverta i perfidi nostri nemici, che più terribili, che più felici ne rende l' aura d' alto favor'; che a noi sorridono le stelle ancor'. Cammarano, 30.

13. Andrew Lamb, 'Galop', in *Grove Music Online*, 2001 (accessed 15 May 2023).

14. In the Scott original text, the character Old Alice (Alisa), who is blind and a former servant of the Ravenswood clan, has the ability 'to see' the future. Alice warns both Lucy (Lucia) and Edgar (Edgardo) that their relationship will fail (chap. 19). When Alice later dies, her ghost appears to Edgar (chap. 23). And, similar to the ghost story in *Lucia,* she motions but does not speak before disappearing.

15. 'Oh! qual funesto avvenimento! Tutti ne ingombra cupo spavento! Notte, ricopri la ria sventura col tenebroso tuo denso vel. Ah! quella destra di sangue impura l' ira non chiami su noi del ciel'. Cammarano, 31.

16. 'Lucia è in succinta e bianca veste: ha le chiome scarmigliate, ed il suo volto, coperto da uno squallore di morte, la rende simile ad uno spettro, anzicchè ad una creatura vivente. Il di lei sguardo impietrito, i moti convulsi, e fino un sorriso malaugurato manifestano non solo una spaventevole demenza, ma ben anco i segni di una vita, che già volge al suo termine'. Cammarano, 32. This description of Lucia's appearance in the 'mad scene' is similar to that found on the stages of several European theatres throughout the 1820s, most especially in their depiction of Ophelia from Shakespeare's *Hamlet*. Among the many dramatic portrayals of this tragic figure in the nineteenth century, Harriet Smithson's 1827 debut performance in Paris has garnered the most interest among scholars, owing greatly to the dramatic affect her performance had on Berlioz and other French romantics at the time; see Peter Raby, *Fair Ophelia: A Life of Harriet Smithson Berlioz* (Cambridge: Cambridge University Press, 1982); Elaine Showalter, 'Representing Ophelia: Women, Madness, and the Responsibilities of Feminist Criticism', in *Shakespeare and the Question of Theory*, ed. Geoffrey Hartman and Patricia Parker (London: Routledge, 1985), 77–94 and Sarah Hibberd, '"Dormez

donc, mes chers amours": Hérold's *La Somnambule* (1827) and Dream Phenomena on the Parisian Lyric Stage', *Cambridge Opera Journal* 16/2 (2004): 107–32.

17. 'Par dalla tomba uscita'. Cammarano, 32.

18. Ashbrook, 377–80.

19. 'Ardon gl' incensi ... splendono le sacre faci intorno! ... Ecco il ministro! Porgimi la destra ... oh lieto giorno'! Cammarano, 32.

20. Even though Donizetti wrote out a cadenza for the end of this section of the aria, it was still expected for the singer to improvise this characteristic vocal set piece at each performance; see Ashbrook, *Donizetti and His Operas*, 376. For more information on the cadenza and its connection to madness, see Pugliese, 'The Origins of *Lucia di Lammermoor*'s Cadenza' and Smart, 'The Silencing of Lucia', 127–30.

21. Although it is crossed out in the manuscript score (supposedly by Donizetti during the rehearsal period), there is another verse to the *tempo di mezzo* section of Lucia's aria found in the published libretto, which further emphasizes Lucia's weakened health: 'Presso alla tomba io sono ... odi una prece ancor. Deh! tanto almen t' arresta, ch' io spiri a te d' appresso ... già dall' affanno oppresso gelido langue il cor ... un palpito gli resta ... è un palpito d' amor' [I am near the grave ... listen again to my prayer at least insofar as it reaches you ... that I may breathe near you. Already I feel this cold breath, but my heart languishes! A heartbeat remains for him still ... It's a heartbeat of love!], Cammarano, 35. For information on this section of the manuscript, see Dotto and Parker, II, 642.

22. The number of bars composed for the 'mad scene' is based on the critical score edited by Dotto and Parker, but this number increases based on modern performances that add extensions to the vocal cadenzas that end both the *cantabile* ('Ardon gl' incensi') and the *cabaletta* ('Spargi d'amoro pianto') sections of the aria.

23. See Susan Rutherford, *The Prima Donna and Opera, 1815–1930* (Cambridge: Cambridge University Press, 2006), 171–2.

24. Ashbrook, 251–2.

25. 'Tombe degli avi miei, l' ultimo avanzo di una stirpe infelice, deh, raccogliete voi ... Di liete faci ancora splende il Castello! Ah! scarsa fu la notte al ripudio! Ingrata donna! Mentr' io mi struggo in disperato pianto tu ridi, esulti accanto al felìce consorte. Tu delle gioje in seno, io ... della morte'. Cammarano, 35.

26. 'Fra poco a me ricovero darà negletto avello ... una pietosa lagrima non scorrerà su quello! Fin degli estinti, ahi misero! Manca il conforto a me! Tu pur, tu pur dimentica quel marmo dispregiato: mai

non passarvi, o barbara, del tuo consorte a lato ... rispetta almen le ceneri di chi moria per te'. Cammarano, 35–6.

27. 'Edgardo si caccia disperatamente le mani tra' capelli, restando immobile in tale atteggiamento, colpito da quell' immenso dolore che non ha favella. Lungo silenzio'. Cammarano, 37.
28. Ashbrook, 380.
29. 'Ah! se l' ira de' mortali fece a noi sì lunga guerra; se divisi fummo in terra, ne congiunga il Nume in ciel'. Cammarano, 37.
30. *Marche funèbre et Cavatine de 'Lucie de Lammermoor'*, S. 398 (Paris: Latte, 1836).
31. For a discussion of the Picardy third in opera, see Peter Kivy, *Osmin's Rage: Philosophical Reflections on Opera, Drama, and Text, with a New Final Chapter* (Ithaca, NY: Cornell University Press, 1999), 288–92.
32. Ashbrook, 263. The Act II *finale* in *Maria Stuarda* (1835) is the only other sextet finale Donizetti wrote. In the case of *Maria Stuarda*, when Queen Mary of Scotland confronts Queen Elizabeth of England at the end of Act II (originally Act I), the sextet is structured in a similar manner to the one in *Lucia*, where it is set to a *larghetto* tempo in <3/4> meter in major but begins first as an aria (Elizabeth), then a trio (Elizabeth, Mary and Talbot) and then morphs into the sextet proper (Elizabeth, Mary, Talbot, Cecil, Leicester and Anna). In addition, the sextet from *Maria Stuarda* is shorter than the one in *Lucia* and is filled with more words of declamation than of contemplation. For a discussion of the Act II *finale* in *Lucia* as compared to Donizetti's other ensemble finales, see Ashbrook, 263–82.
33. According to a letter from Donizetti to a theater administrator in Naples, he began working with Cammarano on 25 May 1835. Work progressed on *Lucia* throughout the month of June with the last page of the autograph score dated Monday, 6 July 1835, or 42 days; see Dotto and Parker, I, xxv–i.

RECEPTION AND LEGACY

'Lucia di Lammermoor' has been performed ...
It has pleased and pleased very much.

(Donizetti, letter to Ricordi)[1]

On 29 September 1835, Donizetti wrote the following to Giovanni Ricordi, his Italian publisher and friend:

Lucia di Lammermoor has been performed, and kindly permit me to shame myself and tell you the truth: It has pleased and pleased very much, judging by the applause and compliments I received. I was called out many times, and a great many times the singers [were called out as well]. The king's brother Leopoldo [1790–1860], who was present and applauded the work, paid me the most flattering compliments ... Every number was listened to in religious silence and spontaneously hailed with shouts of '*Evviva*' [Hurrah]![2]

The reviews that followed the premiere appear to support Donizetti's claim of success. For example, the Napoli newspaper *L'omnibus* was the first to present its evaluation of the work, which appeared on 3 October 1835:

Of the 49 scores written by Donizetti in the past 15 years, no more than three or four have made a big impression on opening night ... But for this *Lucia di Lammermoor*, from the very first evening, applause without ceasing has crowned the famous *maestro*, leaving no doubt of the opera's success. The pieces that have given the greatest pleasure are – in addition to a shadowy *introduzione* and a grandiose [Act II] *finale* – the very brilliant *cavatina* [from Act I, 'Regnava nel silenzio'/ 'At dead of night'] by the *prima donna* [Tacchinardi-Persiani]; a delightful [love] duet between her and the tenor [Gilbert Duprez] that closes the first act and the final two scenes in the third act (although it seems to be the fault of the *maestro* or the poet for putting these two [final] arias side by side, and even still, having the woman precede the tenor). But among the many merits within the score, one above all must be mentioned, which was completely ingenious and one that could only be attempted by a great *maestro*. In the tenor's *cabaletta* [from Act III, 'Tu che a Dio spiegasti l'ali'/ 'You who have spread your wings to God'], everyone knows that the entire effect of this set piece is due to the customary repeat of the opening verse. The *maestro* could not do this however without contradicting the supremely pathetic and decisive act of Edgardo stabbing himself in between the two verses. Donizetti composes the verse the second time through with different harmony and phrasing and places it within the cello, which is joined from time to time with sobbing words from the voice of the dying man. One must hear it to imagine its magnificent effect! Another example to mention but which is no less regarded is the duet that closes the first act. After a delightful *cabaletta* ['Verrano a te sull' aure'/ 'On the breeze will come to you my ardent sighs'], sung separately by the soprano and then the tenor, the two voices come together to repeat the verse, not at the customary interval of a third, as the vocal melody of a duet usually lends itself but at the octave. This unusual distance is one that does not often express vehement passions, incite desire or cause the ear to welcome the *rapprochement* of the two voices with pleasure. It would take a long time to list all the other exquisite numbers by this famous *maestro*, who in contrast to the German school never stifles the singing or diverts our attention from the voice. Everyone knows how much progress Donizetti has made in this very important, though often modest part of the art; and in our judgement, this *Lucia* is sister to that of *Anna Bolena* [1830] for its strength and expression of song and of *Parisina* [1833] for its dramatic effect and richness in instrumentation.[3]

This first review, the majority of which is translated here, reflects the prevailing opinion of the Italian press. Owing much to the success of the opening night, the opera was performed twenty-two times in its first season at the San Carlo. It was produced again with the original cast in Florence and then later in Genoa, where it ran for twenty-one performances. By the end of 1836, in a span of fifteen months, *Lucia* would enjoy six productions in six different Italian cities.[4] Although these first revivals serve as evidence of *Lucia*'s initial success with Italian audiences, it was not until a few years later that the opera would become the international hit that we know today, enjoying performances throughout Europe, the Caribbean (Cuba in 1840 and Trinidad and Tobago in 1844), Indonesia (Jakarta in 1842), South America (Buenos Aires and Rio de Janeiro in 1846), Mexico (Mexico City, 1841) and the United States (New Orleans in 1841 and New York City in 1843).[5]

But as we return to the review presented earlier, one notes that little is mentioned of Lucia's 'mad scene'. The 'mad scene' is of course the dramatic climax of the opera and yet it was continually passed over by most of the press who favored the moments in the opera when the tenor sings. Indeed, one notes that the reviewer and Donizetti's own witness account detail the audience's appreciation for the tenor and not for the lead soprano.

Praise for the music of Edgardo continued as the work found success in other areas of Europe, most especially in Paris, arguably the cultural capital of Europe at the time. For example, as seen in a review article of the 1837 Parisian premiere at the Théâtre-Italien, for the conservative newspaper *La Presse*, Gérard de Nerval makes no mention of the 'mad aria' of Lucia:

The success of Donizetti's opera continues to grow: this score will certainly remain in the repertory … Among the pieces that made the best impression, we must mention first the *finale* of the second act, whose admirable *andante* ['Chi me frena in tal momento?'/ 'Who stops me at this moment?'] is followed by a vigorous *allegro* [the *stretta*], perfect in expression and dramatically well placed. In the duet that closes the first act, one cannot over-admire the simple and touching melody in triple meter that forms the *cabaletta* ['Verrano a te sull' aure'/ 'On the breeze will come to you my ardent sighs'] and the original and expressive *addio* thrown in at the end. In the third act, everything is savored and applauded with reason … the *andante* of the final air of Giovanni Battista Rubini [the tenor who premiered the role of Edgardo in Paris] and the majority of the funereal choir that follows are admired for their great scenic effect.[6]

Writing for the working and middle-class consumer, de Nerval seemed to share the same opinion of the Italian critics' circle, who, once again, favored Edgardo and his sacrifice and not the madness and subsequent death of Lucia. Even the most prestigious music journal in Paris, *La revue et gazette musicale de Paris,* in its own review of the 1837 premiere, made no mention of Lucia's madness as a key dramatic element in the work, simply stating that in Act III 'a cavatina by the dying Lucia' is presented.[7]

Equally so, when the opera reached New York City (Niblo's Garden, 15 September 1843) via an Italian troupe of singers on tour with the Havana Opera Company, the critic for *The Evening Post* viewed the tenor as the main attraction:

The leading tenor [Cerilo] Antagnini, already favorably known to our citizens as an artist of fine method and good cultivation, last evening added to his reputation, by the display of considerable dramatic powers. The [love] duet with [Amalia] Mejocchi, in the [first] act, and the concluding aria [of Act III] were received with rounds of applause. Signora Mejocchi, the *prima donna*, though somewhat inferior in her pretensions as an actress, has a voice of striking flexibility and compass; she was in the highest degree successful in the famous quintette ['Chi me frena in tal momento?'/ 'Who stops me at this moment?'] of this opera … The *primo basso*, [Attilio] Valtellina, produced a very favorable impression as Lord

Ashton . . . In the duet with Antognini, [at the start of] the third act, both performers
were recalled after they had retired, to receive the plaudits of the audience.[8]

Once again, the 'mad scene' is not mentioned, only an oblique
reference to the failed acting ability of the *prima donna*. Perhaps
because of the reception of Lucia's 'mad scene', the subsequent
revivals of *Lucia*, either in Italian or in French,[9] contained several
cuts and additions. Although this was common practice throughout Donizetti's time, most of the changes that were made to the
opera were connected to the music of Lucia, so much so that the
music of the 'mad scene' was replaced (on four occasions alone in
1837) with music from another Donizetti opera (the *rondò-finale*
from *Fausta*, 1832), while even the beloved *cavatina* from Act
I suffered changes due to the predilections of various singers.[10]
Although in time these changes reverted back to what Donizetti
originally wrote in the score, the music for Lucia's 'mad scene'
was continually seen and heard as lacking somehow.[11]

The question remains then, why was the 'mad scene' of *Lucia*
dismissed in the years following the premiere, by critics, singers and
audience members? We know from Chapter 1 that *Lucia* is one of
several Italian *bel canto* operas in the 1820s and 1830s that present
a woman succumbing to madness. Unlike other *bel canto* operas
from the first half of the nineteenth century, however, Lucia is the
only one who kills, which must have caused many sopranos to think
twice about performing a role that would certainly require some
theatrical ability and one that displayed a level of moral depravity.
Indeed, as the report from *The Evening Post* makes clear, the acting
ability of the lead soprano was one of the shortcomings of the
production. The same sentiment was also expressed by a reviewer
who saw the opera in Paris at the Théâtre-Italien in 1837:

In the third act, after a scene of provocation between Asthon [sic] and
Ravenswood, comes the inevitable scene of madness. The theatre, which abuses
everything, has above all made quite an exorbitant use of scenes of madness: to be
sure, in our modern theatre, any woman who has an unexpected annoyance or
violent grief occur will turn mad with deplorable ease. The symptoms of this
cruel dramatic epidemic are frighteningly simple: a white dress, a pale face, hair
that falls and leaves a few strands to float haphazardly over the shoulders . . . As to
its musical merit, and especially as to the manner in the which the air in question
was sung by Madame Persiani, that is another matter! Such a voice could have

Example 7.1 Soprano Cadenza with Flute Obligato, Paris Opéra, 1889 (Paris, Bibliothèque de l'Opéra, MS A.549); trans. Pugliese, 33.

conveyed much more! And would have had many other banalities applauded a hundred times more than a scene of madness![12]

From such evidence, it seems that the 'mad scene' in *Lucia* was all too common and perhaps all 'too real' in the everyday consciousness of opera goers in the first half of the nineteenth century for it to be fully appreciated (see Chapter 1). The 'mad scene' then, for it to be viewed as the true climax of the opera, would have to go beyond the common, into a more heightened and virtuosic realm for it to be appreciated by opera audiences. This is exactly what occurred in the latter half of the nineteenth century, when the 'mad scene' was lengthened to accommodate an extreme vocal performance that eclipsed Edgardo's sacrifice at the end of the opera.

Nellie Melba (1861–1932), an Australian lyric soprano, came to Paris in 1889 with a cadenza for Lucia's 'mad scene' (see Example 7.1). She was one of the first to perform an extended and highly virtuosic cadenza with flute in performance.[13] In fact, the cadenza was such a point of concern for Melba that according to an article in *L'Art musicale* (15 December 1889), she and the directors devoted ten weeks of rehearsals to the 'mad scene' alone. The following is a review that appeared in the French newspaper *Le Ménestrel* on 15 December 1889:

Mme. Melba's performance [on 9 December 1889] was a great success. This is to be expected, for such a delightful voice has never been heard with such virtuosity. After the mad aria, which is a page of immeasurable boredom, ovations were heard from all sides of the room. It is here that it has a dizzying cadenza [*un point d'orgue vertigineux*], where it follows the flute of [Paul] Taffanel [1844–1908] in all its acrobats with incomparable mastery. We can even say that it is because of this moment in the work that the directors of the Opéra have thought it necessary to snatch Donizetti's opera from the repertoire of the Château d'Eau [a Paris theater in the 13th *arrondissement*].[14]

After her opening performance, Melba's cadenza with flute became so popular that it was sung by other sopranos throughout Europe; the cadenza with flute/harmonica is still performed and even expected by audiences today.

By lengthening the music of the 'mad scene', one finds that the 'madness' reflected in the opera was no longer rationalized by the libretto and the staging of the opera but by the vocal virtuosity of the *prima donna*. In this new guise, the soprano voice transcended the theatrical display of madness that compromised her in the first half of the nineteenth century (see Chapter 1), making the 'mad scene' at the end of the nineteenth century and beyond the heroic voice of a woman who challenged the status quo. This point is well argued by the opera scholar Romana Margherita Pugliese, who, after comparing the 'vocal excess' of Melba's cadenza in 1889 to other madwomen arias in the repertoire at the time (e.g., Dinorah in Meyerbeer's *Le Pardon de Ploërmel*, 1859; Ophélie in Thomas's *Hamlet*, 1868; and Anita in Massenet's *La Navarraise*, 1894), as well as citing it among the Parisian public's fascination with hysteria patients in general, concludes:

At a time when most works by Donizetti and his contemporaries were falling out of the performing repertory, elbowed aside by brasher verismo spectacles, *Lucia di Lammermoor* retained a central place in the canon by adapting to changed taste … a shift prepared by Charcot's contemporary studies on hysteria and by the army of vampiric madwomen that had begun to populate the decadent imagination … The cadenza ought therefore to be regarded as the symbol of Lucia's metamorphosis, a bridge between the romantic madwoman and the *fin-de-siècle* hysteric.[15]

Early Reception outside the Theatre

Before the advent of sound recordings, the salon in the mid-nineteenth century was a space where operas were played in miniature, either as a collection of select melodies or the entire work.[16] Here, in this reduced format, the selections from an opera could be arranged for piano alone, as a piano-vocal arrangement or for any variety of instruments. Like a postcard, which stands as an embodiment of 'the real thing', opera selections for the salon were a great way for composers to have their works appreciated outside the theatre, where they served either to remind listeners of what they heard in the theatre or to create new initiates for the work. Publishing houses would usually employ an individual (who was rarely the actual composer of the operatic work) to provide easy to difficult arrangements or transcriptions to play in the home. Because of *Lucia*'s success with audiences, the work was immediately seized upon by various publishers wherever the opera was performed.

Piano-vocal arrangements of selections from *Lucia* appeared soon after the Naples premiere, the two earliest arrived in shops by mid-October 1835, one by the Girard Publishing firm in Naples and the other by the famous Milanese publisher Ricordi.[17] Both piano-vocal scores published the main parts of the opera, the so called 'numbers', which are self-contained vocal sections of the whole that allow for easy extraction or detachment from the rest of the work. In this way, one especially popular vocal number could be rearranged for the salon by the publisher and not fear that the dramatic context of the number would be lost, thus allowing for all manner of adaptations. For example, the popular tenor aria at the end of *Lucia* could be turned into a *quadrille* for four hands or a set of waltz variations for easy piano, or even an arrangement of the

Act I love duet could be re-written for piano and flute, helping to recall the happy love affair before it turns tragic.[18]

The two numbers that were the most popular with the publishers for the salon – a direct reflection of what drew the most praise from the press – were the sextet from the Act II *finale* and the final tenor aria from Act III. The famous piano virtuoso and composer Franz Liszt took these numbers to new heights with his pianistic reflections of the opera: *Réminiscences de Lucia di Lammermoor* (S. 397) and *Marche funèbre et Cavatine de 'Lucie de Lammermoor'* (S. 398). Both piano pieces were published in Paris in 1836, a year after the premiere and a year before its first performance in Paris, with variations of the *cantabile* section of the Act II *finale* ('Chi me frena in tal momento?') and Edgardo's final aria at the end of Act III, respectively (see Example 7.2).[19] Other famous pianists of the day also seized upon what Donizetti's score could provide for the salon market, such as Sigismond Thalberg (1812–71), who, along with Liszt, was one of the most well-known pianists of his day. Like Liszt, Thalberg wrote a brilliant set of variations on the *cantabile* section of the Act II *finale*: the *Andante final de Lucie de Lammermoor, varié pour piano*, op. 44, published in Paris in 1842.[20]

As evidenced by the piano transcriptions of Liszt and Thalberg, as well as the copious press reviews, 'Chi mi frena in tal momento?' ['Who stops me at this moment?'] was popular among performers, arrangers and publishers throughout the nineteenth century (see Figure 7.1). The Act II sextet (see Chapter 5 for an analysis) could be well adapted for any number of instruments and still capture the grand sweep of the *finale*, including (among many) fantasies for the double bass and piano (Giovanni Bottesini), the harp alone (Elias Parish Alvars), or *cornet à pistons* with piano (Joseph Forestier).[21] And, since Donizetti composed the sextet to be a set of variations as it passed from one set of singers to another, the structure of the composition made it easier than other vocal numbers to arrange it for the salon. In fact, the sextet became so popular by the twentieth century that it was often used in films to reference Italian culture or opera more generally (see Appendix C). While the earliest cinematic presentation of the sextet dates from a 1911 silent film (*Chantant*, dir. Georges Mendel), the most dramatic reference to the vocal number is found in the gangster film genre, such as in

Example 7.2 Franz Liszt, *Réminiscences de Lucia di Lammermoor,* S. 397.

the 1932 classic black-and-white film *Scarface* (United Artists, dir. Howard Hawks), where the lead actor (Paul Muni) whistles 'Chi me frena in tal momento?' right before he guns down his victims. And, more recently, in the 2006 Academy Award-winning film *The Departed* (Warner Bros., dir. Martin Scorsese), where the sextet is heard as a ring tone on a blood-stained mobile phone near the end of the film.

Figure 7.1 Adolph Baumbach, [title page] *Celebrated Quartettino 'Chi mi frena in tal momento' from Donizetti's Opera 'Lucia di Lammermoor', arranged for the Piano Forte* (Boston: G. P. Reed & Co., 1849).

Early Reception in the Novel

Further evidence of the opera's popularity with the public can be found in the pages of Gustave Flaubert's famous novel *Madame Bovary* (1857).[22] *Lucie de Lammermoor* (the French version of the Italian opera) appears in the middle of the novel (Part 2, Chap. 15) after Emma's husband suggests that they visit the opera house at Rouen in order to restore her health. Emma's sickness is brought on by the emotional and physical strains of an affair. Her lover was an older man who after four years began to tire of Emma's child-like fantasies, which were fueled by popular romance novels she read. On the day they were to run off together, Emma received a note from her lover that he was ending the relationship. When Emma arrives at the opera house several weeks later with her husband, the affair had finally receded from memory. Flaubert describes the scene at the opera house as follows:

The theatre was beginning to fill; opera-glasses were taken from their cases, and the subscribers, catching sight of one another, were bowing. They came to seek relaxation in the fine arts after the anxieties of business; but 'business' was not forgotten; they still talked cottons, spirits of wine, or indigo. The heads of old men were to be seen, inexpressive and peaceful, with their hair and complexions looking like silver medals tarnished by steam of lead. The young beaux were strutting about in the pit, showing in the opening of their waistcoats their pink or apple-green cravats, and Madame Bovary from above admired them leaning on their canes with golden knobs in the open palm of their yellow gloves ... She felt herself transported to the reading of her youth, into the midst of Walter Scott. She seemed to hear through the mist the sound of the Scotch bagpipes reechoing over the heather. Then her remembrance of the novel, helping her to understand the libretto, she followed the story phrase by phrase, while vague thoughts that came back to her dispersed at once again with the bursts of music. She gave herself up to the lullaby of the melodies, and felt all her being vibrate as if the violin bows were drawn over her nerves. She had not eyes enough to look at the costumes, the scenery, the actors, the painted trees that shook when anyone walked, and the velvet caps, cloaks, swords – all those imaginary things that floated amid the harmony as in the atmosphere of another world. But a young woman [Lucie] then stepped forward, throwing a purse to a squire in green. She was left alone, and the flute was heard like the murmur of a fountain or the warbling of birds. Lucie attacked her *cavatina* ['Que n'avons-nous des ailes?'/ 'Why don't we have wings to fly?'] in G major bravely. She pained of love; she longed for wings. Emma, too, fleeing from life, would have liked to fly away in an embrace.[23]

Emma's fascination with the opera continues to grow throughout the chapter as she begins to hear within the voices of Lucia (Lucie) and Edgardo (Edgard) her own desire for an all-consuming love. At the end of Act II, the curtain falls and allows the audience to mingle for refreshments before the start of the last act. As Emma reclines in her chair, overwhelmed by the whirlwind of emotions that stirred within her, she receives word from her husband that a young male acquaintance is in attendance. Unknown to her husband, Emma was in love with this young man who left before they could begin an affair. The young man is now grown up and comes to Emma's box to greet her. Just as she becomes flustered by his appearance, Act III begins. Flaubert uses the opera's final act to provide tension between Emma's desire to hear the opera and to reconnect with her old flame. As Edgardo (Edgard) and Enrico (Asthon) sing the duet, Flaubert writes that Emma 'listened no more', for she was now fully enthralled with the young man, who motions to her that they should leave. When Emma's husband protests, Flaubert writes: '"Oh, not yet; let us stay", said Bovary. "Her hair's undone; this is going to be tragic." But the mad scene did not interest Emma, and the acting of the singer seemed to her exaggerated: "She screams too loud", said she.'[24] In the midst of the 'mad scene', Emma, her husband and the young man all get up and leave the theatre. Later, as they sit down at an outdoor café, they overhear various attendees humming Edgardo's final aria of which Emma's husband confesses 'they say that he is quite admirable in the last act. I regret leaving before the end, because it was beginning to amuse me.'[25] The next day, Emma and the young man begin an affair. And with that, the opera disappears from the novel.

While traveling to the Middle East, Flaubert heard *Lucia di Lammermoor* in Constantinople in 1850.[26] The opera must have made a significant impression upon the author for him to include the work so prominently in his 1857 novel. The opera not only brought a splash of realism to the novel's setting but also provided a foil to the life of Emma. By the end of the novel, Emma is so consumed with shame and self-loathing that she decides to end her life tragically by swallowing arsenic. Following her death, her husband also dies but of a broken heart after he finds the love letters Emma received from her former lovers. His death leaves their daughter abandoned to relatives, who send the young girl off to toil in a workhouse. Here, in Flaubert's novel, the opera is a painful reminder of the penalty of forbidden love and giving oneself up to literary-based fantasies.[27]

Lucia's Legacy Today

The success of *Lucia* did not happen overnight but interest in the opera continued to grow as it was performed throughout Italy and then later in France in translation. By the mid nineteenth century, the work could be heard throughout Europe and the United States, either on stage, in the salon or the recital hall. The fact that Donizetti's opera was quickly seized upon by publishers and performers alike attributed much to the continual success of the work, especially particular numbers such as Edgardo's aria 'Tu che a Dio spiegasti l'ali' ['You who have spread your wings to God'] and the adagio sextet 'Chi me frena in tal momento?' ['Who stops me at this moment?'].

Just as the opera was achieving world-wide success, the composer was hospitalized (see Appendix A). When *Lucie de Lammermoor* premiered at the Paris Opéra on 20 February 1846, Donizetti was suffering from symptoms later diagnosed as neurosyphilis, which included 'fierce headaches, neck pain, convulsions, high debilitating fevers, nervous complaints, mental disorientation and personality changes'.[28] His afflictions were so acute that Donizetti was checked into the Maison-Esquirol in the Ivry-sur-Seine region outside of Paris, a sanatorium for the mentally ill founded by the famous French psychiatrist Jean-Étienne Dominique Esquirol (1772–1840). Donizetti would remain there for nearly seventeen months (January 1846–June 1847), before being allowed by his doctors to return to Bergamo, his birthplace, where he died on 8 April 1848.[29] As Harris-Warrick points out, news of Donizetti's poor health became known to the Parisian critics' circle at the time of the Paris Opéra premiere, which coloured some of the responses to such a degree that when they heard the 'madness' in *Lucie* they also heard the suffering of the composer, who was described by one member of the press as 'a harmonious lyre that had been broken before its time'.[30]

In the end, the fascinating thing about the legacy of *Lucia* is that after the 'mad scene' was extended with vocal virtuosity, the opera gained even more success at the end of the nineteenth century. Perhaps it was Donizetti's own brush with a debilitating illness and later admittance into a mental asylum that endeared the 'mad scene' to later audiences. Or, simply, the vocal changes to the 'mad scene' allowed for the opera to be included among late-nineteenth-century repertoire that demanded larger voices, such as the operas of Verdi and Puccini. Or, perhaps even still, the 'mad scene' and its heightened vocal virtuosity was seen and heard as part and parcel of the rise of domestic violence, mental illness and degeneracy that was occurring in the so-called *fin-de-siècle* era, thus making the opera decidedly 'modern'.[31]

This last possibility for the mad scene's later success is a particular intriguing one, which portrays Lucia as a type of *femme fatale* who inspires horror rather than sympathy. The *femme fatale*, as understood in literature, psychology, visual culture and philosophy, was a direct result of the late-nineteenth-century outgrowth of the fears surrounding the loss of patriarchal control in European society, when women went against the gender norms of the time, which were exasperated by new technologies such as the typewriter and the bicycle, and the new-found respect garnered to women by the medical community after the Crimean War (1853–6).[32] We see this same display of the autonomy of women in opera in the late nineteenth and early twentieth centuries, such as in Wagner's Kundry (*Parsifal*, 1882), Bizet's Carmen (*Carmen*, 1875), Puccini's Tosca (*Tosca*, 1900), Strauss's Salome (*Salome*, 1905) and Berg's Lulu (*Lulu*, 1935), and then later in the popular *film noir* genres of the 1940s and 50s.[33] Unfortunately, the paths of such 'monstrous women' often led to their own death, which some might argue as a possible warning to all those who would subvert the status quo (note that all the composers mentioned above are men). And yet, in the context of Lucia, despite her murderous act and later death, she continues to live on in recording after recording, on the stages of opera theatres today, beguiling listeners still with her bold display of vocality and violence. Lucia was not the first *femme fatale*, but the character came along at a time when the cultural imagination was ripe to see and hear a strong woman who challenged the weakness attributed to her.

As mentioned in the Introduction, this relatively new assessment of the character of Lucia and her 'mad aria' has become a central focus for feminist scholars since the 1990s, many of whom have been cited throughout this study, including Susan McClary (*Feminine Endings: Music, Gender, and Sexuality,* 1991), Ruth A. Solie (*Musicology and Difference: Gender and Sexuality in Music Scholarship,* 1993), Mary Ann Smart (*Siren Songs: Representations of Gender and Sexuality in Opera,* 2000), Hilary Poriss (*Changing the Score: Arias, Prima Donnas, and the Authority of Performance,* 2009), Susan Rutherford (*The Prima Donna and Opera, 1815–1930,* 2006) and Sean M. Parr (*Vocal Virtuosity: The Origins of the Coloratura Soprano in Nineteenth-Century Opera,* 2021). Such research has inspired opera directors to present the character of Lucia as a powerful domineering figure that no man can tame. Whether we see Arturo literally fall prey to Lucia's on-stage violence (e.g., Katie Mitchell, The Royal Opera House, 2016) or have her appear as a ghost who guides Edgardo's knife to his chest (Mary Zimmerman, The Metropolitan Opera, 2007) or even becomes so obsessed with death that she cuddles the blood-soaked body of Arturo on their wedding bed (Simon Stone, The Metropolitan Opera, 2022), opera productions today are so fixated on Lucia's madness that the horror-tinged scene of Act III has the appearance of being the main reason the opera remains in the repertoire today. But as I hoped to have shown, *Lucia di Lammermoor* goes beyond mere definitions or anecdotes provided by production, score and libretto. It is a work that celebrates the power of love. In this way, the opera's continual success is not bound up in a certain time, country, style of music or composer but in the simple hope that love can conquer all.

Notes

1. '*Lucia di Lammermoor* andò, e permetti pure che amichevolmente mi vergogni e ti dica la verità. Ha piaciuto, e piaciuto assai'. *Le prime rappresentazioni delle opere di Donizetti nella stampa coeva,* III,

518. Giovanni Ricordi (1785–1853) was the owner and founder of Ricordi & Co. (1808), the leading music publisher of Italian opera throughout the nineteenth century.

2. '*Lucia di Lammermoor* andò, e permetti pure che amichevolmente mi vergogni e ti dica la verità. Ha piaciuto, e piaciuto assai se deggio creder agli applausi ed a' complimenti ricevuti. Per molte volte fui chiamato fuori e ben molte anche i cantanti. Il fratello di S. M. Leopoldo che vi assisteva ed applaudì, mi fece i più lusinghieri complimenti ... Ogni pezzo fu ascoltato con religioso silenzio e da spontanei evviva festeggiato'. Binni and Commons, 518.

3. 'E veramente di 49 *spartiti* scritti da lui in 15 ani, non più de tre o quattro han fatto un grande incontro alle prime sere ... Ma per questa *Lucia di Lammermoor*, dalla prima sera applausi senza interruzione han coronato il celebre maestro e son venuti crescendo sempre più, ed oggi nessun dubbio ci ha del suo favorevole incontro. I pezzi poi che hanno fatto massimo piacere sono oltre ad una vaghissima introduzione, ed un grandioso finale, la *brillantissima* cavatina della prima donna, un delizioso duetto tra lei e' l tenore, col quale chiude il primo atto, e le due scene di costoro nel terzo; sebbene vogliosi che sia colpa del maestro o del poeta aver messo queste due arie di seguito; e più, aver fatto che la donna preceda il tenore. Ma fra tutt' i pregi si dee ricordare un novità affatto ingegnosa, e che poeta tentarsi soltanto da un gran maestro. Nella cabaletta (di quest' aria del tenore) siccome ognun sa che è ristretto tutto l' effetto del pezzo, ed una consuetudine oramai radicata vuole che indispensabilmente si replichi, il maestro che non poeta far ciò senza un controsenso della posizione sommamente patetica e decisiva per la risoluzione presa di un suicidio, sublimemente immaginò fare che *Edgardo* si trafigga tra le due repliche affidando peraltro la seconda volta con armonia e movimento diverso il canto a' violoncelli, cui si unisce appena di tratto in tratto con parole singhiozzanti la voce del moribondo. E fa d' uopo sentirlo per immaginarne il magnifico effetto. Un altro artifizio è a notarsi non meno pregevole. Nel duetto che chiude il primo atto dopo una deliziosa cabaletta cantata separatamente dalla donna e dal tenore, le loro voci si riuniscono per ripeterla, non già in *terza*, come si presta la cantilena, ma in *ottava*. Ora questa distanza inusitata ove non si vogliano esprimere passioni veementi, incitando il desiderio fa sì che l' orecchio accolga con trasporto di piacere verso le ultime battute il ravvicinamento delle due voci. E lungo sarebbe dire altre preziose astuzie del celebre maestro che a' pregi della scuola tedesca aggiunge quello di non mai soffocare il canto o anche distogliere l' attenzione. Si sa da ognuno quanti progressi abbia fatto Donizetti per questa parte importantissima, benché spesso modesta dell' arte; e l' augurio non

sembri sconsigliato se diremo che questa *Lucia* sarà tutta sorella dell' *Anna Bolena* per la forza e l' espressione del canto, e della *Parisini* per l' effetto drammatico e la ricchezza di strumentale'. *L'Omnibus*, 3 Oct. 1835.

4. Ashbrook, 'Popular Success, the Critics and Fame', 67–8.

5. See http://opera.stanford.edu/Donizetti/LuciaDiLammermoor/history.html; accessed 25 June 2024.

6. 'Le succès de l'opéra de Donizetti se consolide plus en plus: cette partition restera au répertoire assurément, et nous y reviendrons volontiers encore après plusieurs auditions. On reconnaît là-dedans l'habilité et toute la facilité de l'auteur d'*Anna Bolena*, l'œuvre qui approche le plus des beaux ouvrages de Rossini. L'instrumentation, riche et claire, relève fort heureusement ce que les motifs one parfois de pâle et do commun. Les chœurs nous ont paru en général bien traités, et parmi les morceaux que nous avons le plus remarqués, il faut citer en première ligne le finale du deuxième acte, dont l'*andante* admirable est suivi d'un vigoureux *allegro*, parfait d'expression et di situation. Dans le duo qui termine le premier acte, on ne peut trop admirer la simple et touchante mélodie à trois temps qui en forme la *cabalette*, et l'*addio* original et expressif jeté à la fin. Dans le troisième acte, tout est goûté et applaudi avec raison … Du reste l'*andante* de l'air final de Rubini et la *majeur* du chœur funèbre qui suit sont admirables de facture et d'effet scénique'. Gérard de Nerval, 'Feuilleton de la Presse: Théâtre-Italien: *Lucia di Lammermoor*', *La Presse*, 28 December 1837.

7. 'Une cavatine pour la mourante Lucia'. A. Z., 'Théâtre-Italien: *Lucia di Lamermoor*, musique de Donizetti', *La revue et gazette musicale de Paris*, 17 December 1837.

8. *The Evening Post*, 16 September 1843, 2. *Lucia* was first performed in the United States in a French-language version on 28 May 1841 in New Orleans. For information about the Havana Opera Company, see Katherine K. Preston, *Opera on the Road: Traveling Opera Troupes in the United States, 1825–1860* (Urbana, IL: University of Illinois Press, 1993), 116–22, 320–1.

9. The French-language version of the opera (*Lucie de Lammermoor*) first appeared in Paris at the Théâtre de la Renaissance on 6 August 1839 with a libretto written by Alphonse Royer and Gustave Vaëz. For a discussion of *Lucia* in France, see Harris-Warrick, '*Lucia* goes to Paris' and Fauquet, 'Donizetti: *Lucia di Lammermoor*'.

10. See Poriss, 'Aria Substitution in *Lucia di Lammermoor*'.

11. The most famous of these changes of course is the addition of a vocal cadenza with flute in the 'mad scene' at the end of the *cantabile* section (see Chapter 3). For a list of the cuts and aria substitutions

that took place after the premiere of the opera, see Dotto and Parker, I, xxviii–xxxiii and Carol J. Money, 'The Musical Alternatives of Donizetti's *Lucia di Lammermoor*: An Analysis and Guide for Performance Practice', DMA diss., University of Northern Colorado, 2016, 71–122.

12. 'Au troisième acte, après une scène de provocation entre Asthon et Ravenswood, arrive l'inévitable scène de folie. Le théâtre, qui a abusé de tout, a surtout fait des scènes de folie un usage tout à fait exorbitant; soyez surs que sur notre théâtre moderne, toute femme à qui survient une contrariété imprévue ou un chagrin violent, tournera à la folie avec une déplorable facilité. Les symptômes de cette cruelle épidémie dramatique sont effrayants de simplicité – Une robe blanche, un visage pâle, un peigne qui tombe et qui laisse flotter au hasard un maigre chevelure sur les épaules ... Quant à son mérite musical, et surtout quant à la manière dont l'air en question a été chanté par madame Persiani, c'est une autre affaire! Une pareille voix eût fait passer, bien plus! eût fait applaudir bien d'autres banalités cent fois plus démonétisées encore qu'une scène de folie'! *Le Temps*, 23 December 1837.

13. Naomi Matsumoto has argued that there were earlier precedents to Melba's extended cadenza as used in performance, including an 1868 performance at Her Majesty's Theatre in London by the Swedish soprano Christina Nilsson (1843–1921); see Matsumoto, 'Manacled Freedom'.

14. 'Le succès de Mme Melba a été très grand. Il fallait s'y attendre, car, depuis longtemps, on n'avait entendu une voix aussi adorable servie par une pareille virtuosité. Après l'air de la Folie, qui est pourtant une page d'un ennui incommensurable, on lui a fait de véritables ovations de tous les bouts de la salle. C'est qu'elle a là un point d'orgue vertigineux, où elle suit la flûte de Taffanel dans toutes ses voltiges avec une maestria incomparable. On peut même dire que c'est pour ce seul point d'orgue que les directeurs de l'Opéra ont cru devoir arracher l'œuvre de Donizetti au répertoire du Château-d'Eau dont elle constituait le plus bel ornement'. H. Moreno [Henri Heugel], '*Lucie de Lammermoor* à L'Opéra', *Le Ménestrel*, 15 December 1889.

15. Pugliese, 41–2.

16. For a general discussion of European salon culture as well as the practice of music listening in the home, see Derek Carew, 'The Consumption of Music', in *The Cambridge History of Nineteenth-Century Music*, 237–58; Carl Dahlhaus, *Nineteenth-Century Music*, trans. J. Bradford Robinson (Berkeley, CA: University of California Press, 1989), 41–53 and Wolfgang Fuhrmann, 'The Intimate Art of Listening: Music in the Private Sphere During the Nineteenth-Century', in *The Oxford Handbook of Music Listening*

in the 19th and 20th Centuries, ed. Christian Thorau and Hansjakob Ziemer (Oxford: Oxford University Press, 2019), 277–311.

17. Dotto and Parker, I, xxviii.
18. Performing a search on the international Online Computer Library Center (OCLC), an online catalog that displays the holdings of libraries from around the world, I was able to find hundreds of selections from *Lucia* for the salon. Some of the most frequent works that appeared in the database include Carl Czerny, *Fantaisie pour piano et violon concertans sur les motifs favoris de l'opéra 'Lucia di Lammermoor' de C.* [sic] *Donizetti* (Vienna, 1841); Friedrich Bürgmuller, *Divertissement sur 'Lucia di Lammermoor'*, op. 54, no. 1 (Copenhagen, 1846); Joseph Ascher, *Andante de salon sur l'opéra de G. Donizetti 'Lucie de Lammermoor' pour piano*, op. 27 (Milan, 1856); Nicolas Louis, *Variations brillantes à quatre mains pour le piano: sur les motifs de l'opéra 'Lucie de Lammermoor' de Donizetti*, Op. 78 (Mainz, 1847); August Linder, *Morceaux de salon, pour violoncelle avec accompagnement de piano sur des thêmes d'opéras: Thême de l'opéra 'Lucia di Lammermoor'*, op. 19, no. 3 (Offenbach am Main, 1850) and Sydney Smith, *'Lucia di Lammermoor': Fantaisie brillante pour Piano à quatre mains sur l'opéra de Donizetti* (London, 1873).
19. Franz Liszt, *Réminiscences de Lucia di Lammermoor,* S. 397 (Paris: Latte, 1836) and *Marche funèbre et Cavatine de 'Lucie de Lammermoor'*, S. 398 (Paris: Latte, 1836).
20. Sigismond Thalberg, *Andante final de Lucie de Lammermoor, varié pour piano*, op. 44 (Paris: Latte, 1842).
21. Giovanni Bottesini, *Fantasia sulla 'Lucia di Lammermoor' di Donizetti* (Milan, 1840s); Elias Parish Alvars, *Grande fantasie sur 'Lucia di Lammermoor' se Donizetti* (Vienna: Artaria, 1845) and Joseph Forestier, *Fantasie pour cornet à pistons avec accompagnent de piano sur les motifs de 'Lucia de Lammermoor' de Donizetti* (Paris: Latte, 1845).
22. The novel was first published as a literary serial in *La Revue de Paris*, from 1 October to 15 December 1856 and then published the next year as a novel in three parts by Michel Lévy Frères. Set in Normandy in the mid 1840s, the work highlights the life journey of a young woman escaping her provincial origins to find the love and happiness she only read about in the romance novels of her youth.
23. Gustave Flaubert, *Madame Bovary*, trans. Eleanor Marx-Aveling, *Project Gutenberg eBook* (2021), www.standardebooks.org/ebooks/ gustave-flaubert/madame-bovary/eleanor-marx-aveling/text/chap ter-2-15 (accessed 12 June 2023). The *cavatina* mentioned in Flaubert's novel appears in the French version of the opera, which is a French translation of the Italian aria 'Perché non ho del vento

l'infaticabil volo?' ['Why don't we have wings to fly?'] from Donizetti's *Rosmonda d'Inghilterra* (1834). The aria first came to be used in place of Lucia's original *cavatina* 'Regnava nel silenzio' ['At dead of night'] at a performance by Tacchinardi-Persiani at the Teatro Apollo (Venice) on 26 Dec. 1836. For more information about this aria substitution, see Poriss, 'A Madwoman's Choice'.

24. Flaubert, *Madame Bovary.*
25. Flaubert, *Madame Bovary.*
26. Newark, *Opera in the Novel*, 97, 232 (n. 62).
27. For a critical discussion of the opera within the novel, see Newark, 78–109; Graham Daniels, 'Emma Bovary's Opera – Flaubert, Scott and Donizetti', *French Historical Studies* 32/3 (1978): 285–303 and Pierre Han, '*Le romantisme corrige*: Emma Bovary and *Lucie de Lammermoor*', *Journal of Comparative Literature and Aesthetics* 30/1–2 (2007) (accessed 12 June 2023).
28. Enid Peschel and Richard Peschel, 'Donizetti and the Music of Mental Derangement: *Anna Bolena, Lucia di Lammermoor*, and the Composer's Neurobiological Illness', *The Yale Journal of Biology and Medicine*, 65 (1992): 190.
29. See Peschel and Peshel, 191–2.
30. Harris-Warrick, '*Lucia* goes to Paris', 214, 227. According to letters dating from 1829, Donizetti was already complaining of the symptoms that would eventually claim his life; see Peschel and Peschel.
31. The *fin-de-siècle* or 'end of the century' is a phrase that refers to the heightened fear, optimism and ennui that occurred throughout Europe in the 1880s, 1890s and early 1900s. The period is marked by rising inequality; political unrest; philosophical debates concerning race, gender and class; technical and scientific innovation and the exploration of new styles of artistic expression. For more information about the *fin-de-siècle* and its connection to *Lucia*, see McClary, *Feminine Endings*, 80–111; Showalter, *The Female Malady*, 10–16, 145–64; Clément, *Opera, or the Undoing of Women*, 87–93; Pugliese, 38–41 and Smart, 'The Silencing of Lucia'.
32. For further discussion on this topic, see Bram Dijkstra, *Idols of Perversity: Fantasies of Feminine Evil in Fin-de-Siècle Culture* (Oxford: Oxford University Press, 1988); Margery W. Davies, *Woman's Place is at the Typewriter: Office Work and Office Workers, 1870–1930* (Philadelphia, PA: Temple University Press, 1982); Sarah Hallenbeck, *Claiming the Bicycle: Women, Rhetoric, and Technology in Nineteenth-Century America* (Carbondale, IL: Southern Illinois University Press, 2016); Helen Rappaport, *In Search of Mary Seacole: The Making of a Black Cultural Icon and Humanitarian* (New York: Pegasus Books, 2022); and Terry Tastard,

Nightingale's Nuns and the Crimean War (London: Bloomsbury Academic, 2023).

33. See Mary Ann Doane, *Femme Fatale: Feminism, Film Theory, Psychoanalysis* (New York: Routledge, 1991).

APPENDIX A: TIMELINE OF DONIZETTI
AND *LUCIA*

1797

Gaetano Donizetti is born in Bergamo, a city in northern Italy (near Milan).[1] Although his family is poor, with six children to support and no money for music lessons, the boy's talents are soon evident, whereupon he receives a scholarship to study music at the cathedral of Santa Maria Maggiore in 1806. The school was founded by Johann Simon Mayr, a German-born composer, who would become a major influence on Donizetti's life and career.

1811

The music school at Santa Maria Maggiore puts on a musical farce, *Il piccolo compositore di musica* ['*The Little Music Composer*']. Donizetti, only thirteen years old, is cast in the lead role. His solo vocal part includes the lines: 'Vasta ho la mente, rapido l'ingegno, pronta la fantasia, e nel comporre, un fulmine son io' ['I have a vast mind, a quick wit, a ready imagination, and in composing, I am like a thunderbolt'].

1815

Donizetti travels to Bologna to continue his studies at the Liceo Filarmonico, one of the top music schools in northern Italy.

1819

Sir Walter Scott completes his novel *The Bride of Lammermoor* in April. The book is published in June and soon becomes one of the most popular novels of the nineteenth century. The book is translated into Italian as *La promessa sposa di Lammermoor* by Gaetano Barbieri in 1824.

1822

Donizetti, not quite twenty-five years old, is invited by the impresario Domenico Barbaja to compose for the theatres in Naples, which includes the Teatro di San Carlo, the oldest and one of the largest opera houses in Europe. The theatre would eventually serve as the site of the premiere of *Lucia*.

1827

Donizetti signs a new contract with Barbaja, committing himself to composing four new operas per year for the Neapolitan theaters. The following year, he marries Virginia Vasselli, the nineteen-year-old sister of his best friend, Antonio ('Toto') Vasselli, who shared a long correspondence with the composer. Upon return from his honeymoon, Donizetti is appointed musical director of the royal theatres of Naples, a position with considerable power and prestige.

1830

Anna Bolena, Donizetti's opera about the doomed English queen Anne Boleyn, premieres in Milan. The opera is a tremendous hit and when it is performed in Paris and London, it gives Donizetti his first taste of international fame. A number of successful operas follow, including *L'elisir d'amore* (Milan, 1832), *Lucrezia Borgia* (Milan, 1833), *Rosmonda d'Inghilterra* (Florence, 1834) and *Maria Stuarda* (Milan, 1835).

1835

At the end of May, Donizetti writes to the Neapolitan theatrical censors for approval to compose an opera based on Scott's *The Bride of Lammermoor*. Donizetti completes the opera on 6 July; from beginning to end, he has composed the work in less than six weeks. Unfortunately, the Teatro di San Carlo is on the verge of bankruptcy. The soprano cast as Lucia (Fanny Tacchinardi-Persiani) threatens to go on strike until the singers are paid; rehearsals do not begin until early September. After this rough start, *Lucia di Lammermoor* premieres on 26 September at the San Carlo.

1837 🇫🇷 🇬🇧

Lucia di Lammermoor premieres in Paris at the Théâtre-Italien; the opera's first performance outside of Italy. The following year, the opera is performed in London at Her Majesty's Theatre in the Haymarket.

Appendix A: Timeline of Donizetti and *Lucia*

1838

Following the tragic death of his wife and a series of disappointing professional setbacks, Donizetti moves to Paris and begins to write operas for the French public, including *La fille du régiment* (1840), *Les martyrs* (1840), *La favorite* (1840) and a French-language version of *Lucia* [*Lucie de Lammermoor*], with a revised libretto by Alphonse Royer and Gustave Vaëz (1839, Théâtre de la Renaissance).

1841

On 28 December, *Lucia di Lammermoor* is performed for the first time in the United States, in New Orleans; this first American performance is sung in French.

1842

After living in Paris for four years, Donizetti is offered the prestigious position of music director at the Hapsburg court in Vienna and court composer to the Emperor of Austria, Ferdinand I. This position comes with an enormous salary, allowing Donizetti to split his residence between Vienna and Paris, make regular trips to Italy and compose operas at an incredible rate, including *Linda di Chamounix* (Vienna, 1842), *Don Pasquale* (Paris, 1843), *Dom Sébastien* (Paris, 1843) and *Caterina Cornaro* (Venice, 1844).

1846

Suffering from neurosyphilis (i.e., a latent bacterial infection that spreads to the brain), Donizetti is confined to a hospital bed in the suburbs of Paris. Meanwhile, *Lucie* premieres at the Paris Opéra to great acclaim. The reviewers, knowing of Donizetti's medical condition, hear in Lucia's 'mad scene' the suffering of the composer. The following year, his doctors allow him to be sent back to Bergamo to live out his days.

1848

Donizetti, a successful composer of sixty-five operas, dies in Bergamo on 8 April.[2] He is buried in a local cemetery but in 1875, his remains are moved to Santa Maria Maggiore, where he began his music studies as a child; his body remains there today.

Notes

1. Information compiled from a number of sources, including articles in *The New Grove Dictionary of Opera*, ed. Stanley Sadie (New York: Macmillan Reference Ltd., 1997); William Ashbrook, *Donizetti and His Operas* (Cambridge: Cambridge University Press, 1982); Raoul Meloncelli, 'Donizetti, Gaetano', in *Dizionario Biografico degli Italiani*, ed. Alberto Maria Ghisalberti (Rome: Instituto della Enciclopedia Italiana, 1960–2020), 41 (1992), 185–200 and James P. Cassaro, *Gaetano Donizetti: A Research and Information Guide*, 2nd ed. (New York: Routledge, 2009).
2. Donizetti wrote over seventy operas during his lifetime, a handful of which were never performed or remain incomplete.

APPENDIX B: COMPOSITIONAL STRUCTURE OF *LUCIA*

Preludio			B♭ minor

Act I

Introduzione

Scena	Coro e Normanno	'Percorrete le spiaggie vicine'	B♭ Major – B♭ minor
Cavatina	Cantabile	'Cruda, funesta smania'	G Major
[Enrico]	Tempo di mezzo	'Il tuo dubbio è omai' certez'	B♭ Major
	Cabaletta	'La pietade in suo favore'	G Major

Cavatina Lucia

Scena		'Ancor non giunse!'	E♭ Major*
Cavatina	Cantabile	'Regnava nel silenzio'	E♭ minor – G♭ Major*
	Tempo di mezzo	'Chiari oh Dio!'	E♭ minor – E♭Major*
	Cabaletta	'Quando rapito in estasi'	A♭ Major*

Scena e Duetto Finale [Edgardo e Lucia]

Scena		'Egli s'avanza'	C Major – A minor
Duetto	Tempo d'attacco	'Intendo!'	A minor – B♭ minor
	Cantabile	'Sulla tomba che reinserra'	G minor – G Major
	Tempo di mezzo	'Qui di sposa eterna'	B♭ Major
	Cabaletta/Stretta	'Ah! Verrano a te sull'aure'	B♭ Major

*Transposed a semitone lower in the vocal scores of
Schirmer and Ricordi

Act II

Duetto [Enrico] e Lucia

Scena		'Lucia, fra poco a te verrà'	D Major – B minor
Duetto	Tempo d'attacco	'Il pallor funesto, orrendo'	A Major – F# minor*
	Cantabile	'Soffriva nel pianto'	C Major*
	Tempo di mezzo	'Che fia'	F Major – E Major/minor*
	Cabaletta	'Se tradirmi tu potrai'	A Major*

Scene edAria [Raimondo]

Scena		'Ebben?'	A minor – C minor
Aria	Cantabile	'Ah! Cedi, cedi'	F Major
	Tempo di mezzo	'Taci, taci … ' [L] 'No, no, cedi' [R]	D♭ minor – C Major
	Cabaletta	Al ben de'tuoi qual vittima'	F Major

Finale Act II

Scena	Coro e Arturo	'Per te d''immenso giubilo'	G Major – D Major – G Major
Finale	Tempo d'attacco	'Dov'è Lucia?'	A Major – C minor – A♭ minor
	Cantabile – Sextet	'Chi mi frena in tal momento?'	D♭ Major
	Tempo di mezzo	'T'allontana sciagurato'	D Major – D minor – A Major – A minor
	Cabaletta/Stretta	'Esci, fuggi, il furor'	D Major

*Transposed a whole tone lower in the vocal scores of Schirmer and Ricordi

(cont.)

Act III

Scena e Duetto [Edgardo ed Enrico]

Scena		'Orrida è questa notte'	D minor
Duetto	Tempo d'attacco	'Asthon!' [Ed] 'Sì' [En]	D Major – A minor
	Cantabile	'Qui del padre ancor respira'	D Major – A minor – D Major – F Major
	Tempo di mezzo	'Al primo sorgere'	A minor
	Cabaletta/Stretta	'Ah! O sole più ratto a sorger'	D Major

[Coro e] Scena Lucia

Coro e Raimondo		'D'immenso giubilo'	E Major – B Major – E Major
Scena		Il dolce suono'	D minor – B♭ Major – F minor*
Aria	Cantabile	'Ardon gl'incensi!, . Alfin son tua'	F Major*
	Tempo di mezzo	'A'avanza Enrico'	D♭ Major – G minor – A♭ Major – F minor*
	Cabaletta	'Spargi d'amaro pianto'	F Major*

[Recitativo] Dopo la Scena di Lucia

Recitativo		'Si tragga altove' [En]	A♭ Major – A Major – C minor

Ultima Scena [di Edgardo]

Scena		'Tombe degli avi miei'	E♭ Major – C minor
Aria	Cantabile	'Fra poco a me ricovero'	D Major
	Tempo di mezzo	'Oh meschina'	B minor – B Major – G minor – A Major
	Cabaletta	'Tu che a Dio spiegasti l'ali'	D Major

*Transposed a whole tone lower in the vocal scores of Schirmer and Ricordi

APPENDIX C: *LUCIA* GOES TO THE MOVIES

Selections from Donizetti's tragic romantic opera have been heard on the silver screen since the early days of film, when the opera was often presented as a sonic cue for Italian opera writ-large or for ironic commentary. By no means exhaustive, here is a list of some of *Lucia*'s most memorable 'appearances':

Chantant (1911), Silent Film, dir. Georges Mendel: 'Chi me frena in tal momento?' ['Who stops me at this moment?'] (Act II *finale – cantabile*)[1]

Scarface (1932), United Artists, dir. Howard Hanks: 'Chi me frena in tal momento?'

I Love to Singa (1936), Merry Melodies, Warner Bros., dir. Fred Avery: 'Chi me frena in tal momento?'

Gaslight (1944), MGM, dir. George Cukor: 'Verranno a te sull'aure i miei sospiri ardenti' ['On the breeze will come to you my ardent sighs'] (Act I, love duet – *cabaletta*)

Three Stooges in 'Micro-Phonies' (1945), Columbia Pictures, dir. Edward Bernds: 'Chi me frena in tal momento?'

The Whale Who Wanted to Sing at the Met (1946), Disney and RKO Radio Pictures, dir. Jack Kinney et al: 'Chi me frena in tal momento?'

Long-Haired Hare (1946), Loony Tunes, Warner Bros., dir. Chuck Jones: 'Chi me frena in tal momento?'

Three Stooges in 'Squareheads of the Round Table' (1948), Columbia Pictures, dir. Edward Bernds:'Chi me frena in tal momento?'

The Money Pit (1986), Amblin Entertainment and Universal Pictures, dir. Richard Benjamin: 'Chi me frena in tal momento?'

Beetlejuice (1988), Warner Bros., dir. Tim Burton: 'Regnava nel silenzio alta la notte e bruna' ['At dead of night, in the silent darkness'] (Act I, Lucia's aria – *cantabile*)

Where Angels Fear to Tread (1992), Rank Film and Sovereign Pictures, dir. Charles Sturridge: 'Lapietade in suo favore' ['In vain do you plead for pity'] (Act I, Enrico's aria with chorus – *cabaletta*) and 'Spargi d'amoro pianto' ['Shed bitter tears'] (Act III, Lucia's 'mad scene' – *cabaletta*)

The Fifth Element (1997), Gaumont and Buena Vista International, dir. Luc Besson: 'Il dolce suono' ['The sweet sound'], (Act III, Lucia's 'mad scene' – *scena*)

The Departed (2006), Warner Bros., dir. Martin Scorsese: 'Chi me frena in tal momento?'

Note

1. When this early silent film was presented, the theatre synchronized the actors on film to the playing of a 1908 Victor Co. recording (96200) of the sextet featuring the legendary tenor Enrico Caruso.

BIBLIOGRAPHY

Primary Sources

Barbieri, Gaetano, *La promessa sposa di Lammermoor o Nuovi racconti del mio ostiere* (Milan: V. Ferrario, 1824).

Berlioz, Hector, *Grand traité d'instrumentation et d'orchestration modernes* (Paris: Schonenberger, 1844).

Cammarano, Salvadore, *Lucia di Lammermoor, dramma tragico in due parti* (Naples: Tipografia Flautino, 1835).

Cammarano, Salvadore, '*Lucia di Lammermoor' di Salvatore Cammerano* [sic]: *Lucy of Lammermoor, A Tragic Opera in Three Acts, the Music by Donizetti, as Represented at Palmo's New York Opera House, January 1847*, trans. Joseph Attinelli (New York, NY: Piercy & Houel, 1847).

D'Amiens, Dubois, *Histoire philosophique de l'hypochondrie et de l'hystérie* (Paris: Deville-Cavellin, 1833).

Donizetti, Gaetano, *Lucia di Lammermoor* [critical edition], ed. Gabriele Dotto and Roger Parker, 2 vols. (Milan: Ricordi, 2021).

Donizetti, Gaetano, *Lucia di Lammermoor* [piano-vocal score], ed. and Eng. trans. Natalia Macfarren (London: Novello, Ewer and Co., 1871; New York, NY: G. Schirmer, 1898).

Donizetti, Gaetano, *Lucia di Lammermoor* [piano-vocal score], ed. Mario Parenti (Milan: Ricordi, 1973).

Flaubert, Gustave, *Madame Bovary*, trans. Eleanor Marx-Aveling, *Project Gutenberg eBook* (2021), https://standardebooks.org/ebooks/gustave-flaubert/madame-bovary/eleanor-marx-aveling/text/chapter-2-15 (accessed 12 June 2023).

Scott, Walter, *Tales of My Landlord, 3: The Bride of Lammermoor* (Edinburgh: Archibald, Constable and Co., 1819).

Scott, Walter, *The Bride of Lammermoor* (Edinburgh: Adam & Charles Black, 1886, 1893).

Newspapers

L'Art musicale (Paris), *I Curiosi* (Naples), *The Evening Post* (New York), *Journal des débats* (Paris), *Le Ménestrel* (Paris), *The New York Times* (New York), *L'Omnibus* (Naples), *La Presse* (Paris), *La revue et gazette musicale de Paris* (Paris), *Le Temps* (Paris).

Bibliography

Secondary Sources

André, Naomi, *Voicing Gender, Travesti, and the Second Woman in Early Nineteenth-Century Italian Opera* (Bloomington, IN: Indiana University Press, 2006).

Arnaud, Sabine, *On Hysteria: The Invention of a Medical Category between 1670 and 1820* (Chicago, IL: University of Chicago Press, 2015).

Ashbrook, William, *Donizetti and His Operas* (Cambridge: Cambridge University Press, 1982).

Ashbrook, William, 'Popular Success, the Critics and Fame: The Early Careers of *Lucia di Lammermoor* and *Belisario*', *Cambridge Opera Journal* 2/1 (1990): 65–81.

Ashbrook, William, 'Lucia di Lammermoor', *The New Grove Dictionary of Opera*, Vol. III, Ed. Stanley Sadie (London: Macmillan, 1992), 69–72.

Ashbrook, William, 'Elisabetta al castello di Kenilworth (1829)', *The Opera Quarterly*, 14/3 (1998): 116–19.

Bini, Annalisa and Commons, Jeremy, eds., *Le prime rappresentazioni delle opere di Donizetti nella stampa coeva* (Milan: Accademia Nazionale di Santa Cecilia per i testi per le immagini, 1997), III, 513–32.

Black, John, *The Italian Romantic Libretto: A Study of Salvadore Cammarano* (Edinburgh: Edinburgh University Press, 1984).

Brittan, Francesca, *Music and Fantasy in the Age of Berlioz* (Cambridge: Cambridge University Press, 2017).

Camilletti, Fabio, 'Gothic Beginnings, 1764–1827', in *Italian Gothic*, ed. Marco Malvestio and Stefano Serafini (Edinburgh: Edinburgh University Press, 2022), 19–29.

Cassaro, James P., *Gaetano Donizetti: A Research and Information Guide*, 2nd ed. (New York, NY: Routledge, 2009).

Celletti, Rodolfo, *A History of Bel Canto*, trans. Frederick Fuller (Oxford: Clarendon Press, 1991).

Charlton, David, ed., *The Cambridge Companion to Grand Opera* (Cambridge: Cambridge University Press, 2003).

Charna Lynn, Karyl, *Italian Opera Houses and Festivals* (Lanham, MD: Scarecrow Press, 2005).

Chesney, Sarah, 'Gothic Imaginations in Primo Ottocento Opera', MMus thesis, New Zealand School of Music, Victoria University of Wellington, 2010.

Cipriani, Nicola, *Le tre Lucie: Un Romanzo, un melodrama, un caso guidiziario* (Varese: Zecchini Editore, 2008).

Clément, Catherine, *Opera, or the Undoing of Women*, trans. Betsy Wing (Minneapolis, MN: University of Minnesota Press, 1988).

Dahlhaus, Carl, *Nineteenth-Century Music*, trans. J. Bradford Robinson (Berkeley, CA: University of California Press, 1989).

Daniels, Graham, 'Emma Bovary's Opera: Flaubert, Scott and Donizetti', *French Historical Studies*, 32/3 (1978): 285–303.

Bibliography

Davies, James Q., *Romantic Anatomies of Performance* (Berkeley, CA: University of California Press, 2014).

Davies, Joe, *The Gothic Imagination in the Music of Franz Schubert* (Woodbridge: Boydell Press, 2024).

Davies, Margery W., *Woman's Place is at the Typewriter: Office Work and Office Workers, 1870–1930* (Philadelphia, PA: Temple University Press 1982).

Demata, Massimiliano, 'Italy and the Gothic', *Gothic Studies* 8/1 (2006): 1–8.

Dijkstra, Bram, *Idols of Perversity: Fantasies of Feminine Evil in Fin-de-Siècle Culture* (Oxford: Oxford University Press, 1988).

Doane, Mary Ann, *Femme Fatale: Feminism, Film Theory, Psychoanalysis* (New York, NY: Routledge, 1991).

Downing, Lisa, 'Murder in the Feminine: Marie Lefarge and the Sexualization of the Nineteenth-Century Criminal Woman', *Journal of the History of Sexuality* 18/1 (2009): 121–37.

Esse, Melina, 'Donizetti's Gothic Resurrections', *19th-Century Music*, 33/2 (2009): 81–109.

Facci, Serena, and Garda, Michela, eds., *The Female Voice in the Twentieth Century: Material, Symbolic and Aesthetic Dimensions* (New York, NY: Routledge, 2021).

Fauquet, Joël-Marie, *L'Avant-scène opéra, no. 233: Lucia di Lammermoor, Donizetti* (Paris: Éditions Premières Loges, 2006).

Fillerup, Jessie, 'Lucia's Ghosts: Sonic, Gothic and Postmodern', *Cambridge Opera Journal* 28/3 (2016): 313–45.

Fischer, Jens Malte, 'Wagner and *Bel Canto*', *The Opera Quarterly*, 11/4 (1995): 53–8.

Foucault, Michel, *Madness and Civilization: A History of Insanity in the Age of Reason*, trans. Richard Howard (New York, NY: Vintage, 1973).

Gilman, Sander L., *Seeing the Insane* (Lincoln, NE: University of Nebraska Press, 1996).

Gossett, Philip, *Divas and Scholars: Performing Italian Opera* (Chicago, IL: University of Chicago Press, 2006).

Grey, Thomas, 'Music, Theatre and the Gothic Imaginary: Visualizing the "Bleeding Nun"', in *Art, Theatre, and Opera in Paris, 1750–1850: Exchanges and Tensions*, ed. Sarah Hibberd and Richard Wrigley (Burlington, VT: Ashgate, 2014), 77–106.

Hadlock, Heather, 'Sonorous Bodies: Women and the Glass Harmonica', *Journal of the American Musicological Society*, 53/3 (2000): 507–42.

Hallenbeck, Sarah, *Claiming the Bicycle: Women, Rhetoric, and Technology in Nineteenth-Century America* (Carbondale, IL: Southern Illinois University Press, 2016).

Han, Pierre, '*Le romantisme corrige:* Emma Bovary and *Lucie de Lammermoor*', *Journal of Comparative Literature and Aesthetics*, 30/1–2 (2007): 29–40.

Harris, Ruth, *Murders and Madness: Medicine, Law, and Society in the Fin de Siècle* (Oxford: Oxford University Press, 1991).

Bibliography

Harris-Warrick, Rebecca, 'Lucia Goes to Paris: A Tale of Three Theaters', in *Music, Theater, and Cultural Transfer: Paris, 1830–1914*, ed. Annegret Fauser and Mark Everist (Chicago, IL: Chicago University Press, 2009), 195–227.

Harwood, Gregory W., 'Verdi's Reform of the Italian Opera Orchestra', *19th-Century Music*, 10/2 (1986): 108–34.

Heuer, Jennifer, *The Family and the Nation: Gender and Citizenship in Revolutionary France, 1789–1830* (Ithaca, NY: Cornell University Press, 2005).

Hogle, Jerrold E., ed., *The Cambridge Companion to Gothic Fiction* (Cambridge: Cambridge University Press, 2002).

Hull, Isabel V., *Sexuality, State, and Civil Society in Germany, 1700–1815* (Ithaca, NY: Cornell University Press, 1996).

Hustvedt, Asti, *Medical Muses: Hysteria in Nineteenth-Century Paris* (New York, NY: Norton, 2011).

Innace, Gino, Ianniello, Carlotta, Maffei, Luigi and Romano, Rosana, 'Objective Measurement of the Listening Condition in the Old Italian Opera House "Teatro di San Carlo"', *Journal of Sound and Vibration*, 232/1 (2000): 239–49.

Izzo, Francesco, 'Donizetti's *Don Pasquale* and the Conventions of Mid-Nineteenth Century Opera Buffa', *Studi muscali*, 33/2 (2004): 387–431.

Jaffee Nagel, Julie, 'Psychoanalytic and Musical Perspectives on Shame in Donizetti's *Lucia di Lammermoor*', *Journal of the American Psychoanalytic Association*, 56/2 (2008): 551–63.

Jander, Owen, 'Bel Canto', in *The New Grove Dictionary of Opera*, ed. Stanley Sadie (New York, NY: Macmillan Reference Limited, 1997), 380–1.

Jenkins, Anna, 'Perceptions of the Murderesses in London and Paris, *1674–1789*', PhD diss., University of Sheffield, 2015.

Kimbell, David R., *Italian Opera* (Cambridge: Cambridge University Press, 1991).

Kivy, Peter, *Osmin's Rage: Philosophical Reflections on Opera, Drama, and Text, with a New Final Chapter* (Ithaca, NY: Cornell University Press, 1999).

Lacombe, Hervé, *Les voies de l'opéra français au XIXe siècle*, Eng. trans. Edward Schneider, *The Keys to French Opera in the Nineteenth Century* (Berkeley, CA: University of California Press, 2001).

Macdonald, Hugh, *Berlioz's Orchestration Treatise: A Translation and Commentary* (Cambridge: Cambridge University Press, 2002).

Macy, Laura, ed., *The Grove Book of Opera Singers* (Oxford: Oxford University Press, 2008).

Mancini, Franco, *Il Teatro di San Carlo, 1737–1987*, 3 vols. (Naples: Electa, 1987).

Manén, Lucie, *Bel Canto: The Teaching of the Classic Italian Song-Schools, Its Decline and Restoration* (Oxford: Oxford University Press, 1994).

Margherita Pugliese, Romana, 'The Origins of *Lucia di Lammermoor*'s Cadenza', *Cambridge Opera Journal* 16/1 (2004): 23–42.

Bibliography

Marshall, Rosalind K., *Mary Queen of Scots: Truth or Lies* (Edinburgh: St. Andrew Press, 2010).

Massie, Allan, *The Royal Stuarts: A History of the Family that Shaped Britain* (New York, NY: St. Martin's Griffin, 2013).

Matsumoto, Naomi, 'Manacled Freedom: Nineteenth-Century Vocal Improvisation and the Flute-Accompanied Cadenza in Donizetti's *Lucia di Lammermoor*', in *Beyond Notes: Improvisation in Western Music of the Eighteenth cand Nineteenth Centuries*, ed. Rudolf Rasch (Turnhout: Brepols, 2011), 295–316.

McClary, Susan, *Feminine Endings: Music, Gender, and Sexuality* (Minneapolis, MN: University of Minnesota Press, 1991).

Meloncelli, Raoul, 'Donizetti, Gaetano', in *Dizionario Biografico degli Italiani*, ed. Alberto Maria Ghisalberti (Rome: Instituto della Enciclopedia italiana, 1960–2020), 41, 185–200.

Miller, Richard, *The Structure of Singing: System and Art in Vocal Technique* (New York, NY: Schirmer Books, 1986).

Miron, Janet, *Prisons, Asylums, and the Public: Institutional Visiting in the Nineteenth Century* (Toronto: University of Toronto Press, 2011).

Mishra, Vijay, *The Gothic Sublime* (Albany, NY: State University of New York Press, 1994).

Money, Carol J., 'The Musical Alternatives of Donizetti's Lucia di Lammermoor: An Analysis and Guide for Performance Practice', DMA diss., University of Northern Colorado, 2016.

Newark, Cormac, *Opera in the Novel from Balzac to Proust* (Cambridge: Cambridge University Press, 2011).

Osborne, Charles, *The Bel Canto Operas of Rossini, Donizetti and Bellini* (London: Methuen, 1994).

Pantozzi, Giuseppe, *Storia delle Idee e delle Leggi Psichiatriche: 1780–1980* (Trento: Centro Studi Erickson, 1994).

Parker, Roger, *Leonora's Last Act: Essays in Verdian Discourse* (Princeton, NJ: Princeton University Press, 1998), 42–60.

Parker, Roger, *Remaking the Song: Operatic Visions and Revisions from Handel to Berio* (Berkeley, CA: University of California Press, 2006).

Parr, Sean M., *Vocal Virtuosity: The Origins of the Coloratura Soprano in Nineteenth-Century Opera* (New York, NY: Oxford University Press, 2021).

Parsons, Coleman O., 'The Dalrymple Legend in *The Bride of Lammermoor*', *The Review of English Studies*, 19/73 (1943): 51–8.

Pascoe, Jordan, 'A Universal Estate: On Kant and Marriage Equality', in *Kant's 'Doctrine of Right' in the 21st Century*, ed. Larry Krasnoff, Nuran Sánchez Madrid and Paula Satne (Cardiff: University of Wales Press, 2018), 220–40.

Peschel, Enid and Peschel, Richard, 'Donizetti and the Music of Mental Derangement: *Anna Bolena, Lucia di Lammermoor*, and the Composer's Neurobiological Illness', *The Yale Journal of Biology and Medicine* 65 (1992): 189–200.

Pesic, Peter, 'Composing the Crisis: From Mesmer's Harmonica to Charcot's Tam-tam', *Nineteenth-Century Music Review*, 19/1 (2022): 7–30.

Poriss, Hilary, 'A Madwoman's Choice: Aria Substitution in *Lucia di Lammermoor*', *Cambridge Opera Journal*, 13/1 (2001): 1–28.

Poriss, Hilary, *Changing the Score: Arias, Prima Donnas, and the Authority of Performance* (Oxford: Oxford University Press, 2009).

Pottinger, Mark A., '*Lucia* and the Auscultation of Disease in Mid-Nineteenth-Century France', *Nineteenth-Century Music Review*, 19/1 (2022): 55–83.

Powers, Harold S., '"*La Solita Forma*" and *The Uses of Convention*', *Acta Musicologica*, 59/1 (1987): 65–90.

Preston, Katherine K., *Opera on the Road: Traveling Opera Troupes in the United States, 1825–1860* (Urbana, IL: University of Illinois Press, 1993).

Rappaport, Helen, *In Search of Mary Seacole: The Making of a Black Cultural Icon and Humanitarian* (New York, NY: Pegasus Books, 2022).

Raz, Carmel, 'Music, Theater, and the Moral Treatment: The Casa dei Matti in Aversa and Palermo', *Laboratoire Italien: Politique et société*, 20 (2017): 1–20.

Rutherford, Susan, *The Prima Donna and Opera, 1815–1930* (Cambridge: Cambridge University Press, 2006).

Sala, Emilio, 'Women Crazed by Love: An Aspect of Romantic Opera', trans. William Ashbrook, *The Opera Quarterly*, 10/3 (1994): 19–41.

Samson, Jim, ed., *The Cambridge History of Nineteenth-Century Music* (Cambridge: Cambridge University Press, 2001).

Senici, Emanuele, *Music in the Present Tense: Rossini's Italian Operas in Their Time* (Chicago, IL: Chicago University Press, 2019).

Shapiro, Ann-Louise, *Breaking the Codes: Female Criminality in Fin-de-Siècle Paris* (Stanford, CA: Stanford University Press, 1996).

Showalter, Elaine, *The Female Malady: Women, Madness, and English Culture, 1830–1980* (New York, NY: Penguin Books, 1987).

Smart, Mary Ann, 'The Silencing of Lucia', *Cambridge Opera Journal* 4/2 (1992): 119–41.

Smart, Mary Ann, '"Dalla tomba uscita": Representations of Madness in Nineteenth-Century Italian Opera', PhD diss., Cornell University, 1994.

Smart, Mary Ann, ed., *Siren Songs: Representations of Gender and Sexuality in Opera* (Princeton, NJ: Princeton University Press, 2000).

Smart, Mary Ann, *Waiting for Verdi: Italian Opera and Political Opinion, 1815–1848* (Oakland, CA: University of California Press, 2018).

Solie, Ruth A., ed., *Musicology and Difference: Gender and Sexuality in Music Scholarship* (Berkeley, CA: University of California Press, 1993).

Taruskin, Richard, *The Oxford History of Western Music*, 3 (Oxford: Oxford University Press, 2005).

Tastard, Terry, *Nightingale's Nuns and the Crimean War* (London: Bloomsbury Academic, 2023).

Thorau, Christian and Ziemer, Hansjakob, eds., *The Oxford Handbook of Music Listening in the 19th and 20th Centuries* (Oxford: Oxford University Press, 2019).

Toft, Robert, *Bel Canto: A Performer's Guide* (Oxford: Oxford University Press, 2013).

Tung, Tiffiny A., 'Agency, "Till Death Do Us Part?" Inquiring about the Agency of Dead Bodies from the Ancient Andes', *Cambridge Archaeological Journal*, 24/3 (2014): 437–52.

Veith, Ilza, *Hysteria: The History of a Disease* (Chicago, IL: University of Chicago Press, 1965).

Vellutini, Claudio, 'Fanny Tacchinardi-Persiani, Carlo Balocchino and Italian Opera Business in Vienna, Paris and London (1837–1845)', *Cambridge Opera Journal*, 30/2–3 (2018): 259–304.

Weatherson, Alexander, 'The Stuarts and their Kith and Kin', *Donizetti Society Newsletter*, 106/2 (2009): 13–20.

Weinstock, Herbert, *Donizetti and the World of Opera* (New York, NY: Pantheon Books, 1963).

Wolf, Rebecca, 'The Sound of Glass: Transparency and Danger', in *Performing Knowledge, 1750–1850*, ed. Mary Helen Dupree and Sean B. Franzel (Berlin: De Gruyter, 2015), 113–36.

Wright, Angela, 'Ann Radcliffe and Matthew Lewis', in *The Cambridge History of the Gothic*, I, ed. Angela Wright and Dale Townshend (Cambridge: Cambridge University Press, 2020), 304–22.

Yeadon McGinnis, Pearl, *The Opera Singer's Career Guide: Understanding the European 'Fach' System*, ed. Marith McGinnis Willis (Lanham, MD: Scarecrow Press, 2010).

Zoppelli, Luca, '"Stage Music" in Early Nineteenth-Century Italian Opera', trans. Arthur Groos and Roger Parker, *Cambridge Opera Journal*, 2/1 (1990): 29–39.

INDEX

*page numbers in *italics* appear in the endnotes.